20th Century Avant-Garde Composers
David Cope (Editor, *The Composer Magazine*)

20TH CENTURY AVANT-GARDE COMPOSERS
DAVID COPE

Contents

INTRODUCTION

During the years 1969 through 1981, I edited and published (with the help of many friends, who contributed interviews with composers, and so on) *The Composer Magazine* (sometimes referred to as The Composer or TCM). This ambitious enterprise joined two other similar projects: *Composer Autograph Publications* (CAP), a music publishing house and, with the help of friend John Tanno, *CAPRA RECORDS* (a contemporary recording company). These three different non-profit organizations persisted for different lengths of time, but the latter two longer than the original CAP. This book will concentrate on *The Composer Magazine* since it's best suited for literature and not musical scores or $33^{1/3}$ recordings.

Many times over the forty years since TCM ceased publication, it occurred to me that editing a book of many of the interviews found there, would be a valuable resource, since most of them were never published elsewhere. The priceless interviews and articles by composers of high stature such as Schoenberg, Varèse, Ives, Cage, Xenakis, Penderecki, Oliveros, Berio, Boulez, Carter, Crumb, Ligeti, Partch, Reich, and so many more, provide an extraordinary coverage of the birth, growth, and (to some degree) death of the 20th century avant-garde.

I am occasionally asked about my book *New Directions in Music*, with the question usually centering around someone whose work I describe there, Ichabod Angus Mackenzie. I. A. Mackenzie was a composer/sculptor who lived, at least when I knew him, in the small town of Angels Camp, California, along legendary Highway 49 in gold mining country. Mackenzie created musical sculptures, variations of wind chimes but much larger and more elegant, placing them in remote locations where humans would not ordinarily go. Like the adage 'Does a tree falling in the forest with no one around to hear actually make a sound?,' his work begged the question of both existing and not existing at the same time, along the same general lines of quantum theory and Schrödinger's cat. Since no one else writes much about Mackenzie, the question usually posed is whether or not he actually existed, or did I make him up.

My answer to that question typically relates the idea of how interesting Mackenzie would find this question. After all, the notion that he might not exist puts him in the same status as the tree in the forest, Schrödinger's cat, and his own instruments. If he didn't exist, how did his instruments get where they are? If we cannot find his instruments, did they exist in the first place? Or, if we cannot find any of his instruments, does it simply mean that we haven't looked hard enough. And on, and on. He would have certainly enjoyed this circular conundrum, for I knew him as a man of infinite jest. And his house, still standing alongside Highway 49, at least the last time I drove by there on the left going northward, and looking like the man himself — old, gnarled, and brimming with the curiosity of a thousand cats, and with, no doubt, a thousand lives as well.

I wish to also thank the following people for their contributions to this book:

> Mary Jane Cope (for her endless help with my editing)
>
> Zachary Myers (for his labors as joint editor)
>
> Tom Everett (his two contributions of 187-268)
>
> Andrew Brown (wonderful interview of Steve Reich)
>
> David Felder (interviews with Berio, Erb, and Penderecki)
>
> Halsey Stevens (interview with Arnold Schoenberg)
>
> Galen Wilson (interview with Pierre Boulez)
>
> and many, many others along the way.

David Cope

PREVIEW

The principal thing that started this collection of "hawks" was a letter from Wallingford Riegger, May 1932. This is now a desultory scrapbook (= 'memos' — not memoirs — no one but the President of a nice Bank or a Golf Club, or a dead Prime Minister, can write "memoirs"). Many of these things are of no interest to anyone but a stray and distant cousin or so — or to me — sometimes. When you get started putting things down (a good deal was dictated offhand and not looked over), one thing would come up from another thing — incidents that I or Mrs. Ives or someone of the family, or old friends, might remember or refer to — various family scrapbooks, old letters, programs, clippings, margins in old books, music and manuscripts, even a quotation over the wood house door. Some of the remarks may be rough, but they're the way I feel about things, right or wrong, and I don't apologize for them as such — only for the bad spelling, punctuation, et al.

This introduction is just put in, now and later, to be more polite — (the "memos" originally started with the letter on page 1) — that is, when I got W. R.'s letter, I naturally started to look around to collect things and found, over a letter to E. R. Schmitz, these remarks to an "old lady," a typical type. This and other similar remarks have a right to be — for the same reason it is right to throw a bottle at the umpire who closes his eyes and yells "Foul!" And then they all [have] a double use, in getting something off the chest and over the garden wall, where it may disturb a pansy.

Dear Sirs and Nice Ladies: — (This is not for publication, but anybody who can read can read it.) The following statement is made, not because it's important to anything or anybody, but because there are "lilies" taking money from newspapers and other things, whose ears and brains are somewhat emasculated from disuse. They have ears, because you can see them — they may have brains, but you can't see them (in anything they write). Every so often, an article or a clipping or a "verbal massage" is sent to a man (see name on dotted line), which shows that Rollo has a job, writing his opinion about the facts of which he doesn't know and doesn't try to know — or about music he doesn't hear or try to know. If he can't hear and doesn't know it, he's a mental-musico-defective (from his neck up) — if he doesn't try to hear and knows he doesn't know, then he is getting money under false pretenses! In other words, these commercial pansies are either stupid or they are liars (mean word, but put there after careful consideration). For instance, see the following letter written to E. R. Schmitz by C. E. Ives:

"West Redding, Conn., August 19th, 1931.

"My dear Mr. Schmitz:

"In writing you yesterday, I meant to have put in the enclosed. The Paris concerts given by Slonimsky were better received than I expected they would be; the only unfavorable comment which I saw was by a Prof. Prunières — it wasn't so unfavorable as unfair or weak-eared. He says that I know my Schoenberg — interesting information to me, as I have never heard nor seen a note of Schoenberg's music. Then he says that I haven't 'applied the lessons as well as I might.' This statement shows almost human intelligence. It's funny how many men, when they see another man put the 'breechin' under a horse's tail, wrong or right, think that he must be influenced by someone in Siberia of Neurasthenia. No one man invented the barber's itch.

"But one thing about the concerts that everyone felt was that Slonimsky was a great conductor. I will now say good-by. You have more to do than listen to a poem like this.

Sincerely, Chas. E. Ives"

Another instance: — a nice and dear old lady in Boston (with pants on, often) who sells his nice opinions about music and things to the newspaper and the paper to the public (see editorial entitled "Mr. Slonimsky in Paris"). In this editorial, there are two principal subjects of statements that need attention:

1) Hale is speaking of the modern American composers represented in the two Paris concerts. Eleven names were on these programs. He says they are influenced by — — — — (naming European composers etc. — see above article). I don't believe his statement is wholly true of any of the other ten composers, any more than it is of me or my music. But I'm speaking here of what I actually know of the facts, and what they have to do with his implied opinion (an opinion implying that he knows the facts underlying his opinion), and as far as I'm concerned the facts are as follows. All of the music that I have written, with the exception of a dozen or fifteen songs, was completed before I had seen or heard any of the music of European composers he cites as influencing all of the above American composers.

And besides this, it is interesting (and perhaps funny) to know that I (as I am concluded included in his sweeping statement) have been influenced by one Hindemith (a nice German boy) who really didn't start to compose until 1920 (according to an article [in] Modern Music, March-April 1928, page 18) and several years after I had completed all of my (good or bad) music, which Aunt Hale says is influenced by Hindemith. It happens that the music of mine on this particular program, *Three New England Places*, was completed and scored (for large orchestra) almost a decade before Hindemith started to become active as a composer.

In other words, the gist of Aunt Hale's remarks is that the music of one man was influenced by the music composed by another man ten years after the music so influenced was composed by the man who was influenced by the other man (or see Mark Twain's story about his nice funeral, or any other funny story). Now all this may have been quite all right if Rollo was paid as a humorist by the weak but snappy management of a nice magazine, which hires grave decorators to sell uninteresting premises made interesting to the disinterested.

Again, up to the present writing (August 1931), I have not seen or heard any of Hindemith's music.

2) Another inference given in this more or less sweeping statement (see same clipping) is that conductors of American orchestras do not like the music of modern American composers. To have this statement taken as even comparatively true would have to have for its basic premise that all these conductors agreeing with this statement had examined (and carefully enough to be able to play) the greater part of these eleven composers' music, or a large enough part of it, covering the different periods of their life and the varying types and forms of their music — enough to be fairly representative of their general ability as composers. (To this, I can only say, from my experience, that not enough conductors have seen enough of my music to be able to get even a good impression of how bad it is.)

I imagine that what I give as my actual experience is, to a great or some extent, true of some of the other composers. During the twenty years ending in 1919, only one conductor had seen any of my music. One (in 1910) did try over a part of a *First Symphony*, which was completed in college (1896). In the ten hears ending [in] 1929, two other conductors saw one score (and the same score) of mine — Mr. Schmitz asked me to send the *Three Places in New England* to Monteux, when he was with the Boston Symphony — and Mr. Eugene Goossens played one movement of the *Fourth Symphony* in 1927. In January 1929, New Music (Henry Cowell, Editor, San Francisco) published the score that Goossens played. In other words, in this thirty-year period, only four conductors, as far as I know, have seen any score of mine — and, with the exception of this one movement published in 1929, it is safe to say that at least 90 percent of my orchestral music has been seen by no conductor. Nicholas Slonimsky in 1929 saw the score *Three Places in New England*, and he is the only conductor (at present writing, August 1931) that has made any adequate and comprehensive study of my music for orchestra.

Take the above facts in detail, and then take the statement the old lady makes — and all a man can say is that she, Philip Nathen Hale, is either musically unintelligent or deliberately unfair. To say it quickly, he is either a fool or a crook.

Chas. E. Ives August 1931, March 1932.

1.

A CONVERSATION WITH ARNOLD SCHOENBERG
Halsey Stevens

The seventy-fifth birthday of Arnold Schoenberg occurred on September 12, 1949. To celebrate the occasion, the Los Angeles County Museum planned a concert of Schoenberg's music, to be given in a hall in which an exhibition of the composer's early paintings would be displayed.

Schoenberg had been drawn to the graphic arts, especially painting, in 1907. For a considerable number of years, he was closely associated with Kandinsky, Marc, and other painters of the German Expressionist movement, joining them in the Blaue Reiter group; and later on, when the celebrated Bauhaus moved to Dessau in 1925, he served — along with Albert Einstein, Gerhart Hauptmann, Adolf Busch, and others — as a board member of the Society of Friends of the Bauhaus. The first Blaue Reiter exhibition, held in Munich in the last half of December 1911, had a self-portrait of the composer, seen from the back, and two Visions.[1]

H. H. Stuckenschmidt says of Schoenberg's paintings, "Pushed on by the same daemonic compulsion as that governing his music, some extremely odd pictures resulted, visions of a fantasy world resembling that of Alfred Kubin: masks; a portrait of a woman; several self-portraits — one of them of his back."[2]

That Kandinsky considered Schoenberg seriously as a painter is shown by the chapter on the paintings he contributed to a symposium edited by Alban Berg in 1912. This was the same year Schoenberg composed Pierrot Lunaire, and one may assume a relationship between the point of view expressed in this epoch-making work and that of the visual Expressionism to which the composer had turned his interest.

While he intensified his exploration of new musical resources from this time on, establishing a full-fledged dodecaphonic technique in the mid-twenties, he continued nevertheless to paint for some years.

In the summer of 1949 I was beginning a series of intermission interviews, taped in advance and broadcast during the County Museum concerts by radio station KUSC at the University of Southern California. The first of these was with Schoenberg, and the recording took place in July in the composer's home in Brentwood, with Mrs. Schoenberg and Richard Hoffmann present. Schoenberg had been quite ill and received us in bathrobe and pajamas; but he was alert and cordial. Until we arrived he had apparently not been informed that his paintings were not to be shown: for some reason the exhibition could not be arranged, and the concert took place without visual accompaniment. This came as a surprise to Schoenberg, who was prepared to discuss his graphic work in preference to his music.

The tape of the interview has been preserved — the only one of the series still extant, so far as I know — and because of its peculiar interest it is transcribed below, verbatim. My own questions and comments have been somewhat edited, in the direction of compression.

H.S.: ". . . Mr. Schoenberg's music has stimulated a great deal of discussion and controversy. For the past several years[3] he has been living and teaching here in Southern California . . . It may not be generally known that Mr. Schoenberg is also a painter as well as a composer, and it is particularly appropriate, I think, to have his music performed in the atmosphere of a museum of art. Mr. Schoenberg, was it not originally intended to exhibit some of your paintings at the same time as the performance of the music?"

A.S.: "Yes, it is right. But I have to correct something: I was a painter, perhaps, but I am not any longer a painter. I didn't paint for many, many years — for at least two or three decades. But here still the whole afternoon I was under the impression that I will be asked about my paintings and have to speak about them. So, I have a little prepared about my capacity of improvisation.

"In thinking about this subject — or because all my ideas centered around this subject — so I planned to tell you what painting meant — means — to me. In fact, it was the same to me as making music. It was to me a way of expressing myself, of presenting emotions, ideas, and other feelings; and this is perhaps the way to understand these paintings — or not to understand them. They would probably have suffered the same fate as I have suffered; they would have been attacked and scolded and I don't know what else I should say: I mean, the same would happen to them what happened to my music. This, I mean, would (be) understood or not understood.

"In fact, as I said, I never was very capable of expressing my feelings or emotions in words. I don't know whether this is the cause why I did it in music and also why I did it in painting, or visa versa. That I had this (way[4]) as an outlet, I could renounce expressing something in words. Does this answer some of your questions?"

H.S.: "Yes, it does. But I wonder, Mr. Schoenberg, whether you encountered problems in painting similar to those you found in music, taking into consideration, of course, the complete difference in technical media."

A.S. "It's a very good question. I must answer that as a painter I was absolutely an amateur; I had no theoretical training and only a little aesthetic training, and this only from general education, but not from an education which pertained to painting. In music it was different. But I was also an — was it 'self-made'? — an autodidact. I had always had the opportunity to study them in quite a professional manner, so that my technical ability grew in the normal manner. That is the difference between my painting and my music."

H.S. "Suppose you had pursued the profession of a painter: you have already said that you would have expected the same sort of reception, the same sort of surprise and occasional condemnation that your music has received; but do you feel that your career as a painter might have paralleled that as a composer?"

A.S.: "Yes, I am sure it would have had. So, I must say, technically I possessed some ability, at this time at least, and I'm afraid that I have partly lost it. For instance, I had a good sense of relations, of space relations, of measurements. I was able to divide, let us say, a line rather correctly in three, four, five, six, seven, even eleven parts, and they were quite near the real division. And I also had a good sense of other such measurements, of many measurements. At this time, I was able to draw a circle which deviated very little from when you checked it with a compass. I could draw really very well, but I think I lost this capacity. But I had the idea that this sense of measurement, of measurements, is one of the capacities of a composer, of an artist. It is probably the basis of correct balance and logic within, if you have a strict feeling of sizes and their (word indistinguishable) relationship."

H.S.: "Certainly the feeling for relationship to which you refer is very important in music and has been demonstrated thoroughly in your own music. There is hardly any composer of importance now writing who has not been touched in some measure by the tonal explorations which you have conducted. I wonder if you feel that the techniques you have developed in musical composition will become more significant as time goes on."

A.S. "I think that one can — there is a possibility to learn something of my technical achievements. But I think it is even better to go back to those men from whom I learned them: I mean, to Mozart, Beethoven, Brahms, and Bach.[5] I can really — you can really tell that I owe very, very much to Mozart; and if one studies, for instance, my way in which I have for string quartet, then one cannot deny that I have learned this directly from Mozart. And I am proud of it!"

H.S.: "Then your advice to a young composer, Mr. Schoenberg, would be to base a foundation upon the same composers —"

A.S.: "Yes, yes, yes. Of course, you cannot imitate it directly; you have to take the essence and amalgamate your ideas with them and create something new."

H.S.: "It would be impractical, of course, to imitate any past style —"

A.S.: "No — yes — it's out, yes, yes."

H.S. "Unfortunately our time is about up, Mr. Schoenberg —"

A.S.: "Aha!"

H.S.: "Thank you for being with us on this first interview —"

A.S.: "I was afraid that I would speak too much!"

H.S.: "By no means; it has been a great pleasure and an honor to have you with us . . . "

At the close of the interview we stayed a few minutes to chat informally, but Schoenberg had grown visibly fatigued during the recording session, and we gathered up the recording equipment, and excused ourselves. It was the last time I saw Schoenberg, though he lived almost exactly two years longer, dying at his home on July 13, 1951. The exhibition of his paintings, postponed from the seventy-fifth anniversary celebration, never took place.

---

1. W. Grohmann: *Wassily Kandinsky, Life and Work*. New York: Henry H. Abrams, Inc., 1958. PP:66-67.

2. H. H. Stuckenschmidt: *Arnold Schoenberg*. Translated by Edith Temple Roberts and Humphrey Searle. New York: Grove Press, Inc., 1959. P. 35.

3. In 1934-35 he was on the faculty of the University of Southern California, occupying the Alchin Chair; from 1935 to his retirement in 1944 he taught at the University of California in Los Angeles.

4. The word is not clearly enunciated and cannot be certainly recognized.

5. It is especially interesting that Schoenberg did not name either Wagner or Mahler, from both of whom he must have learned a good deal.

2.

CHRONICLES OF A CAUSE: I. A. MACKENZIE
David Cope

I.M.: I am tired of criticism, of disparagement, of spitefulness of nihilism, in short. It is essential to condemn what must be condemned, but swiftly and firmly. On the other hand, one should praise at length what still deserves to be praised. All Art is good. Like the missionary, however, the creator more often than not must inflict his works on those bent on destroying not only the object, but the spirit. It is time for loving all things of Love, leaving to the gods among us the right to judge. Art is Love.

D.C.: Because many readers may not know of you and your work, could you possibly tell of your background and experience?

I.M.: I was born in the mid-west in 1894 and migrated to Northern California when I was seventeen. I worked at odd jobs (blacksmithing was my favorite) and even managed a year of college (mostly philosophy and metallurgy) before settling in San Francisco as a clock maker in 1921. During the next twenty years or so, I sat in on many music classes at area universities and began composing about 1925. [Camus, Albert. *The Artist and His Time: The Wager of Our Generation*. "Resistance, Rebellion and Death" (New York: Alfred A. Knopf 1961, p. 239)].

D.C.: Could you analyze your style of this period?

I.M.: Yes. Experimental, at least in the sense that no composer I then knew of was using the same materials. Basically, I was curious about the fundamental concept of whether I, or mankind for that matter, was really important in the functioning of music

D.C.: How did this realize itself in your music?

I.M.: Mostly in the area of performance. I still followed traditional notation, etc., but demanded less and less skill for the performer since it was not to be had anyway. I suppose my interest in inventing new instruments paralleled that of other composers of the time, though my preoccupation seemed to be with creating instruments which played themselves.

D.C.: Was this a reaction against bad performances?

I.M.: More a reaction against no performances.

D.C.: Was this due to your being relatively removed from the music world?

I.M.: Partly, I think. Musicians and composers, on the whole, are very "in-groupish." They seem to delight in creating codes and systems that will separate them more from the common man and, I'm afraid, their audiences.

D.C.: I take it, then, that your music was more not received than badly received.

I.M.: Both, but more of the former. I entered contests (composition) but soon found that I was becoming overjoyed if the judges even returned my scores — my hope of winning was soon destroyed. I discovered that, while contests may spur the one or two winners on to better things, they created ten times as many losers. That's a lousy percentage.

D.C.: Was publication possible?

I.M.: Out of the question. By 1927 my music had become so involved in new instruments of my own invention, the publisher would have had to publish the instrument with the music. By 1930, I abandoned the written music completely anyway, believing that I should be more interested in sound than codes.

D.C.: You mentioned that during this time you were studying in universities in the area. What was your and their reaction?

I.M.: My reaction was harsh (it continues so today, I might add). The teachers were very dull; more interested in talking about sound than in sound; mostly more interested in themselves. Many times I would hear visiting composers lecture on their works; afterwards I would struggle through the many young composers waving their flags and patting each other's backs, only to find that the lecturer was just flesh and blood, not a god (what a shock to find that Stravinsky goes to the bathroom, too). I found quickly that for me, at least, the university and its intellect and pomposity was creatively bankrupt: it offered nothing but security (both style and financial) and the same old traditional claptrap. The university, on the other hand, did not react to me at all. My job kept me from participating in the all-important but dull coffee sessions. Except for one professor calling me "a curious fellow," I am afraid I posed no threat to the "system."

D.C.: You sound as if, at this time, you were fairly disgusted with the music world around you.

I.M.: I was and still am. It offers no real solutions to problems, because it recognizes no real problems. As long as people continue to raise gods, not people, the situation won't change. As long as so-called "great" performers are regarded as towering musical figures, instead of rather grotesque finger gymnasts, the situation won't change. The university has contributed to this as well, creating a caste system. I am sure there are people who will read this and subject me to this idiocy: "Certainly Professor So-and-So must be a greater composer; why, Mackenzie hasn't even taken Theory I-A!"

D.C.: Certainly educational institutions have more recently become involved in experimentation.

I.M.: That's worse! There is no such thing as academic freedom; the words are contradictory. If you must achieve freedom (whatever freedom we can achieve) it will have to be outside of the institution, not within it by changing it. If I take the stripes from my zebra, I may get what I want, but it won't be a zebra anymore, etc., etc., ad nauseum.

D.C.: I take it then that you have never been interested in teaching.

I.M.: God, no. Plato was right. Truly there is only one teacher: oneself.

D.C.: Getting back to your composition: you say that around 1930 you began just creating instruments.

I.M.: Yes. But, more important, instruments without human performers. By 1934, early spring, I had created my first wind-sound sculpture.

D.C.: Would you define that?

I.M.: A wind-sound sculpture is simply a sculpture upon which wind creates sound.

D.C.: How did you come by this type of creation?

I.M.: Well, obviously it is not new. It is an elaboration of the old Chinese wind chimes that you can get in the 'Five-and-Dime;' in fact, that's where I got the idea: watching and listening to the soft and eternal ringing of the set of bells my parents owned when I was young. I used to listen to storms approach through their sound and somehow felt I was "tuning in" on nature (nature being something I have always felt to be more impressive and profound than man or myself, to be exact).

D.C.: How large was your first such work, how much time did it take to construct it, and what materials did you use?

I.M.: About eight feet square. Two and a half years. Metal and gut. I soon found, however, that gut rotted and metal rusted (I've had to completely reconstruct that first one). I now use aluminum and non-corrosive wire.

D.C.: What was the reaction to your work?

I.M.: Very little. A composer friend was mostly concerned about what to call me. "Certainly not a composer," said he. He figured me as an artist or sculptor and a bad one at that.

D.C.: What do you consider yourself?

I.M.: I don't. Categorizing, defining and such limit creativity. Like a postman, he discovered that my box didn't have a number on it. He of course chose a number for me: Artist! Sculptor! A number which would represent the least amount of threat to his neat pseudo-mind. Such minds, again, would rather avoid problems than seek real answers. Whether one thing is a work of art, and another not, is unimportant. This is cataloguing, not problem-solving. Problems are: God, beauty, nature; creating with or without them, or to them or from them. Creating is solving; cataloguing is avoiding.

D.C.: You have mentioned your dislike of systems and codes. Would you....

I.M.: In themselves, I don't dislike systems or codes any more than money; but, as before, if these are used by someone to catalogue their own or someone else's work, they have become destructive rather than helpful.

D.C.: You use these then in your own works?

I.M.: I don't know. Consciously, I create what I like, in hopes that God, nature, and people (in that order) may like some or all of them.

D.C.: As you can see, I made a sketch from one of your sketches (to include in the magazine) of one of your wind-sound sculptures.

I.M.: Yours is more of a drawing of my sketch.

D.C.: You're cataloguing.

I.M.: Defining.

D.C.: Anyway, was this sketch ever realized?

I.M.: My sketches are, I suppose, my musical notation. However, they are different in one respect: when I create the work, I let it go its own way, and I sort of follow along. Problems of balance and so forth are worked out as I go along; intonation is achieved through experimentation until I have what I want. To answer your question, yes, I made the sculpture from that sketch; no, you wouldn't even slightly recognize it as being a result of that sketch.

D.C.: Obviously, you are in control of some aspects of the resultant sound and in less control of others.

I.M.: Yes. I am in complete control of pitch, timbre and, hopefully, length.

D.C.: Hopefully?

I.M.: Well, I hope the sculpture will last forever, though forever is a long time (I think).

D.C.: How do you regard the partially controlled aspects?

I.M.: With joy. Certainly rhythm is partially controlled (by controlling weight and so forth, I can determine the amount of wind necessary to move a certain part of the instrument to create sound, and by gradation of sizes, I can at least control some of the rhythmic possibilities), and the same with harmony and melody, which are the least controlled.

D.C.: Does it disturb you when, leaving the instrument alone, it is performing without human audience?

I.M.: Human audience? That's up to humans. It's never without an audience.

D.C.: What other types of creating have you done?

I.M.: All related to this: light-sound sculpture, water-sound sculpture, fire-sound sculpture, among others. With each one, the first word defines the material used as performer to create sound on the instrument.

D.C.: How many sound sculptures have you accomplished over these last forty years?

I.M.: Fifty-three wind-sound sculptures and three to seven of each of the others.

D.C.: Where are they located now?

I.M.: Mostly in the back yards of friends, some of the very small ones inside homes, a couple with businesses, and I still have ten or twelve around my home here, as you can see.

D.C.: And all these years you have avoided traditional notation?

I.M.: Not avoided! That implies negation. No, I have been moving toward something, not away from something. I have never maintained that I am right or even important; I am just doing what I think I can do best (best in a personal sense, not best in relation to others, necessarily). In itself, my work is no better or worse than anything traditional; it's just different. It is, however, too bad that many people never have had the chance to find out about it — for their sakes, not mine. You see, I have learned two very important things about sound: 1) it exists, period. No more, no less. There is no good or bad except in individual terms. (One can say Michelangelo worked longer and harder on the Sistine Chapel, and with more intellectual prowess perhaps, but it is still no better or worse than the sound of a nightingale, except in individual terms.) Like and dislike go in cycles; today I like what tomorrow I may dislike; round and round, going nowhere); and 2) music (sound) communicates nothing. If I were to define (not categorize) Art, I would have to say it is that which communicates nothing. Rather, it incites or creates something new in each of us (I can say "Hello" and you can reply "Hello." This is communication, bad as it is, but it is not Art. Art's beauty and importance is that it does not communicate!).

I was asked once if I felt my 'music' had any value. I answered, "No." "Then why do you compose it?" I was asked. "Then why do you ask?" I replied.

D.C.: Certainly with the advent of recent trends in avant-garde music, your sculptures will possibly achieve more fame and importance.

I.M.: I don't care. The 'avant-garde' is just as corrupt and cliche-ridden as the traditional. I am very old and very tired and too set in my ways to worry one way or the other.

D.C.: Does electronic music interest you?

I.M.: Sounds hold an interest for me; I don't give a damn how one produces them. If you mean composing it, no. It's far too late for that. However, even if I were younger, I doubt I would be interested. The fascination of a storm coming or a bird singing is too much, I'm afraid.

D.C.: What does the "I.A." stand for?

I.M.: The "I" is Ichabod; the "A" . . . well . . . I don't think I'll tell you.

D.C.: No?

I.M.: It's a type of bull, anyway.

D.C.: What does the future hold for you?

I.M.: More work. Death. Obscurity. One last thing: if one should consider the nightingale and its music and inspect closely the battery of technique in use, he might reconsider his own bloated self-view: certainly music is sound (the existence of the former term owes to social implications only) and man, or even his life, has contributed little enough to expand its vocabulary.

Author's Note: This interview was conducted on December 28, 1968. On March 3, 1969, word was received that Ichabod Angus MacKenzie had died of a heart attack at age 75, two days after his birthday. His works are presently held by his grandnephew, George Andrews of New York City.

"Consequently, I strive to forget, I walk in our cities of iron and fire, I smile bravely at the night, I hail the storms, I shall be faithful. I have forgotten, in truth: active and deaf, henceforth. But perhaps someday, when we are ready to die of exhaustion and ignorance, I shall be able to disown our garish tombs and go and stretch out in the valley, under the same light, and learn for the last time what I know."

3.

HENRY COWELL
Theldon Myers

"It is a sign of health that we in America also have our radicals in the persons of George Antheil, Roger Sessions, Henry Cowell . . . but Cowell is essentially an inventor, not a composer." This was Aaron Copland's observation of the musical contributions of Henry Cowell in his article "America's Young Men of Promise" which appeared in the March-April 1926 issue of Modern Music.

In "America's Young Men - Ten Years Later" (Modern Music, May 1936) Copland states: "Cowell remains the incorrigible 'experimenter' of the twenties." A more recent publication expounds ". . . This Californian allowed enthusiasm to out-run discretion so that his fame depends, rather doubtfully, on his use on the pianoforte of forearm and fist. The harmonic results have been described as chords of the dominant with appoggiaturas . . . Cowell has essayed most styles, without, however, finding one of his own. He has probed the rhythmic extremes . . ., has tried the Honegger-mechanical . . . (and) the pure and immaculate. He is an experimenter."

Certainly a musician who spent a lifetime of obviously tireless and super-energetic activity in the creation of hundreds of compositions ranging from piano pieces through symphony and opera, authored books and scholarly articles, edited a music quarterly, delivered lectures or taught courses at institutes, conservatories, music societies and universities on an international basis, has played piano recitals of his piano music (often sponsored by musical 'greats') in the principal cities of the world, and in general has campaigned unceasingly for the cause of modern music cannot be dismissed simply as 'a revolutionary' or as an 'experimenter.'

It appears that the earliest critics of Cowell's music mistook what was actually the serious presentation of an innate talent and sensitive musician as the show-off antics of a young radical seeking attention by the most outlandish means. Many of his recitals during this period were accompanied by riots or near-riots, sometimes calling for police intervention, with a concert in Havana effecting the assigning of a bodyguard to protect Cowell from possible adverse audience reaction.

These 'outrageous' performances were not so much created by the material presented, which was unconventional to be sure, but more by the extremely unconventional techniques used in the performance of his piano works. This, of course, was his 'shocking' inventiveness of playing inside the piano rather than on the keys in which he used pizzicato, stopped strings, harmonics, muted strings and glissando effects in such works as *The Aeolian Harp* (1923) and later in *The Banshee* (1925) and *Sinister Resonance* (1930).

Time has proved, however, that these were not just startling innovations by an overly-enthusiastic young composer, as Cowell persisted with his experiments and his inquiring mind was constantly seeking new musical means. Many of the techniques introduced in his piano pieces have become part of his orchestral language and devices such as the secundal harmony derived from the tone-cluster can be found throughout his works.

Cowell is often referred to as an autodidact, but this is true only in that he had done rather extensive composing before he sought his first formal training at the age of sixteen. He began private musical studies with Charles Seeger, then head of the music department at the University of California at Berkeley, because his lack of a formal elementary or high-school education kept him from matriculating as a regular student. Seeger arranged that young Cowell be allowed to do theoretical studies with E.G. Strickland at the University and receive instruction in counterpoint with Wallace Sabin, a local organist. Also, regular meetings with Seeger to discuss new ideas and formulate a plan of disciplined study were included.

Cowell seems to have based his life's work on suggestions brought out at his sessions with Seeger, as it was decided that the young composer must always work out intelligently and scientifically a valid set of rules to be substituted for any established rules he wished to break and also that as an innovator he would be responsible for creating compositions which employed his innovations.

Cowell felt that many of the compositional devices he at first employed instinctively could be justified acoustically and scientifically, and in the introduction of his book New Musical Resources explains: "My interest in the theory underlying new materials came about at first through wishing to explain to myself, as well as to others, why certain materials I felt compelled to use in composition, and which I instinctively felt to be legitimate, have genuine scientific and logical foundation. I therefore made an investigation into the laws of acoustics as applied to musical materials. Some of the results of the investigation convinced me that although my music itself preceded the knowledge of its theoretical explanation, there had been enough unconscious perception so that the means used were . . . in accordance with acoustical law."

His compositions date from 1908, and in these early works can be found the lack of prejudice concerning the incorporation of musical materials from a variety of cultures that was to be his trademark and the cause of much severe criticism of his efforts. It has also resulted in statements categorizing him as an eclectic and a composer without style.

Cowell's early life in the San Francisco area had exposed him to such diverse sounds as the Chinese opera, Gregorian Chant, honky-tonk pianos, street musicians, etc. He did have a few years of training on the violin, but not enough formal study to make him suppose that any or all of his aural experiences were not valid or suitable as sources of inspiration for his own pieces.

Such statements by Cowell as, "I do not see at all why a composer's choice should be limited to the musical materials used in Europe for the past three hundred years alone. What interests me is music itself as organized sound, its forms and all the possibilities of a musical idea; to write as beautifully, as warmly, and as interestingly as I can," and "You know, I've done a lot of new things, not just to do something new, but because I imagined that that was the way to find out about music," help to dispel the idea that this man was perhaps impetuous in his musical creations and too easily influenced by external stimuli.

Rather, he used his experiments as a means of giving aesthetic as well as scientific justifications for his attempts at fusion of elements and style, and in the preface to his *United Quartet* (1936), an extremely modal and diatonic work resulting from experiments with various folk musics, he writes: "The quartet should be . . . understood equally well by Americans, Europeans, Orientals, or higher primitives; or by anybody from a coal miner to a bank president . . . The work is original in spite of its simplicity, because the simplicity is drawn from the whole world . . . There are in it elements from every place and period."

The composition accordingly is one attempt to express his concept that music is a single world-wide art which uses the same basic elements everywhere but which has developed these elements to various degrees or has used them in combination differently. He suggests: "Another kind of 'internationalism' seems possible to me (other than twelve-tone) . . . in which musical materials developed in a single culture are carried beyond the customs of that culture according to a logic inherent in the basic materials themselves. In this way a given kind of musical treatment is extended, instead of being eliminated because its purely nationalistic aspects are limited."

In the early 1940s Cowell found in the three-part modal folk hymns of William Walker's shaped-note collection a 'primitive' quality that he seized upon and sought to develop into twentieth century music. He decided to combine this modal style of ballad-like tunes, which were used as hymns in the southern United States, with the fuguing tune idea associated with Billings and other colonial American composers, into what has been described as a highly successful neo-Baroque form. He felt that his hymn-and-fuguing-tune form is especially valuable because it is an almost universally used design (slow-fast), because it presents musical material originating in the British Isles undergoing development up to the present time by way of rural American hymnody and also because the use of imitation in music is so widespread and has such roots in the past.

Separate works in this form are found for various instruments and combinations throughout the Cowell catalog, and although not indicated as such, the hymn-and-fuguing-tune design has been employed in some of his larger works and can be found as the first or last movement in several of his symphonies, the *Violin Sonata* and the *Fifth String Quartet*.

Comparative musicology was a strong interest of Cowell and he spent an equivalent amount of time in the formal pursuit of knowledge regarding the music of other cultures with that spent in his theoretical studies in the traditions of Western music (about a decade, including work with Woodman, Ruggles, and Goetschius in New York). His interest in this area of music seems to stem primarily from his search for a musical 'internationalism' and led him to study with the outstanding Oriental musicologists in Berlin (a Guggenheim Fellowship in 1931), New York, and California. He also spent 1956 and 1957 in Asia on a Rockefeller grant for the purpose of learning first-hand the music of several Eastern cultures. This time was spent at the Academy of Music in Madras, India, in observing the Japanese Imperial Orchestra and in the study of folk tunes, and dances in Teheran, Iran. In the early 1960s he made an official trip to Iceland for folk music study purposes.

Attempts to explain why he used such a variety of forms, styles, and techniques (in many instances in the same work, or even in the same movement) invariably refer to Cowell's personality, which seemed to be completely incapable of rejecting any musical stimulus which happened to catch his fancy: the *Symphony No. 13* (1957-58, Madras Symphony) uses ragas, talas, jalatarang, and tablas as well as Western adaptations of Indian stringed instrument techniques; *Ongaku* (1957) presents sounds involving quarter-tone and third-tone effects played in the Japanese Imperial Orchestra; the *Persian Set* (1956-57) uses mixed East-West instruments; the *Symphony No. 16* (1962 Icelandic Symphony) resulted from his absorption with the music of that land.

In composing these works of foreign cultural influence Cowell was careful never to make use of authentic themes from the culture, but creates his own material which he likes to think of as a Westerner's interpretation of the spirit, style, and techniques of the culture represented. This holds true not only in his works of Eastern inspiration, but also in those of Celtic tradition, which include some of his most popular compositions. The Irish songs and stories that he heard from his father are never quoted or described; rather, the aura of their qualities are presented (an ability rather uniquely Cowell's), as in the case with the spirit of the jig being the substance of the Cowell *Scherzo*.

For sheer impressiveness of numbers, the Cowell catalog would be difficult to duplicate. To call him a prolific composer would probably be gross understatement; he produced works for most conceivable combinations of voices and instruments, with dissatisfaction of a certain composition resulting in a new creation rather than a revision of the old (often a miniature in a certain style or one based on a timely idea becoming the generative force or included in some other manner in a larger work).

Cowell's experiments sometimes resulted in innovations in musical notation such as his tone-cluster indication which was developed before 1920. Pieces calling for physical contact with the piano strings used notations involving letters coded to a list of directions.

The type of rhythmic complexity incorporated in *Fabric* (1917) resulted from theories and studies presented in New Musical Resources which deal essentially with the ". . . relationship of rhythm to sound-vibration and, through this relationship and the application of overtone ratios, the building of ordered systems of harmony and counterpoint in rhythm, which have an exact relationship to tonal harmony and counterpoint. Notation for works in this vein include differently shaped notes indicating the basic number of tones to be played by each voice within a measure. He purposes "that all . . . irregular time values be called by their correct names according to the part of a whole note they occupy," and then presents the 'third note series' of triangular shaped notes, 'fifth note series' of square notes, etc.

The problems arising from attempted performances of complicated rhythmic studies such as *Fabric* led Cowell to collaborate with Leon Theremin on the invention of an instrument which they called the rhythmicon. This device was able to accurately produce all relatively impossible rhythmic combinations such as four against three or nine against five. For demonstration of the rhythmicon Cowell composed a four movement suite, *Rhythmicana,* and another composition which called for rhythmicon accompaniment to a set of movements for violin. This instrument had some general acceptance and proved of value in the training of musicians and dancers.

Until more recently critics have been baffled in attempts to categorize works of Cowell because his compositions do not group themselves neatly into periods or styles. Weisgall observes that ". . . what may seem at first a great diversity of musical impulses . . . is . . . the product of a single personality. There is a perceptible consistency in the choice of musical materials, and within a recognizable range there is an equal consistency in the handling of these materials."

And while it is impossible to find a length of time in which Cowell devoted his energies to a single influence in his creativity, two main currents may be traced in his music. The one is a recurrent use of chromatic dissonant techniques often used polyphonically, and the other presents these two basic ingredients of the Cowell style more simply as the first being scientific and technical and the other being subtly simple to the point of naïveté.

Again, Weisgall's study is helpful in that it establishes some sort of chronological sequence to these trends of techniques; 1919 to 1931 finds use with increasing intensity of the dissonant chromaticism and rhythmic concepts that Cowell had presented in New Musical Resources; the mid-thirties to the late-forties shows an adaption of modal material (Eastern and Western); from about 1950 these two 'styles' are found usually combined, however, not in the same manner twice.

Works representing outstanding achievement in these various 'periods' deserve mention. *What's This?* and *Dynamic Motion* (both 1913) are short piano works that utilize his early experiments with 'string piano' and employ dissonant chromaticism and his then new rhythmic approach. Larger and longer works in this vein followed with *Sinfonietta* for Chamber Orchestra (1924), *Synchrony* for large orchestra (1929-30), culminating with the *Piano Concerto* (1930).

Compositions of Cowell's modal period include those which are his most appealing and popular — a fact generally attributed in part to his great use of quasi-folk material during these years. These include the *American Country Set* for orchestra (1937), *Toccanta* (1938) for flute, 'cello, piano, and *Soprano Voice* (1938) and *Celtic Set* (1941).

Cowell was one of the pioneers in the creation of original compositions for band and two of the works from this 'middle' period *Schoonthree* (1933) and *Animal Magic* (1944) are fine presentations for this medium. The latter piece is an exception to his rule of not quoting folk material, as the three note motif on which the piece is based is actually an Eskimo tune from Greenland. *How Old Is Song* (1942), the *Violin Sonata* (1945), the *Fourth Symphony* (1945), and the *Fifth Symphony* (1948) are notable compositions which bring this phase of his creativity to a close. It is of interest to note that Weisgall finds many of the longer works of this period "aggressively redundant" in spots and in some instances the final movements fail to build to the expected tension before their close.

What can be considered as Cowell's third period produced the majority of his symphonies beginning with the *Sixth* (1950). It also includes the *Septet* (1955) and the *Thanksgiving Psalm* (1956).

Cowell was an inveterate champion of American composers and their music, and during the thirties his activities in this and related areas were observed by Paul Rosenfeld: "His activities include . . . perseverance as a composer, a pianist, an editor of new music, both in score and in record form, a promoter of performances of music, a director of musical activities, a lecturer, an author, a teacher, a musicologist, and . . . inventor. Wherever in his steady whirl he has set foot on the earth...concerts have sprung up, like flowers about the feet of Flora, and they invariably included performances of the works of the leading American moderns. And he has got these revolutionary scores not only played but printed and recorded as well. And he has been writing about this music and getting his articles published. He has indeed become very influential." Some of his enterprises and projects referred to in the above are the New Music, a quarterly for the publication of modern compositions and articles of which Cowell was the owner-editor and which was initiated in 1927, the New Music Orchestra Series, established in 1932 for the publication of new works, the New Music Quarterly Recordings, originating in 1934, issued recordings of many new works, the symposium American Composers on American Music, edited by Cowell and first published by Stanford University in 1933, and the more recent Charles Ives and His Music (1955) (in collaboration with his wife, Sydney Robertson Cowell), a study which helped greatly in bringing recognition to this outstanding creative spirit. His musical theories presented in New Musical Resources (written in 1919) have been mentioned previously.

It must be noted that none of these activities was for the purpose of his own gain. Rosenfeld presents an insightful statement: ". . . Indeed there is something almost saintlike in this activity. Cowell is after all quite disinterested. He has always been, and he remains a poor man. What little money he has derived from his concerts, his symposiums, his critical articles, has immediately been reinvested by him in new concerts, new symposiums, new musical publications and recordings. He doesn't even push his own work forward at his recitals . . . nor does he ever print or record his own work."

Other related activities of the 'saintlike' bustle include his being at one time or another on the faculties of the University of California, Stanford, Bennington, Mills College, Columbia, The New School, Adelphi College, and the Peabody Conservatory. He was director of musical activities at the New School for Social Research where he established the first composer's forum and organized concerts of modern music. He was an official or member of such groups as the New Music Society of California, the Pan-American Association of Composers, the International Composers Guild, the National Institute of Arts and Letters, and the International Society for Contemporary Music to mention a few.

One of his activities that had considerable influence on the trend of contemporary composition was the west coast experiments with percussion orchestra which were followed enthusiastically by the younger composers John Cage, Ray Green, and Gerald Strang.

Surely Cowell's experiments and theories have had a decided effect on contemporary music and some of his works may become standard repertoire because of their intrinsic musical value. But he will perhaps be best remembered by future generations for his wholehearted support of modern music at a time when young American composers most needed a helping hand in establishing a place in the world culture for their relatively new creative ventures.

4.

AN INTERVIEW WITH PIERRE BOULEZ: FEBRUARY, 1969
Galen Wilson and David Cope

G.W.: In an article in Contemporary Composers on Contemporary Music, Milton Babbitt suggests that the composer is a specialist; that there are levels of music appreciation, and we recognize now that some people are not at the level of the contemporary composer. We no longer have to worry about the crowd, the common man. We have our own audience, which may consist of other composers and close friends, very much like the medical researcher who works in his laboratory for his own little crowd. Do you agree with this outlook?

P.B.: No, I don't agree with that, because the invention of music had nothing to do with the invention of science or medicine. Medicine is a specialty to be shared by only a few, because most do not have that special knowledge. Science is one thing and expression is another. They can have links, of course, but they are not of the same nature.

I think that since the beginning, you can very often find extrovert and introvert works in the same composer. If you take Beethoven, for example, the last quartets will never be as popular as the Ninth Symphony. The Ninth Symphony is consciously extrovert; on the contrary, the last quartets tend to be like a diary of himself searching ideas. I think in the life of a composer there are always these two tendencies, not for an audience of specialists, but for himself. He tends to glorify his own thoughts and put them in a kind of musical research. After he grasps something, maybe he wants to enlarge the possibilities and not feel so constricted by the technical medium and compose a work which is more extrovert, more towards pure expression.

There is always for me a mirroring between the two things the technical more than the scientific: to confuse science and music is really very bad for science.

First, science is so far in advance of music in the process of thinking, and on a different track. It is impossible to have them on the same track; it would be a pseudo-track, something which is not real, pure idealism. Science as its purpose has its own kind of imagination. Scientists have an extremely sharp and amazing imagination, but this is not at all the same type of imagination of men who express themselves through music or painting. Therefore I think to make scientific purpose the same as musical purpose is to parody science and not do it justice.

To make science practical and then apply it to music (applied science) is not, I find, necessary for me at all. I myself studied science when I was younger and find now that musical imagination is on a completely different wavelength. I like scientific vocabulary, but that is the wrong type of security. Musical imagination does not have this type of security that people like to have from science; they have the "impression." Many composers feel that if they apply certain scientific vocabulary (there are very many fakes; however, Babbitt's knowledge is reliable), a certain scientific environment to their music and writings, they achieve security. They think they are safe; they no longer have to work in the insecurity of musical invention.

I want that uncertainty. I find it necessary to discover my own way of imagination. One must find his own way and not rely on some analogies. It is much more difficult to find something which is not shaped after this or after that which gives a kind of security, but you must invent. I have not found aesthetics in computers yet; these aesthetics cannot be reduced to any scientific formula. Aesthetics in any form of expression escape any kind of definition. One must not be blind to this. One cannot keep away from aesthetics through some kind of scientific blanket.

D.C.: You are defending, in a way, live performance?

P.B.: No, I am not defending especially. I am not against electronic music. I just say, at the moment, that there are no aesthetics about the sounds. They have picked up the scientific ways in which a sound can be made, but who knows , for instance, if this sound will be musically good? Who can tell you that? That is exactly the point for me. I have read an analysis by one of Babbitt's students of the Schoenberg *Fantasy for Violin and Piano*. The analysis was good and everything there, but at the end the main question was not answered: Is this Fantasy good or not? Here is where they are blind because they refuse to answer the main question, the aesthetic point of view.

D.C.: It seems that, particularly in America, most composers are working in colleges and universities as teachers, and therefore already in an academic environment.

P.B.: Yes, academic, and in the strong sense of the word. It does not matter whether the academic is after Schumann, after Bach, after Wagner, or after a new serial type; the academic is something which I cannot accept at any time. The main problem, to my mind, is to find a purely musical way of thinking and not something which is parascientific. I don't mean to say that instinct is the only way. There are always musical techniques, but these must be thought of by themselves and not always by comparison. One must have a genuinely original way, and not always derived. Mathematics derives, but it is wrong to say that because they do it we should do it as well. After all the analysis, you still have to go to the main question: Is this work valuable or not? And for what reasons? And there you get no answers at all because these analysts are unable to give you answers.

D.C.: You were speaking a moment ago about Babbitt and science. Would this also be true of, say Karlheinz Stockhausen?

P.B.: No, it would not. For him it would just be on the side. Living in America, one of our only sources about structure and composition technique has been in Die Reihe, and what we read in Die Reihe is analysis.

But you can see my name only twice in Die Reihe, and only one article. I disagree with this pseudoscientific information and I was away from it after the very first days, as I don't like this type of caricature.

G.W.: Would you care to comment on Ligeti's analysis of your *Structures*? It seems so mathematical.

P.B.: This work was a kind of automatic relationship to be tried just to see how far one can go with the automation of language. They did not analyze the other two pieces because these were beyond their possibilities and were not based on the same principles. One must not isolate these pieces. This was just a border of a system for me.

D.C.: Recording seems to be the main source of disseminating music of Europe in America and vice versa; this would give a very small and prejudiced view of the differences and similarities of contemporary music here and abroad. Is there now still a nationalism, not of country but of continent?

P.B.: I am sure that there is. I am not very involved in it, but I am sure there is an idiotic form of nationalism still present. I arranged for Babbitt to visit Darmstadt, and it was probably a waste of time for him because nobody would accept his ideas and, of course, there was a great difficulty with language. He is difficult to understand even with a solid grasp of English, but with the little understanding of the students it probably brought more misunderstanding than was present before. When American composers come to Europe they feel that they are neglected and not taken seriously. They feel that European musicians know only the American iconoclasts who they feel are not at all important. Europeans who come to America feel that at the universities they are just a drop of water in the middle of the ocean. That is the misunderstanding. The musical life of Europe and America is quite different. Here there is a lot of teaching and university activity; most of the composing is done in the university life, which is absolutely not the case in Europe. Universities there have very little to do with contemporary music. The composers work from commissions and small jobs, etc.

D.C.: There are a great many musical pessimists who believe that live performance is dead, both because of the vast dissemination of recordings and the advent of tape music. Is the "music audience" dead and/or dying?

P.B.: Audiences are not dying, they are only uncertain of the future.

In America you have the type of musical culture which does not encourage people to come. If you want live musical organizations you have to build up your musical culture in another way. We have those audiences who go to reminisce over their youth, and not for the music itself. It will bring them their youth again. Young people are not interested at all by this type of establishment.

I think a great deal could be accomplished by having professional musicians have regular explorations into contemporary music. In America, the musical life is still run by the academic life for the most part, and therefore stiff, while in Europe the cultural life is run by the city or state where you know you waste money, so that it doesn't matter so much. Here they care about the wasting of money. If you give money to taxes for state or city as in Europe, you already know that it is wasted and you don't care, whereas here, if you give a large sum of money for culture you care in what way it is spent.

Here you also have the still stronger reaction by certain people who just refuse to mix themselves with the 'official' musical life, because they think that it is hopeless and they are not strong enough to change it, so they escape it in small circles where they are accepted. In New York, for example, you can always find 300 to 500 people who will come to anything. This is not convincing. Avant garde composers are laughing about those specialists who only go to hear Baroque music, but they are exactly the same, because they are composing for the same type of specialized audience, but on the other side. You don't fight them, because you know that you have your 300 to 500 people, and that these people are for you before you begin. They may be disappointed in you, but not against you. These are the "in" groups isolating themselves into these ghettos. What happens in the ghetto doesn't come out of the ghetto. When they are sure of a certain response when they allow themselves to do anything, and they no longer have discipline or control of themselves.

There is much more of a future if you try to fight this situation which is frozen. It is much more important to take a certain work (even through pedagogic steps) which is not accepted by, say, three thousand people, to performance rather than let them once more hear Brahms, etc. and the 200 hear their contemporary music, etc. I want to shock them out of their nests. If you are hunting, you can wait a lifetime for your prey, but if you want to get them, you must go to their nests and flush them out. That is the reason for giving concerts. These nests are nothing more than new versions of salon music.

G.W.: Is this what you were trying to do with Domaine Musicale?

P.B.: With Domaine I tried to do this on a very narrow basis, but that was fifteen years ago. I started with 200 people but it grew to 2000. But I did not continue because I didn't think that that is the right way to go about it now.

D.C.: Why do contemporary composers dislike each other so much? Is it ideas or personalities? One particular comment I would like your reaction to is this quote from Morton Feldman in an interview with Robert Ashley: "There is only a total insecurity because people don't know who they want to be. This is not only true of the young people. This is true of Boulez. This is true of Stockhausen. You can see this in the way they have approached American 'chance' music. They began by finding rationalizations for how they could incorporate chance and still keep their precious integrity."

P.B.: I have no reaction except that this is certainly a part of this American nationalism of which we were speaking earlier. American composers, of this type especially, are very bitter about Stockhausen and me because we are in both places, Europe and America. They are not the same way. I have done my best to perform American works in Europe, and I am not responsible if there is no response here. I cannot think that Mr. Feldman is a very first class American composer; he has to do it by himself. You don't gain in personality by attacking other personalities. You must give your personality first. Just saying the others are nothing does not make you something; in fact, it brings you still further down.

G.W.: Feldman refers to "chance" here. Do you feel that you conceive of "chance" in the same way that, say, John Cage conceives of it?

P.B.: No, not at all. I find that so highly unproductive, because "chance" is not an aesthetic category. "Chance" can bring something interesting only one time in a million and that is not interesting to me at all. Most of the time you do not get that one time which would be interesting, and, if you do get it, you get it in the midst of a hundred thousand possibilities which are not interesting.

G.W.: Going to a "chance" concert, then, you feel it would be like going to a baseball game, gambling for excitement?

P.B.: Yes, but even a baseball game has rules. Card games, which have much more chance, I suppose, still have rules. Can you imagine a card game with absolutely no rules?

D.C.: Like Mallarme saying, "A throw of the dice will not abolish chance," which you have been quoted as saying that, "While nothing can be totally chance, nothing can be totally without chance." (Schwartz, Elliott, and Barney Childs, eds, *Contemporary Composers on Contemporary Music*. New York. Holt, Rinehart and Winston. C. 1967. p. 3)

P.B.: Exactly. With the combination of the two, you must integrate, and it is much more difficult to compose in this way, integrating on a high level than in more traditional ways. Composing by chance is not composing at all. Composing, even from the entomological, means to put things together. I am interested as to what chance sounds occur on the street, but I will never take them as a musical composition. There is a big difference between unorganized sounds and those placed within complete organization.

D.C.: Many composers today seem to feel that they are being left behind, with so many new concepts and techniques. Do you feel that there is "progress" in music?

P.B.: No. That is like fashion, and composition has nothing to do with fashion. They make styles for the winter season, the spring season, etc., and these tricks are dried up in one year. Then it is finished. You cannot think of music in these very coarse and fashionable terms. Even the term "old-fashioned" fails here. I don't care whether I'm "in" or "out!" or "old" or "new," and I have no sense or care for fashion.

G.W.: The young composer is in search of an audience. He sees one group getting an audience and possibly he goes where that audience is.

P.B.: Many times, due to university requirements for students, the young composer is faced with a "forced" audience, required attendance. Which is worse? These are college games, and no longer composition.

D.C.: You once said: 'It is not deviltry, but only the most ordinary common sense which makes me say that, since the discovery made by the Viennese, all composition other than twelve-tone is useless. Would you explain this?

P.B.: Yes. If you want to go through historical processes, you must go through a process, and if you do not go through the process of the Viennese composers, you have absolutely nothing to say. These tricks we were referring to before, this pure junk, most of the time has absolutely no dialectic, no rhetoric, and no vocabulary. These composers have no experience in what articulate vocabulary is. They reject it because they are unable to use it. If you do not go through their mental processes which existed then, I cannot see your necessity of composing. Even with more advanced media, I don't see the necessity of composing. If you want to use noises with instruments, or electronic sounds, it's nothing new, first of all, and nothing modern, second, as long as there is really no dialectic which organizes it with a type of dimension which is not just a pure accumulation of things.

D.C.: You do not feel, then, that twelve-tone construction is a fashion?

P.B.: No. Twelve-tone is not a fashion. One cannot stay on the twelve-tone construction, but it is not just a fashion. That is why I find so many analyses of twelve-tone music a waste of time.

It's like old ladies who make lace. But I have found that if you have not gone through this experience of twelve-tone writing, and tried to enlarge upon it and go forward, you can fall into these traps of "chance" and the parascientific. These latter are mythologies, ways of escaping the real center, the real way of searching the problems. We have a story about a fox who is looking at grapes and, being unable to reach them, he says they are sour. It is the same with these composers of fashion music. They also say they are free. What is freedom? It does not interest me at all.

D.C.: What American composers that are living today do you feel represent an honest approach in your terms?

P.B.: In the older generation, Elliott Carter. I find also that Milton Babbitt has an honest approach, but too esoteric in my opinion. Imagination is another question; you can be honest but not imaginative. The point, I think, is to have in reserve a technical background and at the same time to invent something. Inventing without the background is not the same. It reminds me of what one says of some of the underdeveloped countries in Asia that went from the donkey to the jet age: "They come in in jet planes and leave by donkey." They want to have very modern ideas, but have not the background to apply them. The invention is spoiled, really, because they do not have the background to exploit it. The two sides are necessary, and if you do not have the right balance between them, then you are nothing. If you have only one mirror, you can see yourself only once, but if you have two mirrors, you can see yourself an infinity of times.

D.C.: You have done some work in Pierre Schaefer's laboratory for musique concrete in the early fifties. Was this productive?

P.B.: No, that was not satisfying, and I quit very quickly. The equipment was very poor. Schaefer himself wanted to be the big boss, and even to this day he has absolutely no musical background. He is really illiterate in music. His background is entirely scientific. He really wished his thoughts to be realized by others.

G.W.: Have you ventured into the area of electronic music?

P.B.: Yes, I have done some works of this type but, again, the equipment was not good. I think that you cannot do good work in this area until you have teams working together. You must have composer and technician alike. Four things, really: composer, technician, good equipment, and a company or factory with money to back the operation, as well as performers in some cases, and as long as these elements cannot work together you will have small laboratories without any outstanding results.

D.C.: Are the conditions under which Stockhausen, say, is working any better?

P.B.: Very primitive. The studio in Cologne is exactly as it was before Stockhausen. They have no money.

D.C.: If we were to build a studio that met the qualifications you describe as necessary to a sophisticated studio, would you then be interested in this type of work?

P.B.: Certainly, certainly. But nobody has begun to have an aesthetic point of view on that. At the same time, aesthetic and scientific.

D.C.: Some have said that tape music, per se, has very little future, both because of what you have just brought out, and because of lack of live audience and performers.

P.B.: I think that that is too pessimistic. But I do think that the way in which experiments are done now is a dead end. There is no cohesion or collaboration between teams who are involved in discovery. You have to do the same type and amount of research in each laboratory. You have many really good studios in Germany and Holland which are bringing in things which were discovered ten years ago, and that is not interesting at all. One must have cohesion and a team effort, and very strict collaboration, for success. The great problem, of course, is taking the individuality of the composer and putting him with a team of other individualities, and this is not only not solved at this time, but not even seen.

D.C.: Do you have any qualms about teaching composition?

P.B.: No, I am not against it, but I am not very interested in teaching. After two years I had had enough, I must say. I like the change for very short periods. I want to communicate my experiences and to talk with young people, and that is the interest of teaching, but more than that I would not do.

D.C.: Does conducting for a living leave little time for composing?

P.B.: Yes, and therefore I want to concentrate in one city, to change the musical life of that city, and have the time to compose more. That is education for me: performing a work for an audience that has never heard it before. That is my way of teaching because you teach the orchestra to play it and the audience to listen to it.

You must always have your own room, and then you can throw bombs from your own room. You must preserve your own privacy and personality; you are much more respected, and you can much more act on changing this life. That's my point of view.

5.

NOT A SPECIAL DAY
Karlheinz Stockhausen

I do not keep a diary. This is an exception. Traveling from Würzburg to Cologne on 28 June 1968 I rode in a train which had first class only. I sat beside the writing compartment. After I had seen two gentlemen going in and coming out again I felt the desire to "dictate" a little, too. I went in. The stenographer told me when I should return. About twenty minutes later I was sitting across from her and telling about yesterday and today. Certainly not a special day, unless every day is a special day.

* * *

Würzburg-Cologne, 28 June 1968

27 June 1968. Got up in the Hotel Climat in Vienna -- 6:00 a.m.
Flew to Frankfort --   7:30 a.m.
Traveled on from Frankfort to Würzburg --   9:55 a.m.
In the new hall of the Bavarian Conservatory of Music testing
the loudspeakers --   12:00 noon-2:00 p.m.
Hotel Würzburger Hof. Conversation with Mr. Flackus in his private
apartment --   3:45-6:00 p.m.

He told me about his years of efforts to impel the mentally ill and those with memory disturbances to spontaneously loosen up their closed-in state with my music ("Contacts") or "music therapy." But he is mixed up and wants only to restore the "recognition of tonal structures" expressed in speech (the people are to "describe what they experience, what they hear, what pictures they see, etc."). He told me of many fellow specialists who are attempting similar things. A week ago -- the International Congress of Psychologists, Psychoanalysts, and Medical Men in Würzburg. Many critical opponents with words like "shock music."

"What we did not achieve with any other music is succeeding with your electronic music." I explained to him that the unrecognizability of the sounds, the unfamiliarity of the sound waves, factors out the recognition activity of the mental and that therefore the music reaches the subconscious more directly. He asked me to make the acquaintance of his friend, the medical superintendent of the asylum in Bethel, as well as of his superior, the medical superintendent of the Würzburg Clinic. He dwelt for a rather long time on the description of his one-time friend, the Darmstadt composer Hermann Heisz, who he said had suffered much from fits of depression. He depicted in detail a special case of one of his patients, saying that the patient kept on describing how he had five bullets in his head. Flackus said he was now trying to find acoustic models with the same organization and formation and always played them. Only with an excerpt from my "Contacts" had he evoked spontaneous and in part extraordinarily eruptive utterances, which previously had not been successfully done in many sessions. I tried to make it clear that it did not seem sensible to me to use excerpts for such purposes, but that the organic whole of a work should be presented for hearing undivided. Although I knew that most of my works need not absolutely end where they do, nevertheless there was a "higher" dispensation, I said, which had brought about the conclusion of a work. He argued that in his opinion exposing such people to longer periods of this music was extraordinarily critical since they "exploded" and "became aggressive," and he did not yet see any practical chances of keeping patients from such "dangerous" eruptions. Above all, the music could not in any case be played to groups of patients, although he really considered that proper.

At 7:20 p.m. in the Conservatory hall. After a short introduction by the composer Bertold Hummel I spoke on the gradual change from informal and monochromatic music to a music in which the found and the newly produced, ancient and modern, known and unknown, are combined with each other to an increasing degree. The attempt to reach a higher consciousness than that of the collage. Explanation of the process in *MICROPHONY I*. Presentation of *MICROPHONY I*. The hall in complete darkness. Description of work on *TELEMUSIC*. Explanation of the "intermodulations." Examples given of how the rhythm of a musical *objet trouvé* has been modulated with the envelope curve of a second *objet trouvé*, with the harmonic structure of homemade electronic sounds, and finally with the melodic line of another *objet trouvé*. Presentation of *TELEMUSIC*.

The vibrations in the hall unusually heterogeneous and mutually disturbing (about 450 in the audience, very many students). Bertold Hummel, who organized the series of events, announced to me that in the most pluralistic fashion possible he wanted "everyone to have his say." Perhaps that is one of the reasons that the public is quite statistically shaped and that an open attitude ready for self-experience does not come about in the longer pauses of *MICROPHONY* I heard finger snapping, repeated clapping, imitation by some listeners of sound heard shortly before. The imitations stereotyped and very primitive. I said that it was not the acoustic reaction as such which was unusual, but, on the contrary, the signal for attention; that, however, the type of reaction was too unconscious and therefore resulted in nothing really complementary. Very lively reaction at the end. Afterwards a group of students came with very practical questions about where records, scores, and printed commentaries could be obtained and where the next performances would take place. Afterwards taken to a restaurant, still with a group of Hummel's friends. Among them the concertmeister of the Würzburg Theater Orchestra, who is apparently a good astrologist and by several remarks induced me to recommend him books by Sri Aurobindo. Among those present, the extraordinarily congenial percussionist Finck. He told me that he works a lot with Riedl in Munich, who, he said, often presents *TELEMUSIC* on his programs and who always sets the loudspeakers up at ear-level (which I consider very questionable). Early this morning, 28 June 1968, I wrote Riedl a letter that he should not present *TELEMUSIC* on his program any more (he uses a copy of a copy which he once requested for a short time for a Munich performance). Furthermore I wrote him that at the next opportunity I should like to explain to him just how loudspeakers are properly placed in an auditorium (a procedure which is becoming better and better known to me and which demands the greatest care in the particular place in question, as well as often up to four hours of time from me and several other collaborators sitting in various parts of the hall; in Madrid, for example, Kontarsky, Fritsch, Gehlhaar, Alings, Boje, and I took several hours to set the loudspeakers up; some of them were lying on their backs up in the balcony, and others were on stands on the stage, and we had put pieces of wood under the front edge of each speaker so that they were pointed up at the ceiling and the sound was only reflected into the house at an angle at a greater distance; we set up two loudspeakers contrary to the usual way with their diaphragm sides at an acute angle directly toward the wooden walls in order to prevent hiss and to enable the people sitting right in front of these loudspeakers -- at a distance of about 5-7 meters [$16^{1/2}$ to 23 feet] -- to hear also the loudspeakers standing on the opposite side, as well as those which were diagonally opposite; in principle we try to send the sound of the loudspeakers, particularly when instrumentalists are playing at the same time, as high as possible into the house and to achieve a smooth acoustic match, especially in four-track reproduction).

This morning, 28 June 1968 -- saw Tiepolo's ceiling frescoes in the palace. The most surprising thing is the great surfaces left free in the whole middle region in the ascending stairwell. The hardly perceptible transitions of two-dimensional painting into three-dimensional plastic continuations, the setting of whole sculptures into the painted surrounding, and the optical illusions of seemingly plastic surface painting are very humorous after the rediscovery of similar effects in pop art. In the view from the balcony of the imperial hall into the garden the arches of the arcade in a semicircle are interesting -- they are entirely overgrown with ivy and at first look like overgrown walls, but when I went down out of curiosity they proved to be overgrown wooden scaffoldings. The idea of making similar walks with views around my house. Longish talk with two stucco-workers who from photographs fully restored all the 32 rooms formerly used as living rooms in the palace for the Fuchs company in Würzburg. I made inquiries about methods of working, technique, and time taken for such work with the thought of composing certain rooms in my house with stucco reliefs. I would make the photographic models myself, or provide them. Bought a copy of Freeden and Lamb's book on Tiepolo at half price, as this book is being closed out. Short conversation with a bright art student who was taking a school through the halls and knew many details about the life and customs of the persons depicted. His remarks interesting about the anachronism in historical representations by combining the persons of a certain time with the costumes and objects of an entirely different era. Explanation of conventions between spiritual and secular dignitaries. The necessity of reciprocal ceremonial abasement. The impossibility of personages who under certain assumptions are regarded as equally important (bishop and prince) going up the same staircase together (who walks on the right, who on the left?). Therefore two parallel staircases were built in the palace and the two dignitaries only meet in the upper reception hall, entering by different doors.

A MOUTHPIECE
Karlheinz Stockhausen

In the May 1968 issue of Art International (pp. 27-29) appears an article by Professor Harley Parker, a collaborator of Marshal McLuhan, entitled "Waning of the Visual," which absolutely every musician should read. The article implies that in our time, in which the visual (television, the flood of advertising and printed matter, etc.) seems to be suppressing everything else, the visual itself is beginning to lose its total domination. That paper also sketches the social significance of art criticism in its historical rise and attacks its function today with convincing arguments.

The statement about the helplessness of art criticism -- that a conscious person scarcely lets an art critic (particularly a music critic) prescribe to him any more what he should find good or not good -- confirms what has long since become a fact. More and more people long for their own experience and remove themselves from doctrinaire formation of opinion. They simply drop what does not set them into higher vibration and with increasing frequency they seek contact with artistic and generally human events -- without a classifying system of values -- which "touch" and awaken them. The function of the professional "critic," to express an aesthetics that is approved for all, dates back to times in which most people were considered to be adolescent sheep and were treated like that in increasing degree. Today we need no "critics" any longer, but personalities who in the service of everyone are always going in quest of events in which people are set into higher vibration and transported beyond their previous consciousness. Reporters who in the least self-centered manner possible give inspiring news so that their readers and hearers drop everything and seek out these experiences.

Very soon a rather large number of people will become conscious of what great significance attaches to music during the "waning of the visual," and chiefly to certain new music of universal orientation that stirs the whole man right down into his atoms, massages him, and sets him vibrating so that higher consciousness can penetrate the layers of the subconscious and unconscious. This is perceived clearly in the difference between people, mostly older, who want to listen to the new music (principally electronic music) in relative quiet and young people who preferably listen to music in large rooms as "loud" as possible and with many sources of sound distributed around them.

The artists most advanced in consciousness have made the step from the fixed art·object, produced in individual detachment, to the planning of open processes in which IT can happen. The picture of the artist as the "antenna" of society or as an "early warning system," as the siren of the supraconscious that we commonly call the future, no longer suffices. A modern artist is a radio receiver with self-consciousness in the supraconscious. Today, however, only a few are such receivers. The "artist" is generally still distinguished as the "able" who has practiced and trained with unprecedented discipline and has let himself be caught in the worldwide competitive process of rivaling with professional colleges to see who, after all, makes the greatest impression on people.* Like other professionals he became more and more a specialist -- painter, sculptor, composer, poet, circus artiste, magician, etc. -- because he subjected himself to the instrumental nature of the world governed by systematizing reason and because what he produced was to be sold to a certain stratum of consumers. The "instruments" were nothing more than extensions, sharpenings, further refined developments of the individual bodily sense organs, and from the all-controlling development of these instruments resulted the increasing inability to perceive and communicate the world to oneself without these instruments. The majority of people has, for example, unlearned that tones can set everything into motion, even interior sight, taste, touch, olfaction, the accurate sense of time and space, the feeling for "inanimate matter," for plant, animal, human, and suprahuman presence of living beings, and so on.

What, then, is to be done? First, as much as possible make "works" which stay open all the time for the direct reception of vibrations of the supramental which are always "in the air." Therefore as much as possible produce no objects which harden, chill, and thus segregate that which has become conscious from the process of continual increase in consciousness. This is not easy, of course, since it is only with difficulty that we can detach ourselves from the set of instruments and the preference for "solid" material and since the frozen art object is still generally regarded as worthy of being striven after because at bottom it matches the drive for possessions.

The artist must therefore plan processes in which practitioners and media participate that can manage the presently unavoidable set of instruments and the fixed materials and always connect them to the current of universal electricity. If "finally" fixed objects are involved in a process, they must then be opened, commented upon, subjected to current, and used as material for flight.

The hectic search for "total works of art"# is to be quieted. It must become increasingly clear that in every field of vibration -- acoustic, optical, tactile, etc. -- the whole consciousness, which is basically undivided, can be set vibrating insofar as the higher prerequisite is fulfilled that every artistic action be connected to the universal current and be permeated by it so that the artist himself is merely a mouthpiece tuned as pure as possible and he transfers the vibrations going through him to the practicing media, to the set of instruments, to the material, and to everything that gets into the vibration field.

As "unexpressive" as these works may sound, they do indeed not come from the mythic subconscious or from thinking, but from experiences of a progressively intuitive and supramental doing.

Never before have people "seen" so much, as when I have recommended that they close their eyes when listening to electronic music (in which they have no longer been able to get an idea where the sounds really come from).

*Translator's Note. An echo of Goethe's famous etymological aphorism "Art is ability" (in German the words 'art' and 'ability' can be traced to the same ultimate root).

#The German "Gesamtkunstwerk," which nowadays is reflected in the 'multi-media' fashion.

6.

AN INTERVIEW WITH LUCIANO BERIO
David Felder

The following interview with Luciano Berio took place on April 20, 1976, at Severance Hall, Cleveland Ohio, following a rehearsal of his *Calmo* (Homáge a Bruno Maderna), *Folk Songs*, *Différences,* and *Chemins IV* with the Cleveland Orchestra.

David Felder: About 1951 you came to the United States to study serial techniques with Dallapiccola at Tanglewood on a Koussevitzky Foundation Fellowship. In your early works you applied these techniques and since have abandoned them. Would you elaborate on your application of serialism and on your feelings concerning the use of serial technique?

Luciano Berio: My study with Dallapiccola was very short, was very limited, I loved him as a person, but certainly he was not a good teacher. In fact, musically speaking, it was not useful, but was very important culturally, spiritually. Especially being an Italian, Dallapiccola had an important influence, was a very important point of reference for me.

As for the serial technique, no, I don't believe in this type of strict label. I grew gradually, organically into this, and it was a kind of a natural developmental process for me. I didn't fall from the horseback of Saul on the way to Damascus and receive a revelation; no, long before I met Dallapiccola while I was still in the conservatory, I was aware of things, I was developing. Actually, the most important thing is constant growing, constant development. Then more specifically as serial technique goes, what is it? It is a way of thinking in terms of proportions. It's a relative proportion, a method of quantifying things; a quantification that is relevant for the perception, perception as you measure with your own ears. When you can have more abstract forms of quantification, which are also very useful because, dealing with abstract things, one walks in a kind of a "no man's land" in which trust is placed in certain abstract proportions, you can discover very important things.

So your question, strict application of serial technique, if you allow me, is a false question; it doesn't exist. For the moment that you make sense in what you do, it is strict by definition. I would say that in that respect Puccini's as strict as Anton Webern. Then if you go further, the world represented by Anton Webern is completely different than the world represented by Puccini. So you find, perhaps, a more strict, a more natural view of the world through Webern's music than, of course, that of Puccini. The view is different because Webern's music is directed to the intellect, the most complex part of us, while Puccini is more directed toward the emotional, simpler part of us.

D.F.: You've mentioned the simple and the complex, the emotional and the intellectual. Emphasis on the intellectual is suggested in your early serial works, but in some of your later works, emphasis seems to be on the emotional, the dramatic. Do you direct yourself consciously toward one or the other, the intellectual or the emotional?

L.B.: I didn't know that in my later work, I was involved more with emotional implications! No, I would say that I've refined my own instrument enough; now I can look at a wider range of expression. I can combine the most complex with the most simple. That's the point.

D.F.: You began working with electronics sometime around 1954 with Bruno Maderna, whose work, sadly enough, is little known in this country. Could you elaborate regarding your interest in electronic music and your work at the Studio di Phonologie in Milan?

L.B.: I started well before 1955. I must say that my interest for electronic music was triggered in New York, exactly 1952, when I went to the Museum of Modern Art and attended a concert conducted by Leopold Stokowski. He stepped out onto the podium and left a space for a loudspeaker, then played a work by Vladimir Ussachevsky and Otto Luening entitled *Sonic Contours*. It's a kind of elaboration, a transformation of piano sounds, which musically, of course, is absolutely irrelevant. Nevertheless, this was very shocking for me, the first time, in a concert-audience situation, to become aware of this possibility. In fact, just a few weeks later, I went to Milan, I was working for the Italian Radio putting together the first instruments, filters, oscillators, etc.

I started doing my first experiments with electronic sounds at the end of 1952-53. In 1953-54 the studio was more or less decided on, 1954 developed, and 1955 officially recognized and announced after two or three years of preparation. Bruno joined me in 1954. At that time the studio was a conventional electronic music studio, more or less like Cologne. That means comprised of equipment already available for other purposes, not for music; at that time there were no specifically designed instruments for realization of electronic music. Oscillators, filters, sinusoidal generators, pulse generators, echo chambers, tape recorders, these types of devices constituted the basic content of the studio. In the following years we developed more sophisticated filters, different types of other devices and so on.

D.F.: A great deal of your electronic music involves manipulation and transformation of existing sonic material in the classical concréte fashion, for example *Visage* and *Différences*. Do you have a marked preference for permutation and extension of natural sounds electronically over those electronically generated sound sources?

L.B.: I think the most important aspects, the most important results achieved thus far in electronic music are not in the electronic product, but in the thinking involved in the work. As a musical possibility, electronic music is not self-sufficient yet. This is not to deny varied importance to many of the works that have been produced, but I see that as a very important exercise to a future that is not there yet. Electronic music even to this date, to a certain extent, is surrounded by silence; it doesn't connect with musical work, with man's work. When someone hears electronic music it doesn't reverberate to other levels of his experience, as instrumental music has and does. Up to now I feel electronic music has been developing, evolving as a bridge between what we know and what we don't know yet. It is not without reason that the best musical work that has been produced up until now (from the early 50s to the present?) are those that try to make this connection.

For example, works such as *Gesang der Jünglinge* by Stockhausen, which is the first really meaningful work, and other works both in Europe and the United States. You use electronic music to explore a new type of bridge between known sound, known structural, acoustical situations, and new ones.

I think that the computer will be a great help in enlarging the bridge to the moment in which the musical mind might travel back and forth from known objects, old and new instruments, whatever it is, to synthetic sound, so the difference between so-called natural sound and so-called synthetic sound will be irrelevant. There will be no difference. With the computer, for instance, you can analyze sound very well. You know what's happening inside a sound, you can duplicate exactly the sound of a trumpet, for example, and combine the synthesized sound with that of a live trumpet, and you can imagine what kind of connection you can create - - how far you can push the trumpet, how far away from you and how deep inside you can go with this natural sound.

D.F.: You spoke briefly of Stockhausen. He dedicated the last section of *Hymnen* to you, and you have dedicated *Allelujah III* to him. Your relationship stems, I believe, especially from Darmstadt. Did Stockhausen influence your later compositional aesthetic, in that you began exploring "chance" or "performer choice" operations?

L.B.: No, we move in completely different directions, levels of expression. I have a great respect for him. We are very good friends, too. Nothing happens by itself, but I like to think that Stockhausen is there working and thinking about doing something, and I'm sure that he likes to think that I'm somewhere doing something. I'm aware of many things that he is doing, and he's aware also of those things others are doing. Even on the unconscious level there are influences, as sometimes a negative reaction to something. But any specific influence - - none, I would say.

D.F.: What was the significance of the Darmstadt experience to your compositional development?

L.B.: Darmstadt was a necessary thing of the same gender as if one were speaking from a historical point of view. In that sense as Beethoven was necessary, Galileo Galilei was necessary, maybe in the smallest kind of a way one might state that Darmstadt was necessary. It was a kind of spontaneous, authentic meeting. In fact it had a relatively short life; the really good years lasted seven or eight years, ten at the most. After that, everybody went his own way. Yet it was important for the collective feeling, the give and take, mutual exchange of ideas, and reactions to each other.

Darmstadt was an extremely intense type of exchange. It was responsible for, well, in looking back, many developments in what we can now call the "roaring fifties." Many things have been done, many roots have been planted, but I don't believe in the mystique of Darmstadt. Darmstadt cannot be repeated, as other events in history cannot be repeated. It was really a focal point of many different musical thinkers there, and, yet I look at Darmstadt as an extremely important experience for me.

D.F.: In several of your works, notably *Epiphanie* and *Tempi Concertate*, you have employed indeterminate or performer choice operations. Seemingly, after works such as these you abandoned chance as an integral element. What has the composer to gain from chance elements?

L.B.: Well it depends, I personally do not believe in chance - chance doesn't exist. In terms of performing technique, sometimes it is necessary to allow the performer a certain amount of freedom in order to achieve a certain objective which could not otherwise be obtained through, say, metrical notation; to remove obstacles between an ideal result and the performer. Of course, if the performer is good enough other psychological restrictions are placed upon him, but this is another matter.

In the case of *Epiphanie,* the chance element, I would say, doesn't exist. There's a limited number of organized strategies in the two cycles, one orchestral cycle, one vocal cycle, that can be interconnected in different ways. Depending on the ways in which you interconnect and superimpose them, you will take a different attitude toward the content of the text, text which goes from Proust to Brecht. In *Tempi Concertate*, which is a very rigid and severe work, there are instances in which the progression towards different types of harmonic categories is suspended. In these moments a more loose type of activity is present to go beyond a certain harmonic norm, just for a brief moment. Otherwise everything is rather strict. You see, instead of having a 3/4 measure, if you have an organizational plan, perhaps with the conductor, that is equally strict, all that doesn't mean that there is chance present. Chance exists when your action in a musical sense can be completely responsible for the complete change of the structure, the form of the meaning. Your decisions are therefore so strong that you take the place of the composer, as a performer. As for compositional chance, as John Cage used it, it doesn't make any sense, especially now.

D.F.: In a work such as *Circles*, you have directed that the singer should respond to audience reaction.

L.B.: No! Respond to the other performers, yes! It's a very close secret between the three players and the singer. Perhaps you mean *Passagio*, another work, in which the singer attempts to provoke the audience to a certain type of behavior, but not in *Circles*.

D.F.: Let me rephrase. Does the singer react musically to the perceived impact of the work as she feels it, on the audience? Is this an incorrect impression?

L.B.: I think a performer is always aware of the audience. A passive audience can, of course, be very distressing to a performer. In the case of *Circles*, what you've heard is a studio recording with no audience interaction. Everything is completely written out.

D.F.: *Passagio*, which you mentioned in passing a moment ago, has been labeled an anti-opera. Would you care to comment on that?

L.B.: An anti-opera because it uses only one character. It is the story of one woman alone on the stage, addressing the audience at the end. It's a kind of letter to the audience itself, the typical audience of opera theater. In fact the audience itself is surrounded by a kind of "guerrilla group" inside, a speaking chorus scattered in the audience, which represents the audience itself. They are the "bad guys," and there is a constant conflict between the audience (composed) and the action on the stage. I wouldn't say anti-opera, but certainly it is a comment on opera. Because there is a refusal to employ scenography, only the minimal element is used to characterize every situation; and the real stage, in a way, is the audience. There are many political implications inherent in the work also.

D.F.: In your later works you seem to have evolved a more eclectic, personal style in which the drama, especially psychological drama, is extremely important. Have you employed multi-media techniques; and if not, can you foresee this in your compositional future?

L.B.: No, because I wouldn't be able to control those elements. I'm working currently for the theater. I'm preparing a very complicated work for La Scala. I know there is a fashion of so-called multi-media, but I think it's kind of amateurish, dilletante, because each of the separate media by itself is very complex. The result is usually a poor use of the media, instead of probing more deeply into one. So you have a kind of bouillabaise, fish soup. Yes, you might have shocking effects, charming things, gags; but there is no overall, inner scope - at least up until now. I don't know of one.

D.F.: Are collaborative efforts a distinct possibility in media works, for the creation of the artistic?

L.B.: You mean like in San Diego. No, it doesn't make any sense. In fact, look at the results. They've been there for ten years. I don't know, it's kind of squalid. Many wishful thinkers go there, but they usually don't have the necessary technique. For example, Subotnick is an excellent musician and composer. When he works with music, OK, fine. But when he tries to combine laser and this and that, it's a curiosity, kind of nice for a Saturday or Sunday afternoon show, but no more than that.

D.F.: Then it's too much of a task for the composer to master his craft and also the other component art forms?

L.B.: No, it's not just that. Music as an art is very powerful; and through musical thinking, in fact, you can control many other elements besides just music. You can compose musically with many other things besides sound like the sound of a clarinet, so why not with lights or, smell, etc. However, the grammar, the alphabet, the technique necessary to make this type of compositional control possible is not there yet. I don't believe this will be the discovery of an individual; rather, this type of a discovery is a result of slow social process. You don't invent a new grammar, you don't invent a new kind of situation. It's always a collective, very unconscious, often, effort or direction. At least up until now the instruments that have been developed, the musical ideas that have been formulated, have been a result of gradual changes. Monteverdi was not a mushroom that suddenly sprouted!

So many forces arrived there in his work and his thinking; so in Mozart, so in Beethoven, so in anything else of certain importance that happens. It's the focal point of many component directions, many factions. So development in media has a long way to go, I feel, because there's no way for a genius to have control, coordination of this. You can have these for an effect - - smell, an accordion, a symphony orchestra, but so what?

D.F.: You have, since 1968, added a fifth movement to *Sinfonia*, which of course is not present in the recording. What is the significance of this last movement in relation to the entire work?

L.B.: The fifth movement is the most important movement. It is to the four previous movements as the third movement is to Mahler. Everything is included - - for instance, the entire second movement is present as a skeletal framework. Also the text of the first movement is utilized to conclude the work. It's the most complex, and is the culmination of all that has happened before; therefore it's the most important.

D.F.: The third movement employs an "information overload" type of technique with all its complexities and references. Are you planning to utilize this more frequently in forthcoming works?

L.B.: No. Of course, I'm interested in layers of meanings, like the interweaving ideas used in the third movement. There's a lot of information, but each side of what you hear is meaningful in itself. There's a kind of indeterminacy of communication, if you want. Whatever you hear is complete in itself; it is not a fragment of a larger part.

D.F.: In your *Sequins - Chemins* works, for example *Sequins VI* for viola and *Chemins II* and *III* for viola and different ensemble, are closely interrelated. Does this constitute a larger, broader concept, namely, that a single work is incomplete in itself, and other works comprise a larger thought?

L.B.: No, I think that perhaps in the life of a man, in the work of a man, the separate works can be viewed as segments of a larger work, which is your life. So why not go back, why not revisit a work to discover new things. It's a way of analyzing, educating yourself, and also thinking in terms of continuative processes. Everything which one does is never completed.

D.F.: Is this analogous to the Boulez "work-in-progress" concept?

L.B.: No, because his work-in-progress idea is that of open form, as in the *Third Piano Sonata*. No, this is completely different. He doesn't like to look back; and I like to look back - - it's very ambitious.

7.

AN INTERVIEW WITH JOHN CAGE
David Cope

D.C.: After studying a good deal of your music and writing, I find a number of correlations (possible) between the ways in which you describe your listening processes and the methods of composition you employ. On a simple level, it is obviously 'being open to all sounds;' such a statement could be employed both from a point of reception and a point of composition. How much did and does your approach to listening affect your approaches to composition?

J.C.: I'm not sure I understand the question. My composition arises out of asking questions. I am reminded of a story early on about a class with Schoenberg. He had us go to the blackboard to solve a particular problem in counterpoint (though it was a class in harmony). He said: "When you have a solution, turn around and let me see it." I did that. He then said: "Now another solution, please." I gave another and another until finally, having made seven or eight, I reflected a moment and then said with some certainty: "There aren't any more solutions." He said: "O.K. What is the principle underlying all of the solutions?" I couldn't answer his question; but I had always worshipped the man, and at that point I did even more. He ascended, so to speak. I spent the rest of my life, until recently, hearing him ask that question over and over. And then it occurred to me through the direction that my work has taken, which is renunciation of choices and the substitution of asking questions, that the principle underlying all of the solutions that I had given him was the question that he had asked, because they certainly didn't come from any other point. He would have accepted that answer, I think. The answers have the question in common. Therefore the question underlies the answers. I'm sure that he would have found my answer interesting; though he was very brilliant — he may have been thinking of something else.

D.C.: The concept of zero is an important one to understanding both what you say and what you compose. The reference is made in the questions and answers section of this issue of COMPOSER: "I always want to start from zero and make, if I can, a discovery." It is, very honestly, a very difficult problem for me to imagine a zero to start with, no less to begin there in my composition. What techniques does one acquire to achieve this; even more important, how do you renew that zero after a new discovery is made?

J.C.: It's a good question. It's exactly the problem that I face all the time and it's very difficult, because we have a memory. There's no doubt of it. And we're not stupid. We would be stupid if we didn't have memory. And yet it's that memory that one has to become free of, at the same time that you have to take advantage of it. It's very paradoxical. Right now, I am refreshed and brought, so to speak, to zero, I think, through my work with Joyce.

I don't know how he actually worked. I know more than I used to know. Writers like Louis Mink and Adeline Glashine have helped. One of these mentions that you can't understand Joyce unless you have an unabridged dictionary and the eleventh edition of the Encyclopedia Britannica. And if you have both you can then see doors open on passages in *Finnegans Wake*, which are more or less lifted from one or the other. He used these reference texts in a way that facilitated and stimulated his work.

In my way, I do the same thing in my most recent work. The passage about water in the next to the last chapter of *Ulysses*, which was Joyce's favorite chapter, was no doubt taken out of the encyclopedia just as I took some recent work relating to charcoal out of the encyclopedia. I added to it, of course — and I'm sure he did, too — but the skeleton was there for the having, so to speak. The dictionary is a gold mine and so is the encyclopedia. Joyce had that very great one, which I used to have as a child, but unfortunately no longer have. It was put in a garage in Southern California and mildewed, otherwise I would try to get hold of it. Now it's very hard to find that edition.

I had the notion when I was asked to write for the Walker Art Institute in the series on "The Meanings of Modernism," to write a text against the 'march of understanding,' and to make clear the virtues of remaining ignorant in the face of art. Mink says that it is no longer possible to take this naive attitude, that enough is known about *Finnegans Wake* to make it imperative to know more and, ultimately, to destroy it. I work at . . . keeping it mysterious. Instead of understanding it, I would like, if I can, to help keep the work of Joyce mysterious.

Satie has avoided problems of being understood through seeming to people to be too simple to bother to analyze, I think — so that people leave his work alive without analyzing it. But I didn't do that. I analyzed it and I still find it beautiful. I think it was because he had, as I've had, a rhythmic (empty time) structure rather than a structure connected with the surface result (the notes). I'm arguing on the other side of the fence from Steve Reich and from critics in general, many of whom say that my work is trivial since it can't really be analyzed in the conventional sense. What can be analyzed in my work or criticized are the questions that I ask. But most of the critics don't trouble to find out what those questions are. And that would make the difference between one composition made with chance operations and another. That is, the principle underlying the results of those chance operations is the questions . . . the things which should be criticized, if one wants to criticize, are the questions that are asked.

I had the experience, in writing *Apartment House 1776*, of wanting to do something with early American music that would let it keep its flavor at the same time that it would lose what was so obnoxious to me: its harmonic tonality. My first questions were superficial and so resulted in superficial variations on the originals. Not having, as most musicians do, an ear for music, I don't hear music when I write it; I only hear it when it's played. If I heard it when I was writing it, I would write what I've already heard; whereas since I can't hear it while I'm writing it, I'm able to write something that I've never heard before.

The result was that I was working so fast, and against a deadline in the case of *Apartment House 1776*, that my first questions were simply questions about subtraction from the original Billings. Namely, seeing that a situation had four notes, I would ask, "Are they all four present, or only three, or two, or one?" And unfortunately, the first time I did it, I did it with respect to a piece that was interesting in itself, so that when I subtracted from it, it remained interesting. When I played it, it was new and beautiful. And so, not being able to hear them, I then did that with respect to the 43 other pieces, and it took me a long time. When I got to a piano and tried them out, they were miserable. No good at all. Not worth the paper they were written on. It was because the question was superficial. I hadn't found what was at the basis of my trouble with tonal music. I hadn't rid the music of the theory. The cadences all remained recognizable.

Then I thought I should include silence. I did that (asking, "Are four present, or three, or two, or one, or none?") and again wrote a beautiful piece. I again wrote all 44 pieces and again they were not good. So I came back to the problem and saw that I had to go deeper into it. Finally I took — my question was for each line — which tones of fourteen tones in one of the voices were active, and I would get through chance operations an answer like this: number one, seven, eleven, and fourteen. That would mean that the active one was first a sound, then silence.

The first sound I would write from Billings, put it down and extend it all the way up to the seventh tone; and at the seventh tone, a silence would begin that would last to the eleventh tone. I would then write the eleventh tone, and it would last to the fourteenth, and at the fourteenth, a silence. Therefore the cadences and everything disappeared; but the flavor remained. You can recognize it as eighteenth century music; but it's suddenly brilliant in a new way. It is because each sound vibrates from itself, not from a theory. The theory is no longer in power. The cadences which were the function of the theory, to make syntax and all, all of that is gone, so that you get the most marvelous overlappings.

D.C.: The reactions to that piece have been extraordinary, particularly in Los Angeles about two years ago.

J.C.: That's because of the superimposition of so-called spiritual musics, which offended some of the Jewish people in the audience.

D.C.: It was not intended in any way to do this?

J.C.: No. I was concerned. I knew that something might happen because people who sing such music don't have the habit of singing while another person is singing something else. And I had to explain to each singer carefully what was going to happen to get them to accept that before they did it. It was particularly hard with Helen Schneyer, who said that she didn't think that she'd be able to sing while other people were singing; that her work meant too much to her. She said, "I won't like it," and so I used a simple device. I said, "Life is full of things that we don't necessarily like." But now she loves it. They all love it because it is a kind of ecumenical feeling to have everyone, all the churches, so to speak, together. The Indian chief was marvelous; he mostly wouldn't let me talk at all when I first met him.

D.C.: He talked over you.

J.C.: Yes, because for years he had given pow wows in a tourist trap between Montreal and New York and so he didn't know how to stop talking. Finally I said, "Swifty, I must tell you what it's going to be like for you to sing in this piece." He put his hand on my knee and said, "Don't bother, I understand. There are going to be many things happening all at the same time."

D.C.: That piece has been performed twelve or thirteen times since by many major symphony orchestras throughout the country.

J.C.: And it's going to be performed in Europe in all the various radio stations — I've written to find out when — on a program with Ives and Nancarrow.

D.C.: About Nancarrow. I have been for years infatuated with his music. You discovered his work in the '60's, I believe, and quite by accident. Is that correct? You were in Mexico City with Cunningham and . . .

J.C.: Not by accident; I'd known about him for years. We always knew of him as someone who had lost his citizenship. He was 'prematurely anti-Fascist' and I'd always looked forward to meeting him. Then I went on a Latin American tour with the Cunningham Dance Company, and met him with David Tudor in Mexico City.

D.C.: Had you seen the piano roll in Cowell's New Music Edition?

J.C.: I didn't know of that. One of my old friends in New York is Minna Daniel, formerly Minna Lederman, the editor of Modern Music; she was a close friend of Conlon Nancarrow; she often spoke of him. Anyway I was, as everyone is, delighted with his music when I heard it. He was puzzled over my pleasure because he considered himself not on the side of chance operations at all and he couldn't understand why I enjoyed his work so much. But he may be bending a little bit in my direction since he's discovered that it's impossible to synchronize two player pianos.

D.C.: And he won't accept microprocessor control, apparently.

J.C.: Right.

D.C.: It seems to me that there are some interesting correlations between your styles, being in a sense on either extreme: one being so totally organized and the other being 'totally' unorganized (at least in predetermination). Particularly when he uses certain mathematical ratios, decisions are made for him in much the same way as certain chance techniques that I am aware of.

J.C.: He wouldn't agree. The only thing he would agree with, as he told me, was that he couldn't get those two pianos together.

D.C.: Do you agree with my last statement?

J.C.: No. I see what you mean, and I see that that's what's on the surface, but as I said earlier about indeterminate music, the surface is not important. It's the underlying questions that are important and the questions of Conlon Nancarrow are entirely different from mine. Not only that, but the effect upon him is different. And the effect upon me is different. And finally, as I've said, we are working with our minds ultimately. We are changing our minds. And his mind is not changing the way my mind is changing. Nor should it.

Do you know that poem I wrote on his name? That's about that, because he told me once that when he thought of music he didn't think of any other music but his own.

Of course, that's why his music is so marvelous. He's so concentrated, so focused.

D.C.: Is he aware of what is going on elsewhere in the world musically?

J.C.: He's completely aware. But it doesn't mean anything to him. He has a huge library of periodicals about music.

D.C.: A large record library as well?

J.C.: Everything. It's all there. His house is a reference library. He has stacks and stacks of material. I'm sure that he reads and listens a great deal, but none of it means anything to him in relation to his own work. That's what's so astonishing. He says, "When I think of music, I think of my own music."

D.C.: Partch might have said the very same thing.

J.C.: Oh, yes. Certainly. One difference between Partch and myself — also a difference between myself and Lou Harrison — is that he became interested in intonation and control of microtones, whereas I went from the twelve tones into the whole territory of sound. I took noise as the basis of it. I don't try to make the situation between what is musical and what is not musical more refined as both Partch and Harrison do; but I start from the other direction, from noise, and don't use sounds that don't do honor to noise. And I suggest that the same thing might bring about an improvement in society; that instead of basing our laws on the rich as we have, that we would do well to base them on the poor. If we can have laws that make poverty comfortable, then those laws will do well for the rich; but the other way around is oppressive.

D.C.: The title of this new piece you have completed is . . .?

J.C.: *James Joyce, Marcel Duchamp, Eric Satie: An Alphabet.* I wrote it between Thanksgiving and Christmas, 1979. The performance last night here was the first public reading, though I did read it for a group of 35 people at Crown Point Press in Oakland earlier this month.

D.C.: I found it to be an extraordinary experience. The conceptual aspect of the piece is so realistic. I was completely taken in and clearly perceived the visual images which you described, as if I were watching a play. You read it with a compelling rhythmic sense. How do you view rhythm in regard to that particular piece? Is it improvised? Is it somehow organized in any way?

J.C.: I don't use punctuation anymore, which brings about a flexibility in my reading.

D.C.: Is it something that you listen to yourself as you're reading? Is it conscious?

J.C.: It's improvised each time. And the same is true of certain tonal inflections. I have found that those passages written by Duchamp that are so inscrutable, about the fourth dimension and all that, if you slightly sing it, especially if you make long lines out of it rhythmically, singing in a single breath, it becomes very beautiful. This is true of Joyce, too. Joyce himself said that you will enjoy *Finnegans Wake* more if you read it out loud than if you do it silently.

D.C.: In relating this piece to, say, *A Lecture on Nothing*, when you actually marked off the seconds, etc. (sometimes, for example, placing a very few words for ten seconds and at other times a great many for the same duration), rhythm there seems to play a very important part in the performance process.

J.C.: Yes. The same would be true of *Empty Words* if I read that now. I had a very strange experience. When I finished the first part of *Empty Words*, I read that when people asked me to give a lecture. When I finished the second part, I read it instead of the first, the third instead of the second, etc. And then it became necessary to read all four for a projected Tomato recording which hasn't been published yet. I had, through reading excessively the third and fourth parts, forgotten how to read the first and second. Fortunately I had written the introductions, the head notes, which are printed in *Empty Words*, and so I studied those carefully. They told me how to do it. I had written out very clearly the directions. But most people don't read those head notes, so they don't know how to read it. For instance, Jackson MacLow complains that he likes *Empty Words* when I read it but he doesn't himself enjoy reading it. If he would read how to read it, he would enjoy it. What you do is take the stanzas in the first and second parts, and you count them in relation to a total length of time, which is 2½ hours, and you find out what the time length of each stanza is by division. Then ones that have few words in them have silences or opportunities for space, whereas the ones that have many words have to be read very quickly. You then have a rhythmic situation that is absolutely fascinating. If you pay attention, as I say in the introduction, to each single letter, and not to the groups in their ordinary sound, it becomes most interesting. It gets more musical, the more you pay attention to the time and to the sounds.

D.C.: I often state, and believe to be true, that there is no piece of music written in the past thirty years that has not felt the influence in some measure of John Cage. I know of few composers who do not pay full respect to you regarding their own work. How do you react to this?

J.C.: I try to be totally ignorant of that. That's the only way I know of to solve it. I don't think it's accurate, though. I think that when a person does something he does it originally, even if he's thinking of something he calls an influence. I really think that each person does his own work.

D. C.: I guess the kind of influence I am referring to is that of, for example, Lutoslawski, who, when I saw him a few years ago, claimed that his music was radically changed after he heard your *Concert for Piano and Orchestra*.

J.C.: That's a very good example. He does say that he made certain changes in his work after hearing mine. What he did, of course, was original to him and exactly what I'm saying, so I don't feel any problem there at all and I enjoy his work when I hear it, and I enjoy it as his rather than as mine. I think that's what is good about my influence, if there is one, that there are more possibilities open to people than there were when I was young.

When I was young you had either to follow Stravinsky or Schoenberg. There was no alternative. There was nothing else to do. You could perhaps have felt that you could follow Bartók, or you could have translated that Bartók into Cowell or Ives; but we didn't think that way then. We thought Schoenberg or Stravinsky; and the schools certainly felt that way. I think, for example, that folk music was thought of only in the way that Stravinsky thought of it. Now, of course, there are 1001 things to do, and I think that that's partly a result of a kind of step that not only I took, but others took.

D.C.: It would seem to be a more healthy situation now . . .

J.C.: Well, it's certainly more suitable for a larger population, which is the case, too.

D.C.: Most people knowledgeable with your life know that you are an expert in mycology (fungi; especially mushrooms). I even wrote a piece dedicated to you at one time, entitled *Amanita Bisporegera* — though I never sent it to you. How has your study and work with mushrooms paralleled your work with sound; or has it? I ask since I am very involved with writing and studying science fiction, and have found the relationship spectacular.

J.C.: I certainly think that is true in my case with mushrooms. I've had for a long time the desire to hear the mushroom itself, and that could be done with very fine technology, because they are dropping spores and those spores are hitting surfaces. There certainly is sound taking place. I mentioned this in the last article in Silence, in that humorous article. I would still like to do that. It leads, of course, to the thought about hearing anything in the world since we know that everything is in a state of vibration, so that not only mushrooms, but also chairs and tables, for instance, could be heard. One could go to an exhibition of sounds in which you would see something and hear it as well. I would like to do that.

D.C.: Are you familiar with some of the work that was done about eight years ago with wiring plants with electrodes and tying these through synthesizers?

J.C.: Yes; I've done that.

D.C.: What were the results?

J.C.: It was most interesting, and I have a project (unfortunately it hasn't taken place yet) to amplify a city park for children. It was to be done at Ivrea near Torino where the Olivetti company is. There is a marvelous hill in the center of the city that is high and has a beautiful view of the Alps, and is isolated enough from the traffic sounds so that you hear the sounds of the plants. The project fell through, but I was invited to do the same kind of project in Rome and also in Zagreb; but I haven't accepted it until I accept the place. I was spoiled by that marvelous situation in Ivrea where the silence — when you weren't playing the plants — was very audible and beautiful; you could hear it as if you were in a concert hall.

In other words, I wanted the silence of the mountain to be heard by the children after they had heard the sounds that they themselves had made by playing the plants. We were going to have a programmed arrangement so that every now and then the plants were going to become unplayable, and the children would be obliged to hear the silence. Otherwise the children would have been making noises continually.

Did you hear the music with cactus (*Child of Tree*)? That was what that came out of. For a dance of Merce Cunningham's I used cacti. I made the sounds on cacti and a few other plant materials. That led to the idea of amplifying a park, and that's led to the idea that I've found quite fascinating: a piece of music performed by animals, and butterflies, which sounds fantastic now but is almost within reach, I think, of our technology.

D.C.: Santa Cruz is certainly the place for this. We have a Monarch butterfly tree here which collects millions of Monarchs each year. Have you seen this?

J.C.: No, but it must be marvelous.

D. C.: Have you done any other work with computers since HPSCHD; a work which you did with Lejaren Hiller?

J.C.: No, I have not done any work with computers since then. I first have to become educated and to know what has been done in the field, to see if I can invent anything in it. I don't know whether I can, but I wouldn't want to do it unless I could; that is, find something new — come back to zero. Zero there is very hard to find, because people are doing a lot of work.

D.C.: Do you think that technology would get in your way?

J.C.: No, not if I could find what everyone else has done. Then I think I could find something. I would have to be instructed. I haven't had the time yet to do that. I worked at IRCAM to make the *Roaratorio*, and they were disappointed that I didn't use the computers — I simply used the 16 track machines — so they don't really consider it an IRCAM project. On the other hand, since it's won a prize, they've changed their minds. They do now think of it as an IRCAM project.

D.C.: I have for some time been working with *Cartridge Music* and found it to be an unusual experience in many ways. The 'chance' element seems obvious from the beginning, yet as one lays out the various possibilities of the score, there is a kind of extraordinary pattern that develops — it's an amazing contradiction. One sees that the combinations possible are nearly limitless; at the same time, there is clearly a pattern, a logic, almost as if you've already seen each of the results in some way. Every performance is different, yet somehow every performance is the same. I am likewise delighted when I recognize your work from sound and style (though somehow that again seems contradictory). In indeterminacy do you perceive a 'style' or group of performances within a style? Are you surprised by performances of your music? Is that pleasant, difficult, or . . .?

J.C.: Again, I ignore it. I can't recognize *Cartridge Music* from one performance to the next. Somewhere I tell that story of going into a house in Beverly Hills, and the hostess to be nice had put *Cartridge Music* on in another room. We were having drinks in this room and I turned to her and asked, "What is that music?" And she said, "You can't be serious." I said, "It's very interesting; what is it?" And then she told me. I was pleased that I couldn't recognize it.

D.C.: How many times have you heard that particular piece?

J.C.: I don't hear it, you see. I performed it at that time with David Tudor, and we made a recording when Earle Brown was in charge of Time Records. Earle asked David and me both if, when we had recorded the individual tracks, we wanted to hear the end result. Neither one of us wanted to hear it.

D.C.: Did you in the process of recording the piece listen to what you were doing?

J.C.: We did, so to speak, what we had to do. You are usually a bit too busy to listen. And the idea there is that the players confound one another. That's one of the ideas of the piece. So that if you do listen to what you're doing, you're apt to get the wrong attitude toward the piece. What you have to develop is an indifference to whether your work is effective or ineffective; let happen what will. In my mind it arises from the experience that is so frequent in American life, of traffic congestion, and how to take it with what I call a sober and quiet mind, how to remain susceptible to divine influences.

D.C.: I find as I perform that piece that I listen, when I am able, in a very different way than I typically do. My Germanic tendencies of listening to all in respect to what has happened, or what will happen, becomes subjugated, much as with listening to Satie, to merely what is happening. Is that appropriate?

J.C.: Yes.

D.C.: You mention so often how important the questions are that you were asking in the process of creating a composition. Is it possible to paraphrase such questions in regard to such a piece as *Cartridge Music*?

J.C.: I think that those are explained, in a piece like Cartridge Music, in the directions, and by the materials, so that one playing the piece sees that the materials and the directions of the piece do constitute the questions.

D.C.: I understand, I think, and felt that way, but didn't want to seem presumptuous; that is, that I might know your particular questions.

J.C.: But why I made them that way, and why one permits a situation to arise, where one person's action (through changing an amplifier and tone control, etc.) will affect other people who are doing something that is not in his mind, puts the questions in a situation which results in a confusion of intentions and non-intentions. The desire to do that arose from that experience of traffic congestion — because everyone wants to go through the tunnel in order to get along a little bit further. But one doesn't necessarily succeed.

D.C.: In a performance of *Cartridge Music*, does it cross your mind that this is a good performance, a bad performance, or enjoyable . . .?

J.C.: If I think that way then I won't hear very well. The only time that I think that things are good or bad is when some other intentions than are proper to the piece take over. That happens so frequently with orchestral music, where the players don't do what they're supposed to do. Then I don't think that it's good or bad, but has moved out of the realm of music into the world of society and becomes a theatrical situation that was not intended at all. People ask me, "Well, isn't that music, too?" I say, "No, it really isn't."

D.C.: You must have had many of those experiences where, for a variety of reasons, particularly ego on the part of performers (I am reminded of the one with the New York Philharmonic — *Atlas Eclipticalis* with *Winter Music*).

J.C.: What's so annoying about orchestral musicians is their tenure and their lack of shame. They really are shameless. They'll smile and, after playing miserably, they'll say: "Come back in ten years and we'll treat you better . . ."

D.C.: In the performance of *Atlas Eclipticalis*, there are photos of you developing a large 'baton-metronome' to conduct the orchestra: a conducting machine. Is this something you developed after you saw Bernstein attempting to conduct the piece, or before?

J.C.: No. He was there for the rehearsals but the machine was the conductor at the performance.

D.C.: Then his look of perplexity was from something else; not from being usurped as a conductor.

J.C.: No.

D.C.: You used that method because you needed a certain exactitude for the timing sequences?

J.C.: It made it possible for the time to be much slower than it would have been otherwise. It was made by Paul Williams and it took six minutes to make a single sweep.

D.C.: Is it still around somewhere?

J.C.: I don't think I have it anymore. It has gone the way of all machines. All of that equipment may be out at Stony Point; David Tudor may have it up in his attic for all I know. David is a marvelous keeper of things and I'm very careless about objects. That's why I give everything away. That's why I've given my mushroom books away to this university (University of California, Santa Cruz). I keep boxes and put things in them, and give them away almost immediately or send them to places, because I am searching, you see, for this emptiness all the time. I'm a magnet in this society for material. Things are sent to me continually. I have no way to survive unless I get rid of them. It seems ruthless, but it is necessary.

D.C.: There have been three or four years (spent at different times during your career) that you've spent at universities. The ones at the University of Cincinnati and at the University of Illinois I am particularly familiar with. While I know very well that you've spent three or four weeks often at colleges, how have you worked in year-long situations? Especially, how has the reaction been to your stay? How do you feel about the teaching of composition?

J.C.: At Cincinnati I didn't teach. I was in residence and students could come to me if they wanted to, and a few very good ones (Walter Mays was one) did come. But it wasn't encouraged. I didn't encourage it. I didn't teach a class. It was like tutoring; and irregular. I did conduct some classes at Davis, but I didn't do anything at the University of Illinois.

D.C.: Did the students come to you there for instruction on a private level?

J.C.: They were allowed to, but they didn't.

D.C.: They just didn't come?

J.C.: I didn't encourage it.

D.C.: Did you discourage it?

J.C.: Perhaps.

D.C.: So you spent the time working, composing, and . . .

J.C.: Yes. I gave now and then lectures and a performance at the end. But I was very, very busy. And most of them knew that I was, so they did not want to disturb me.

D.C.: Does this suggest a thought on your part that composition cannot be taught?

J.C.: No. I think it can be done, but it is very difficult, and very time-consuming. I think that you probably agree. I think that each student must be honored and, rather than submitting the same body of information to each, you must find out what each one needs to know. Or what they can teach you, as Schoenberg would say. And that's not an easy matter. It resembles psychoanalysis, I think. It can be done; I have done it at times, but I don't think it's the proper use of my time.

D.C.: With the students that you have taught, would there be something that you saw in that student such that you would take them on? Or was it a random situation?

J.C.: It was a question where someone would come to me and say that they wanted to study. People still do that. I receive letters that say that so and so has come to the conclusion that he must study with me, and would I accept this situation. I mostly refuse. Now and then circumstances arise or a letter is such that I break my rule. I then don't teach, but I let the person come as an apprentice. The trouble with that is that when I find out who the person is, I become interested in him or her and I end by teaching a little bit, perhaps.

I have worked recently with a film maker, for example. He wasn't really studying music, rather film making. Therefore he was perfectly willing to help me in my music work because it didn't disturb his film making any more than it disturbed my music making. And he was discovering from something that wasn't teaching, really. He is currently making films with elaborate uses of chance operations, and applying it to every aspect of film making. The results are quite marvelous. One sees films like one has never seen. Rober Rayher is his name.

In 1969 at the University of California at Davis, I taught a course. In the beginning I stated that we didn't know what we were studying. I had also said when they asked me to come and teach, that I would only teach if everyone in the class got an "A." They agreed to that and it became acknowledged that that was happening, so it was a very large class.

Assuming that we didn't know what we were studying, we subjected the entire university library, which included books that you could get from Berkeley, to chance operations, so that each person was reading his book instead of everybody reading the same book. This was pointed out through chance operations. If the book a student was to read wasn't in, the student read the book preceding or following, according to chance operations, in the catalog. If the book he found was too big, he then subjected the book itself, or the parts of it, to chance operations, so that he knew which part to read. The result was that everyone studied and knew different information and was interesting to everyone else in the class. Rather than being in competition with one another, we all became givers of gifts. It was a very happy, pleasant and productive class, and productive of all kinds of things. There were some people who were cooking and other people who were making films, writing music, etc.

D.C.: Some of your critics have mentioned to me that one major factor in being alienated from your thoughts and music is that of a sense of avoiding skills, or avoiding a practiced or virtuoso approach. Their notion of 'skill' and 'virtuoso' is based on deciding something is good and working to intensify that narrowly as a goal until it is spectacular. Do you agree with the criticism (or even believe it to be a criticism), or are such critics simply missing the point of your ideas?

J.C.: That's a mistake on their part. Most of my music is written for virtuosos. The orchestra music is not written for virtuosos because orchestral musicians are not virtuosos. But the *Music of Changes* was written for David Tudor, and he is a virtuoso pianist. The *Etudes Australes* were written for Grete Sultan, and are probably the most difficult piano pieces ever written, demanding skills that include even how to sit at the piano. I receive over and over again letters from virtuoso pianists who find these pieces fascinating, most recently from Roger Woodward. He says that he's fascinated by them. I've heard different pianists play them and I'm delighted to see that the pieces will have a long life; again, in opposition to the general critical thought that my music will evaporate into thin air the day I die — which I don't think is true. If it did, I think there is enough of it around that it would germinate again, that it would come back. But I'm not concerned, really.

The pieces that I'm writing now for Paul Zukofsky, he says are the most difficult violin pieces that have ever been written. He objects to that difficulty and he can't work at them for more than about five minutes at a time. He has to stop and rest. Too difficult. On the other hand, he has explained to me, since I don't play the violin, that the history of violin literature has been one of increased difficulty as time goes on, so that it's only reasonable that these pieces should be more difficult than previous pieces for the violin.

We've worked on these closely now for three years. Now we're revising them, because through questioning me more closely, Zukofsky discovered that he had taught me about the difference of the strings and the practicality of using them; had given me, so to speak, a little bit of knowledge and, instead of letting the chance operations play utterly, I had modified them by what I thought was appropriate, violinistic. So now we are revising them and going back and letting the chance operations play utterly, and only modifying them when, from Zukofsky's point of view, it's literally impossible. The result is that it is a give and take between practicality and chance operations.

And it is this kind of use of chance operations that takes place in choreography, because when we leave architecture or the dance — things that depend on gravity and physicality — and move to something that, as Kierkegaard says, is free from physical problems, then we get into the area of great freedom that we think is characteristic of music. But if you then come back to music, not through its theory but through the playing of an instrument and the attendant virtuosity, then it becomes like dancing or architecture; whether or not the person can do it is the question.

Zukofsky is courageous; he is willing to do the impossible, which is what Schoenberg demanded in the *Violin Concerto*. And Zukofsky is willing at the same time that he is complaining. I keep track of his answers to my questions: of what is possible when you have your finger on such and such a string, and this finger on such and such another string, what you can do with the third finger. And we are going to publish the results. I have quite a card index; it includes all the questions regarding three fingers and what you can do with the fourth. He regrets that he published that article about all the possible harmonics.

Some composers using it have written music that doesn't make sense, he says. I'm working partly with that article but also, again, getting Zukofsky to edit it, or to revise it where necessary. So that these pieces are being made as a choreography on the violinist, which is the opposite of what a reasonable composer would do. Stockhausen, for instance, said to me once, "If you were writing a song, would you write music or write for the singer?" I said unhesitatingly that I would write for the singer. And he said, "That's the difference between us; I would write music." But then he wrote a song for Cathy Berberian and she couldn't sing it, because he asked her to whistle. She can do everything but she can't whistle. It had to be changed.

D.C.: It would seem to me that even on another level there is skill to be necessary in developing the right questions; how and when to ask these questions in the compositional process?

J.C.: I have enormous amounts of energy; I still do. And so I've never made composing easy for myself. Many people discount chance operations altogether as a simple way to make music. But it isn't. It's very time-consuming and very tedious; I've developed it to a high point.

D.C.: In *Music of Changes* you spent at least nine months . . .

J.C.: Yes, and these etudes (*Freeman Etudes* for violin) have taken three years; I'm nowhere near the end of them, and some of them will be literally impossible to play. It's just hopeless to think that they would be played, so we've decided to include them in the series but to synthesize them.

D.C.: Was there any thought to do as Ives mentioned, to have them "remain in the leaf," as in *114 Songs*, where it is suggested that they should not be performed at all?

J.C.: I am going to write them anyway, knowing that they can't be done, because nowadays we can synthesize them. In Ives's case it was just due to his point in time, I think. He would have wanted them performed now, if he were working now. He would be foolish not to. In other words, it would be 'un-Nancarrowish.' What's needed in this case is a 'player violin.'

D.C.: Which exists; a theatre here (in Santa Cruz) has such an instrument. It has a mechanical bow and various mechanical fingering possibilities up to quadruple stops. It can play very fast.

J.C.: Marvelous. It is the speed and the speed of transition from one string to another that is impossible in the *Etudes*, and the change of position on one string.

D.C.: It sounds very possible on this 'player violin.'

J.C.: Or violin four hands! At the same time that I've been writing the *Violin Etudes*, I have been writing pieces that I call "music of contingency," in which there is a rupture between cause and effect, so that the causes that are introduced don't necessarily produce effects. That's what contingency is. One piece, *Inlets*, uses conch shells, for example; if instead of blowing a conch shell, you fill it with water and then tip it, it will sometimes gurgle and sometimes not. You have no control over it. Even if you try very hard to control it, it gurgles when it wishes to . . . when it's ready to. Sometimes if you rehearse with it and think that you've got it down pat, you'll discover as I do, I'm sure, that it foxes you and gurgles when it chooses.

D.C.: Is the fact that recent pieces have taken so long to compose related simply to larger forces and longer pieces or to a deeper relationship with the fact that intricate chance operations take immense amounts of time to work out?

J.C.: In the early '40's I wrote *The Book of Music* for two pianos, which is an extensive piece, and that took me a long time. That, I think, was the first piece that took a great deal of time for me. I had in mind to write a long piece that would last the whole evening. It didn't have a title but it turned into those pieces called *She is Asleep*. The part of the evening up to the intermission was to be the female principle, and the part after intermission was to be the male principle.

That division is the division of *The Book of Music*, too; into two parts. I wanted to do it then with prepared piano, singers, and with chamber music that would make an evening. I only started the first part and then dropped the project. Then the next big work that came was the *Music of Changes*, and then those time length pieces. Things got longer and longer . . . *Atlas*, etc., . . . endless.

My plan, when I finish the violin pieces, is to write for another virtuoso. I'm fascinated nowadays by the virtuosos, not as a musical solution only, but as an example to society of the possibility of accomplishing the impossible, because our society in general now has serious problems. If they aren't solved, we are in, as Fuller puts it, "danger of oblivion."

The example of the virtuoso seems to me more and more necessary to a society that thinks that nothing can be done. Most people don't lift a finger to help the society because they think it is hopeless. That's why I insist upon this virtuoso situation and carrying it to impossible lengths now. Grete Sultan's devotion to the *Etudes Australes* is fantastic. She can now play, I think, the first 24 all the way through, and they are incredibly difficult, and she has had, as I have, bad arthritis. But at my advice she is on the macrobiotic diet and, like me, has shown incredible improvement. Her ability now is amazing. It's extraordinary. She plays beautifully.

D.C.: Is improvisation playing any role in your music at this point?

J.C.: I am very interested in improvisation now. I always fought against it. It seemed to me that improvisation was very related to taste and memory; and those were precisely the things that I was trying to free myself from. Recently, and in relation to what I earlier called music of contingency, where you have no control over the instrument, I can see that it's perfectly possible to improvise if what you do is ineffective. If you can make a faulty relationship between cause and effect, then you can improvise and still make a discovery, because your taste and memory won't have any control over the situation. The reason I didn't want to improvise was that I would be expressing my feelings. I do want a music in which I don't do that. So when I use improvisation now, it must be in situations where I have a low degree of influence.

D.C.: There's a biography being written about you now.

J.C.: He's a journalist from Minneapolis; his name is Roy Close. It's his first book, and he has a grant to do it. He causes me a lot of difficulty, naturally, because he's always asking me questions about my life and my whole need is to be free of that.

He also wanted to actually sit in the room while I was composing and follow me everywhere for a year. He told me he wanted to do this, and I said, "We'll have to alter your plans somewhat, because I need a certain amount of privacy." Then if he couldn't be with me while I was composing, he wanted to be with me when I wasn't. Finally at one point I said, "It would be better for you if I were dead." And he said, "That's not a bad idea."

The only thing that interests him is not me, really, but his own life. The idea that he's writing a book fascinates him, you know. He's absolutely delighted with the project, and the idea of what it will do to him — not what it will do to me. And I'm obliged to save myself in the face of that enthusiasm. He's discovering all kinds of things that upset my feelings. For instance, I had been told by my family (not by my mother or father, but by aunts and uncles) that my mother had two children before I was born, and that both of them died. Both of them had been called after my grandfather rather than after my father. My grandfather was called Gustavus Adolphus Williamson Cage III. These two that died would have been called Gustavus Adolphus Williamson Cage IV, and I've always felt that that was the reason they died . . . because they had such a ridiculous name . . . and that the only reason that I lived was that I had my father's name: John Milton. Close discovered that the second one actually had my name, but died anyway. One was born dead, and the other was a monster whose head was larger than the rest of his body. Fortunately he died after two or three days of life (he had my name). It would have been possible for me, you see, had I lived in Colorado (which I didn't; I lived in Los Angeles and Michigan), as it was for Boulez, as it was for Berio, as a child to go past a graveyard and see a grave with my own name on it. It happened to both of them but never happened to me. What happened to me was that they had my grandfather's name. Roy has now discovered that one of them had my name. I would have had quite a different feeling through my life had I known that I had already died, so to speak.

D.C.: Both Berio and Boulez mention that such knowledge was a very strong influence on their lives.

J.C.: Oh, of course. I think that it's marvelous that I was freed from that whole thing, and it's a little hateful of him to have discovered it. He's finding out all sorts of other things which are contrary to what I've thought all along.

D.C.: And he's telling you these things?

J .C.: With joy!

8.

INTERVIEWS WITH GEORGE CRUMB
Robert V. Shuffett

Interview, 19 July, 1977

R.S.: In music that is very tightly controlled, such as that based on total serialism, how many of the subtleties can even the composer perceive?

G.C.: I think that there are elements in any style that are not perceived consciously or intellectually, but which nevertheless induce a subliminal aural impression on the listener. When I listen to a Beethoven string quartet, I don't consciously follow the tonal scheme or chord progressions — that would merely be an analytical way of listening. We are all capable of hearing music in this way — or of learning to do so — but the effect and understanding of music do not depend on the conscious recognition of its constructional basis. The emotional or expressive force of music exerts itself irrespective of theoretical or analytical considerations. I have always disagreed with the idea that a listener must have an extensive knowledge of theory or analysis in order to enjoy music in the truest sense. I am sure that there are many people lacking in knowledge of the technical side of music, who have a great sensitivity to the most fundamentally important aspects of the art.

R.S.: What is the relationship between analytical validity, and actual musical validity in a given composition?

G.C.: Many compositions have been written which are filled with technical or constructional subtleties, but which are totally lacking in inspiration. One can make detailed analyses of certain traditional works which are not very effective as pieces, but which show roughly the same harmonic and structural characteristics as do masterpieces from the same stylistic period. I think that these questions are often confused. Just think of the countless academic fugues that must exist, many of which would be as intricate as those in *The Art of the Fugue*, though devoid of any really musical impulse. Compositional craft is something that we must assume in any music; what the music does beyond the mere craft is the essential question. Actually, craft is far less important than inspiration; in some cases, such as that of Mussorgsky, an enormously gifted composer, the craft is not always impeccable. With Mussorgsky, this really doesn't matter. The ideas are so striking and powerful that they exert themselves in spite of any technical weaknesses. Actually, the redundancies and awkwardnesses are part of the charm of his music.

R.S.: You once said it was a mistake to separate compositional technique from conception. What do you mean by this?

G.C.: A composer should not elaborate schemes for the sake of elaboration. Viable music requires that such schemes be associated with an expressive impulse. Exercises can be useful, but when one is working with original ideas in his own style, the compositional approach is quite different.

R.S.: Do you think that viable music in the style of Beethoven could be written today?

G.C.: I personally don't think that such music would be viable — it would be second-hand, derivative. Any good composer can of course duplicate the external characteristics of any given style, but it would be impossible for such music to be anything more than an academic exercise. I can imagine using a short passage of traditional music as a quotation or quasi-quotation, juxtaposed with other music, but anything in excess of this would lack validity in my opinion.

R.S.: Would a moment-to-moment approach to composition, in which the form of the work was allowed to evolve from the process of working, be as fruitful as an approach in which the form was arrived at with the very first musical ideas?

G.C.: I suspect that most composers use both methods. I would think any preplanning would have to be very flexible. A composer might very well start with a general idea of what the overall form of a piece will eventually turn out to be, but at the same time he would need to feel free to modify this at any point during the working process — or even after the work had been considered completed, if later — perhaps after the first hearing — the form doesn't seem satisfactory.

It might also happen that a composer might begin working on a piece without any idea as to what the form is going to be; at some point in the piece — perhaps at midpoint — he may suddenly be able to see the appropriate form.

R.S.: Could you comment on the role indeterminacy played in *Echoes of Time and the River*?

G.C.: I think that is a very low order of indeterminacy — considering how indeterminate music can really be. I wouldn't be interested in employing anything more indeterminate than the circle-music in *Echoes*. In this piece the emotional quality, the tempo, the dynamics, and the sequence of events are fixed; the indeterminacy involves simply the spacing between segments, which consequently affects the vertical alignment.

R.S.: Are you sure that such pieces will work before hearing them?

G.C.: Relatively sure, since a very limited use of indeterminacy is involved: the sequence of events is there, the textures are there and the fabric is there. There was in my mind a sense of what might conceivably come together, but the actual coincidence of tones between instruments is not critical.

R.S.: Do you believe that the principle of completion is a valid compositional procedure? What I mean by completion is, if one were working with the total chromatic, one tone at a time might be stated until all but the final twelfth tone had occurred; special structural prominence would then be given to that note. Does the fact that this twelfth tone hasn't been heard give it more prominence, and does the fact that it completes the chromatic scale also give it additional structural value?

G.C.: The effect of saving a fresh note in order to give it structural emphasis is constantly used by both serial and non-serial composers. Merely the fact that a tone completes a given scale would normally not give a tone more significant structural value, but such questions would have to depend on context. It's difficult to speak so abstractly about pitch, since many of the other musical parameters could affect the relative prominence of any given tone.

R.S.: Berg once stated that the greatest music resulted from 'ecstasies of logic.' What would you say about such a viewpoint?

G.C.: I think a kind of tension exists between the expressive impulse and the structural aspects of music, and this tension — this sense of struggling against technical exigencies — can enhance the music.

R.S.: Do you feel that a good composer could conceivably fail to receive recognition as a result of being a careless notator?

G.C.: Certainly bad editing and careless notation would stand in the way; one needs to be as clear as possible. The belated recognition of Ives probably had something to do with the poor editions of his music. Several of his works are still in that state. He was writing so fast that he might have felt spending time with careful editing would have broken the flow of ideas. When he did take time, as in the collection of songs which he published privately, the editing and notation are quite clear.

R.S.: Some composers feel that they need to compose every day to maintain their technique. How do you feel about this?

G.C.: I would have to be doing something each day that is related to composition, even if it weren't actually composing. There are always things such as copying and editing to do, and I would feel the need to at least do something of this nature.

R.S.: Would you include reading a book on notation as part of this compositional activity?

G.C.: (Laughter) No, that somehow seems to be in a separate category.

R.S.: Could you name several traditional pieces which you might regard as personal favorites?

G.C.: That would be very difficult. There are certain special pieces, including some of the late Beethoven works. I, like most composers, regard the *Well-Tempered Clavier* very highly. There are some works which simply stand out; taking Beethoven alone, there must be at least fifty works in this category; of the thirty-two piano sonatas, at least twenty have to be masterpieces of the highest order; of the seventeen string quartets, at least fourteen or fifteen are of transcendental import.

R.S.: How important for you is improvisation on an instrument in composition?

G.C.: It used to be more important than it is now; I used to do quite a lot of improvising as a way of experimenting with ideas. I still sometimes improvise in the preliminary stages of a piece; at other times I work directly on paper, and am not physically involved with an instrument. When I was younger, I frequently improvised solely for pleasure, but now, it has to serve the function of working out compositional ideas. In this way, it can be useful; if you are unencumbered with paper, the flow of consciousness is much more immediate. There are all kinds of precedents for this certainly; it was very important for Beethoven. Even after his hearing deteriorated, he still liked to try out his ideas at the piano, since the tactile sense was always important for him.

R.S.: Stockhausen and Boulez — as well as certain other composers — have called for one-half, one-third, one-sixth, etc. pedal in their piano music. Do you think this is a valid effect?

G.C.: I think there is an effect that you can call half-pedal, but more precise specifications of pedal would seem to be overly fussy. In many contemporary scores, you find overly fussy nuances; these various shadings of pedal are a prime example. The main thing is that the music should project unambiguously. The same thing is true with the specifications of quarter, third, and sixth tones. They are all heard by most listeners merely as different varieties of out-of-tuneness.

R.S.: What year did you begin publishing your scores with Peters?

G.C.: It was right after the completion of *Ancient Voices of Children*, so that would have been about 1971.

R.S.: Do you think other systems of intonation, such as just intonation, have viable compositional applications?

G.C.: I would be skeptical about the importance of just intonation. I would be opposed to fine distinctions that are not practical. Many contemporary composers have become obsessed with scarcely audible refinements.

R.S.: How important to the compositional process are your titles?

G.C.: They are important to the extent that they reflect in some way the spiritual content of the music. In any case, they have a certain symbolic meaning, which in a way focuses the feeling I have about a piece. For example, if one entitles a composition "nocturne," it limits and defines the expressive range; a certain kind of music is necessarily suggested.

R.S.: How strong has the influence of Robert Schumann been on your music?

G.C.: There hasn't been a strong conscious influence from his music, but I would say that I love many of Schumann's compositions. In his day Mendelssohn was considered the premiere composer of Europe; now it has become obvious that Schumann is many times the composer Mendelssohn was. I can't imagine a pianist or a Lieder singer without Schumann's music. Schumann can say so much in very brief pieces, and with such seemingly simple materials. When you get to the really great piano works, such as the *Symphonic Etudes*, the *C-major Fantasie* (one of my favorites - a really fabulous piece), and *Carnaval*, you are talking about incredible literature. The sonatas are fine, but underrated works, and there is an enormous output of miniatures, many of them extremely elegant. You hear so much about the orchestration of the symphonies being defective; basically, I don't feel this is true. I can understand a few modifications, but any drastic overhaul is not necessary. I think Mahler, for example, went a little too far with the Schumann symphonies; his instinct, which was almost infallible in his own scoring, seemed to desert him when he began touching up the orchestration of others. With the Schumann symphonies, the only touching up that needs to be done usually involves the addition of the horns to the woodwinds in certain passages.

But after all, in the Beethoven ninth you have to do the same thing (at this point, the composer hummed a passage from Beethoven's Ninth Symphony). In general, I think Schumann got the sound he wanted. Brahms was a marvelous orchestrator, but nevertheless, you hear criticism regarding the "turgid" quality of his scoring. He wanted a dark, rich fabric, which is an important part of his style. It wouldn't be Brahms without this quality. Even in his piano music, he favored very rich voicings and a prominent use of the lower register.

R.C.: With regard to the Rachmaninoff quotation that you originally incorporated in *Makrokosmos, Vol. I*, do you think you will reincorporate this when it becomes available in the public domain?

G.C.: I'm not really sure — I've become fond of the Chopin which I had to substitute; maybe one day a double version would be the solution. It would be nice to be able to use the Rachmaninoff, since it was part of the initial conception.

R.S.: What do you think of the music of Satie?

G.C.: I think Satie's music is quite droll; it can be amusing at times, but it is so restrained and reserved, with its aristocratic sense of irony, that it becomes tiring to the ear when one hears very much at a time. There is very little basic variety in his music from one piece to the next.

Interview, 11 June, 1979

R.S.: Do you think that a young composer just starting out should consciously attempt to discover an original style?

G.C.: Most young composers are searching for the language which would best project themselves. I doubt if it's a conscious process in most cases; rather, I suspect that most mature styles are a synthesis of all a composer has learned, plus his own unique contribution.

R.S.: Is it not true that just about any composer could come up with an 'original' style, in the sense of employing unusual juxtapositions of combinations, but that such artificially derived originality would necessarily lack sincerity?

G.C.: Yes, if the originality were too much of a self-conscious thing, it would seem arbitrary and capricious. I suppose one could attract attention by doing bizarre things that nobody else is doing, but this is certainly not the equivalent of having a convincing and original personal style.

R.S.: It seems to be different now in terms of achieving originality than it was in the common practice period, when a number of common stylistic elements were assumed.

G.C.: Yes, and as a matter of fact, I would think that it would be easier now to have some kind of immediate originality than it was in the middle of the nineteenth century; then there was a common practice, and, for that reason, originality would have been much more difficult to attain than it is today.

R.S.: Maybe it is a mistake for today's composers to want to establish their own style.

G.C.: I have always felt that originality is very important.

R.S.: Elliott Carter once described his scores as being auditory scenarios. Do you know what he may have meant by this?

G.C.: No; I can imagine that term being applied to almost any music, since all music is auditory, and all music lays out its own landscape and it own 'argument.'

R.S.: Carter also claims that he considers all of the instrumental parts as characters in a kind of drama.

G.S.: As did all the great composers of chamber music. What he is saying is true, but it also applies to traditional music. There is a strong sense within a string quartet by Schubert or Beethoven of the voices being protagonists within a musical drama — of each voice having its own character. Carter is thinking of his own string quartets; even his first quartet isolates the voices. In his third quartet, he ends up with virtually four independent soloists, who nonetheless contribute to a whole. Thus, he carries a traditional concept to its logical conclusion.

R.S.: I think that we once mentioned the fact that the Classical symphony is a kind of chain form, since the four movements are usually not related thematically — hopefully they are related in terms of ethos. Do you think there is a problem with this concept?

G.C.: Well, I think it's a fact that the basic ethos unifies such works. For example, in the *Eroica Symphony*, it's true that the movements are independent, but still the work has a cumulative force, even though the various movements aren't thematically connected.

The sequence of movements always seems inevitable, though it's difficult to determine just why it succeeds. In the later nineteenth century, the motto and cyclical elements used by some composers were intended to unify a series of movements. Beethoven accomplished this just as well without these devices — except for the *Ninth Symphony*, which, of course, does recapitulate in the last movement.

R.S.: We have discussed the term 'mystical' as applied to composers, and, in this context, mentioned Palestrina, Bach, and Medieval and Renaissance composers in general. You stated that you didn't think of yourself as a mystic composer. Why do you think Scriabin has been labeled a mystic?

G.C.: I'm not sure. For one thing, Scriabin had his 'mystic chord,' and he propounded certain metaphysical ideas which were somehow associated with his music.

R.S.: In Scriabin's case, I think the term 'mysticism' has different connotations than it did with the earlier composers we mentioned; in connection with Scriabin, mysticism seems to have to do primarily with non-religious aspects of the supernatural. He had some rather strange beliefs about music and its power to induce certain states. Would you comment on this kind of mysticism?

G.C.: There is a tradition of mysticism in American music, deriving from Charles Ives. Another word for it would be 'metaphysical.' In a work like the *Unanswered Question*, the premises are quite mystical; this is felt in musical terms. And yet, as far as I know, there is no program — only the title. Scriabin's mysticism may relate to Ives's in its basic character.

R.S.: In your own music, because of numerous extramusical references — mainly via titles — some critics have come to the conclusion that you are a mystic composer.

G.C.: Well, my music is in the Ives' tradition to a certain extent, I suppose, but also in the tradition of Debussy. I don't think of my own music as being particularly arcane or cabalistic. I'm not sure what 'mystical' means in today's music. There is the religious connotation, a certain misterioso quality, emphasis on imagery, references to the occult and to ritual — I suppose the term could include any of these aspects.

R.S.: Thompson, in his biography on Debussy, quotes the composer as making the following statement: "I should like to see the creation of a kind of music free from themes, formed on a single continuous theme, which nothing interrupts, and which never returns upon itself." Could you comment on this quotation?

G.C.: Debussy was a very mystical composer; some of his music seems to transcend formal ideas. Several works are of their own nature altogether, and show little relationship to earlier models. The *Sunken Cathedral* is not really athematic, but the themes are in the background: it is a continuum of a kind, and doesn't have the strong sense of being structured according to themes per se. The quotation you have read may also reflect Debussy's rebellion against what he considered to be formalistic Germanic compositional thought. In all senses, he was one of the most truly radical composers in the history of music. There are so many aspects of his music that in essence are antitraditional! It impresses me as having a greater degree of nonconformity than the music of many later twentieth-century composers often referred to as iconoclastic.

R.S.: Why do you think it is that so much serial music seems to be limited in terms of its range of expression?

G.C.: On that, I can only concur with my colleague, George Rochberg, who — of course — was for many years identified with serial music. He feels that there is a whole range of expression that this music doesn't adequately convey, and that most serial music has to do with a super-heated kind of angst. It's true that it does express all of that range: fear, malaise, desperation, and the related inflections; but, it rarely expresses joy, exuberance, playfulness, or a healthy eroticism. The reasons for this are complex. I know that twelve-tone composition arose in conjunction with expressionism, which, of course, existed earlier in atonal, and even in late tonal music. Expressionism in music seems linked intrinsically to the darker range of expression I just mentioned. Later serial music in general seems to have retained this connection. There are signs of expressionism in late Mahler — and in late Wolf and Wagner for that matter. Perhaps one could say that it was invented in its pure form by Strauss, in *Salome*.

R.S.: I've heard Stravinsky termed a 'musical parasite' because of his extensive borrowings. Do you concur with this view?

G.C.: It is true that Stravinsky did often borrow themes, forms, ideas, and techniques. His own saying was that good composers don't borrow, they steal; I'm sure he thought of himself as a thief, and not simply a borrower. In a sense, I think he was right; he did make much of what he borrowed his own. He draws from many sources, more than does almost any other composer I can think of, but the music remains Stravinsky.

R.S.: Most composers today would not consider making such use of borrowed material. Why do you think this is?

G.C.: There are very few composers who would be capable of doing that. Stravinsky had great technical competence, along with a certain ironical detachment, which enabled him to assimilate borrowed materials, alter their character, and use them in an ironical manner. In his Neoclassical music there is an implied irony that always goes beyond the borrowed elements.

R.S.: In looking at Schoenberg's music, I've noticed that — separate and part from the extremely fast harmonic rhythm — there is almost too much harmonic variety, in the sense that almost every vertical simultaneity is intervallically different.

G.C.: Schoenberg's music offers two basic problems to the listener. There is a sense of too much change, and also an overall sense of stasis; in fact, the extremely rapid harmonic rhythm produces a kind of stasis. The idea that repetition of any kind wasn't such a good thing is reflected in much of Schoenberg's music; there is a sense of almost total variation in certain works. The result is an extremely rapid "musical metabolism," which has puzzled many listeners, including Stravinsky.

R.S.: Wagner made the statement that "the secret of good orchestral sound is sustained tone." Would you agree?

G.C.: I think this describes late nineteenth-century orchestral practice very well, with its binding tones in the horns, the prevalent use of pedal tones, the infinitely long string lines, etc.

R.S.: Rimsky-Korsakov wrote in his treatise on orchestration: "To orchestrate is to create, and this cannot be taught." What did he mean by this?

G.C.: I think he is suggesting that the orchestration of an original composition is part of the actual conception, which is, of course, true. It would be less true as one moves back in time, but — even so — there are many older works — the Beethoven symphonies, for example — in which the orchestration certainly seems like an integral part of the conception.

R.S.: In Beethoven's symphonic sketches, does he write in any instrumental indications?

G.C.: I don't think so, but this is no proof that he wasn't making timbral associations. There are so many passages in Beethoven that seem to be conceived for a particular instrument. For example, the famous solo flute passage in the third *Lenore Overture* is constructed according to the flute's particular capacities — and there is the oboe part in the *Funeral March* of the *Eroica*, and of course there are the famous timpani passages in the *Fourth Symphony*.

R.S.: Could you comment on the fact that Brahms stopped composing for over a year in order to learn more of the literature, while — in contrast — Verdi seemed, according to a well known letter, to be almost indifferent to such concerns? (At this point Crumb paused to read "The Verdi letter which appears in *Letters of Composers through Six Centuries* edited by Weiss.)

G.C.: Beethoven made the remark, at one point, that he didn't want to hear works by other composers; he felt that doing so would jeopardize his own originality. It's hard to know how rigorous a fashion composers like Verdi and Beethoven actually avoided hearing other composers' music. Some composers, like Brahms, held a completely different view. Ultimately, such considerations depend on each composer's psychological make-up. And, of course, Beethoven and Verdi would have certainly mastered much of the literature in their earlier years. Maybe there was not much that interested Beethoven after a certain point in his career. Since he was the foremost innovator of his time, maybe there wasn't much he could learn from his contemporaries. He would probably have learned from Schubert, had he known earlier that Schubert existed. It was only during the very last weeks of Beethoven's life that he discovered Schubert's music.

R.S.: You once mentioned that, among contemporary composers, you found the music of Berio to be of particular interest. What aspects of his music have attracted you?

G.C.: The qualities of imagination, and the lyricism present in most of his music. In Berio's music, there always seems to be a genuine musical impulse.

R.S.: In the previous interview, we discussed the fact that in order to evaluate a style, it would be of value to know a few works that relate to that style. Do you think that as a result of the exposure that a serious composer automatically gets to popular music via T.V., radio, etc., that he absorbs enough by osmosis to be a competent judge of popular styles?

G.C.: No. I would be hard pressed to judge quality in the rock or jazz idioms. Such forms of expression are frankly ephemeral, and don't have any pretentions of being any more than that.

R.S.: Could you comment on the importance of unconventional spatial arrangements of instruments?

G.C.: Space has always been important in music, in the sense that an orchestra occupies space on the stage. There was always the sense of music coming from different parts of the stage. From its beginnings, opera utilized off-stage music and spatial effects. And there was the antiphonal tradition of the Venetian School and of the Colossal Baroque. I think that spatial effects are much less important than the actual music, although the spatial dimension can be expressive in itself.

R.S.: When you think about it, any conventional use of spatial effects in music is a form of aleatoricism, since every concert hall has its own construction, space limitations, and acoustics.

G.C.: That's true; in fact, the sounds from the stage itself will differ according to the concert hall, so that certain players deep into the stage will sound much more remote on some stages than on others; on some stages, the entire orchestra sounds as if it is coming from one source — you don't even hear the difference between far right and far left.

R.S.: How did the off-stage trumpet music in *Star-Child* sound at the New York performances as opposed to the Philadelphia performances?

G.C.: I thought the best performance in terms of sound and spatial effects was in Carnege Hall, thanks to its marvelous acoustics; the off-stage music there had the right weight. It is true that the hall does make a significant difference in respect to such effects, and, therefore, you have to design the music so that it doesn't depend on these.

R.S.: Would you comment on the 'work-in-progress' concept as seen in the recent work of Boulez?

G.C.: To me, the concept seems a little unusual. It focuses on the actual involvement with writing, rather than on the finished composition. One aspect of this concept is that if a given work is referred to as unfinished, the possibility then exists of significantly altering it in some way — for example, movements or sections might be added or taken away. The idea seems rather foreign to me.

R.S.: How would you compare German, Russian, and French orchestration of the nineteenth century?

G.C.: In the Russian tradition, which developed first with Glinka, there is a tendency towards separation of all of the choirs of the orchestra, resulting in very clear orchestration. This type of orchestration remained very important in the music of all of the later Russian composers, including Stravinsky. By contrast, the horn melody in Brahms' *First Symphony* is also in the oboe and solo violin — it is doubled in three octaves. This would generally not occur in Tchaikovsky, though you might have a unison doubling. In *Romeo and Juliet*, the D-flat major theme is played in unison by the violas and English horn — and even that seems a little exceptional for the Russian style. German orchestration relies more on mixtures, and also gives more prominence to the strings; in the Russian style, the winds have somewhat more autonomy. As far as French orchestration goes, there seems to be a strong relationship to the Russian technique; in both, as a result of the colors being generally unmixed, the texture is lighter, thinner, and more etched than in nineteenth-century German orchestration.

R.S.: How would you describe the formal construction of Mahler's symphonies?

G.C.: For one thing, Mahler didn't always insist on the total unity of keys throughout a symphony; the *Ninth Symphony*, for example, begins in D major and ends in D-flat major. His treatment of tonality within a large work is analogous to the tonal situation within an opera — there is a great deal of freedom. His treatment of actual forms was very untraditional; he tended to blend concepts.

For example, the first movement of the *Ninth Symphony* is really a mixture of sonata and rondo forms — it's refracted in a strange way. The exposition of the first movement of the *First Symphony* is terribly out of proportion; this movement amounts to a bizarre treatment of sonata form. It's perfectly satisfactory in a musical way; it just happens to be rather outré in terms of form. One might summarize Mahler's treatment of form as a very free elaboration of traditional patterns — so much so that one almost loses the sense of organic cohesion in some cases. There are also what I would call 'fantasy movements,' which have little or nothing to do with traditional patterns. An example is the last movement of the *Ninth Symphony*, which has long orchestral cadenzas interpolated along the way and is formally very free. It's a kind of rondo — as I recall — but with development sections; these can occur anywhere in Mahler. The first movements of the *Fourth* and *Sixth Symphonies* are more perceptible as genuine sonata forms — even though the proportions are quite large.

R.S.: When you listen to a Mahler symphony, are you consciously aware of the form?

G.C.: Normally, no; the form per se seems less important than the 'psychological curve' of the work.

R.S.: Do you enjoy reading Source Magazine?

G.C.: Source Magazine seems to be a sort of Dada organ, and I find few points of contact with my own aesthetic. To redress the balance, I also never read Perspectives of New Music! (laughter)

R.S.: We've talked about the fact that most of the higher ranking composers worked intuitively. Webern strikes me as a rare exception, in that he was obviously fond of elaborate precompositional schemes and planning.

G.C.: Yes, that's true. And in spite of this, the musical impulse is always strong in Webern. It is true that his influence has abated somewhat in recent years, but I think there will be a reappraisal. His best pieces impress me as being very personal and beautifully fashioned. Part of his constructional bent of course stems from his involvement with Medieval and Renaissance music.

R.S.: Why do you think it is that one's evaluation of a piece or a style can change over the course of time?

G.C.: All music has to be reborn for the precise moment in which you are hearing it; I personally am aware of this happening constantly. One remembers music heard previously, and one also responds to that some music as it is heard in the present; when you compare the two reactions, they are rarely identical. You may perceive something different upon returning to a work, and, for one reason or another, you may rank it higher or lower. Comprehension can also change. When I first heard the Bartók string quartets in early student years, I found the style difficult to understand. A little later, what he was doing became very clear. I'm sure this was partially a result of exposure to the quartets, but, it also was a result of psychological change on my part.

R.S.: As a humorous note, could you comment on the use of earmuffs by the string players in the recent performances of *Star-Child* given by the Philadelphia Orchestra?

G.C.: The string players apparently felt that the noise quotient was very high; they were sitting in an unconventional position at the back of the stage (behind the percussion section!) and were subjected to the kind of noise levels that brass players always must tolerate. The earmuffs didn't bother me, since, in spite of their complaints, they played like angels (laughter). The passage they found uncomfortable was a very loud section featuring the percussion; the loudest part was about two minutes in duration.

R.S.: Could you comment on your most recent piece, *Makrokosmos IV*, for piano four-hands?

G.C.: I would have to hear the piece first. When I've finished a piece, I have no idea of what it's about. It leaves my ear altogether until I 'relearn' it from actual performance.

R.S.: It seems appropriate that you have written a piece for piano four-hands, since you are so fond of playing four-hand piano music yourself.

G.C.: Yes, that's right — I am a veteran four-hand player.

R.S.: You have subtitled your new piece *Makrokosmos IV*; have you consciously employed elements from the other Makrokosmos works?

G.C.: There isn't anything literal, although the general style bears a resemblance to the earlier works. It uses the same extended range of timbral effects and I suppose there could also be certain subliminal connections.

R.S.: Why do performers consider Mozart so difficult as compared to Beethoven?

G. C.: Perhaps it has something to do with the transparency of the texture; and also what I would refer to as the 'irony' of Mozart's style. It is so balanced and sophisticated with its grace and elegance. Everything is so delicately balanced in Mozart. Much of his music is not difficult in terms of technical requirements, but getting beyond the notes is the problem — it has to become more that just a play of notes. Because of its special problems, some performers avoid Mozart's music altogether.

R.S.: Do you think it is possible for a really good composer to have lived and not been recognized in his lifetime?

G. C.: Schubert might be an example of this. His reputation was minimal; his music was known by only a few friends. He would probably have been recognized by a much larger public had he lived two or three years longer. Ives also comes to mind. In his case, recognition came very late. There are very few other examples that come to mind.

R.S.: Why do you think there have been so few significant women composers?

G.C.: It is probably related to the fact that, until recently, there have been few women in the profession. Women have contributed so much to literature. Now that so many women are studying composition and participating professionally in the field, I am confident that the whole picture will change.

R.S.: Stravinsky once made the following statement concerning his compositional practices: "My freedom will be so much greater and meaningful, the more narrowly I limit my field of action and the more I surround myself with obstacles." How did he do this?

G.C.: All I can think of is the overall sense of economy that you find in Stravinsky. He seemed to be trying to find the most economical way to express himself musically. He thought of form as being rigorous; he was much influenced by common-practice, especially Baroque forms, which he thought represented ideal types. Perhaps one 'obstacle' for Stravinsky was working within the confines of rigorous formal construction.

R.S.: Do you think this is related in any way to his concept of each new work as a 'new adventure?'

G.C.: In actual fact, I don't see each new work of Stravinsky as a fresh departure at all. There are several dozen Neoclassical works which have very much in common. Of course, Stravinsky is speaking subjectively of a 'new adventure;' in some ways, he probably did approach each new work differently.

R.S.: In a famous article of a few years back, entitled "Who Cares if You Listen," Milton Babbitt propounds the idea that a serious contemporary composer is involved with complexities so far removed from the frame of reference of the general listener that he should not be concerned with reaching any but a few initiates, just as the research scientist doesn't care about his theoretical ideas reaching a large public. Do you agree with such a view?

G.C.: I doubt that Babbitt really feels this way; otherwise, he would refuse to have his music performed at public concerts. I believe that such an attitude would be a kind of defense against criticism — against having your music out in the open where it should be and letting it speak for itself. If all composers actually felt this way, I fear the art would ultimately atrophy.

R.S.: You once mentioned that you felt the music of Gershwin was on quite a high artistic plane. Could you compare him with another composer who did not emphasize jazz elements?

G.C.: It's difficult to find a real equivalent. Gershwin's music is very vital. The source is a kind of pop culture, but the musical impulse is nevertheless very strong; the constant and total vitality is enviable. I believe his musical vitality was equal to any of his contemporaries. I'm speaking now just of vitality — not of range or depth; he obviously didn't have the range of Bartók, but he did have comparable vitality.

GEORGE CRUMB
David Cope

It came as no big surprise to me that George Crumb was as quiet and gentle a man as those who knew him had described him to me. He in fact was something of a legend among those of us wearing "new music" aficionados' hats. It came as no shock that his wife was a boisterous woman who smoked large green cigars and spoke almost as much as George didn't. Nor was it too shocking to discover that his daughter was an actress in New York City that liked to keep her Porsch in George's driveway while she was away. When I visited George in 1980 she was away and the Porsch was in his driveway and what ensued thereafter surprised me very much.

I had come to know George then because Robert Schuffett, one of George's former students, and I were trying to finish an ill-fated book of interviews with George and a lot of re-interviews were necessary in order to finish it. It never reached a point where finishing was possible though I did write George's biography in the C. F. Peters book on his work. The day and one-half I spent in those interviews were uneventful enough. George spoke slowly and carefully, taking long draws on his corncob pipe and re-lived many events of his life in Charleston growing up. He proved to be wonderfully entertaining and insightful as the hours wore on.

Nearing the end of the second day George's wife told him she was leaving and he warned her of my flight plans and of his need to get me to the airport on time. She acknowledged the timing of it and left. If George were to drive me as fast to the airport as he had *from* the airport, she wouldn't have had to get back with much time to spare. George drives like a mad man — as fast as he can and splitting yellow lights from red ones as good as anyone I know.

As time went on, however, George became quite concerned. His wife did not return and my flight, while not yet boarding, was reaching a ticket deadline. She did not come back and George, with great frustration suggested that we take his daughter's car to the airport. I had seen the red Porsch in the driveway the day before and assumed that was the one we were going to take. Since I had never been in a Porsch before, it sounded exciting. That wasn't the word for it.

As we came out the front door, George paused and reached down to pick up what looked to me like a kind of garden watering-can and filled it with water. He then went over to the red Porsch and opened the hood with such a resolve that he appeared to know the car thoroughly. I was wrong. Without pause, he unscrewed the oil cap and began pouring water into the oil spigot. I jumped.

"George," I yelled, "don't do that."

"I know what I'm doing." he answered.

"But, George, you're pouring water into the engine. It doesn't go there."

"How do you know that?" he asked.

"Because it belongs in the radiator in order to cool the engine." He looked a little confused.

Finally, he asked me where the radiator was. I pointed to the front of the engine where it usually is and was.

"Are you sure?" he asked.

"I am, George" I said, "I really am."

He asked, "Well, do you think that my pouring it there has caused any damage?"

"No," I said, "we can drain it out and fill it again. But I don't think that you should leave it out overnight. It is winter and with the freezing temperatures it probably would crack the engine block with the expanding and contracting of the water."

He looked especially pained at my last remark.

I said, "Don't worry, I'll catch another flight and you can get more oil from the gas station when your wife returns."

He still looked pained. I asked him what was wrong. He said that his daughter had told him that the radiator leaked and he should put water in every so often.

"I've been putting water in here every day for the past two weeks," he wheezed. I thought we both would cry.

"Do you think it still might be okay?" he asked.

"I don't know," I replied, "you could always try and turn it over."

"Turn it over?" he asked.

"The engine, George" I said. "Turn over the engine, you know, try and start it up."

"Oh," he said, "do you think I should?" I looked at him for a minute and then shook my head.

"No," I said, "I wouldn't touch that car again," I said.

Just then George's wife returned. George said, "Let's go!" I tried to refuse, but he would have none of it.

To say we made a dash for the airport is an understatement. But I don't think that anyone could have gotten me there faster. As I left him in the street in front of Philadelphia's International Airport I noticed shrubbery caught in his car's front grillwork. I didn't have the time or the inclination to ask him how it had gotten there. Nor will I ever do that. Nor have I ever asked him about the fate of the Porsch. There is something special about my memory of George's semi-connection with the real world.

9.

AN INTERVIEW WITH DONALD ERB
David Felder

D.F.: You studied with Boulanger, among others. How did that study influence your growth as a composer?

D.E.: Well, I think that one of the things that the study in France taught me at that time was a useful kind of reinforcement about my own educational background. The attitude there was that if you were an American you must somehow be under-educated in the theoretical subjects. When I arrived, they tested me to find out if I could do all of the things that they thought the French students could do. I think that all of that has had a certain amount of long range meaning to me. We've always, as a nation, musically speaking, had this feeling of inferiority the moment a European puts us down. I don't think that's true at all. The people that studied with Boulanger in the twenties and thirties went there at that time for good reasons. Those people brought their knowledge back here and were able to transmit it on a national level. Those were important people; and so we were educated by a group of musicians who had been educated in a better way. We were then in less need of the so-called refinements that one used to get in Europe after World War I. We were simply the products of better teachers who had learned their trade in Europe in the beginning of the century and we didn't need the European finishing school anymore. We may be back to needing something again, because I think the educational process in this country is slipping and there may come a time when we either pull up our socks or figure out what else to do.

D.F.: But you specifically . . .

D.E.: I found out that I knew a lot of the things I was about to be taught. Also, she and I were philosophically in different worlds. She believed so strongly in the abstract forms and artifices of certain contrapuntal devices and all of the things she had taught to composers for a long time, and she was down on the kinds of music that, at that time, I admired. She didn't like serial music at all, frequently making rather bad comparisons between the Viennese composers and others. I couldn't quite see that because I'd studied with a very good serial composer and I'd learned a lot from him. I therefore came back to America feeling a lot better about the state of musicianship in my own country.

D.F.: One of the benefits that is frequently mentioned in connection with Boulanger study is her ability to generate lots of music from the students. In other words, the students write and write and write, producing a good deal of music. Did you consider that a positive experience?

D.E.: No, I'd already been through that. At some point in your life, you do have to acquire a certain degree of facility, if only to negate it. In other words, to say, "I could write that piece by next week, but I'm not going to," so that there is a kind of security in knowing that you could do it. When that is turned into facility for its own sake, it becomes the turn-on-the-faucet-and-let-it-run kind of music that I can't stand. There is a type of music that we shouldn't really do, except for movies maybe.

D.F.: You were, and maybe still are, a jazz trumpeter. Can you be specific about the impact that experience has had on your music?

D.E.: I think it's had a lot to do with how my music has developed, because I became interested in jazz at a very early age. I can remember trying it even in elementary school, and was having a really good whack at it by the time I was in the ninth grade. I actually played my first jobs in bars in the ninth grade. I was already making my way through twelve bar blues in B-flat when I was fourteen years old.

The kind of musical gesture I made was formed. Although these haven't had a direct influence on me for the past twenty years, I still can hear my phrases rolling off a kind of blues line. There was a time in my life when I thought about that more consciously than now and I decided that, as the saying goes, you can take the boy out of the country, but you can't take the country out of the boy. So, it's had a deep influence.

I think my music's full of little bluesy gestures sometimes, and it has lines that kind of roll, like Bach does. In addition to that, I think there's also, at its best, in the jazz world, the idea that it's not a bad idea to communicate with your audience. There was a period in the middle fifties where it became so remote that the audience did lose interest in it. But before that, there was nothing wrong with the idea of making people sit up and enjoy. So, given my background, the audience was always somehow in my mind. What kind of impact is the music going to have — it doesn't become just an abstract thing that you're putting on paper, but a sound experience that will have some kind of an impact on other people, maybe not even a nice impact, but an impact.

D.F.: Stylistically, you've gone through several different changes. We don't know your early works — they're not in your catalogue . . .

D.E.: No, they're destroyed, actually.

D.F.: . . . but, there seems to be a very unique Donald Erb style, especially in comparison with more "eclectic" composers. How would you characterize your style and how has it changed?

D.E.: Well, I think that one of the ways to hang onto a style is to not analyze it too carefully. I've really stayed away from self-analysis. I write music by ear. I write trying to give the music form and shape, by tempering it with drama and time. And I don't get too far into analyzing its form, either. So what I really try to do is to deal with music the way I hear it on an instinctual level for climax, coloration, melody, ways of creating contrast, and so on and so forth. Into that pot goes your whole background, which early on was blues, then study with Marcel Dick, and other experiences.

All of those things have an impact. All of that music which has a direct influence of jazz and serial methods was the stuff that I took down to the furnace one day because there was a point at which it all began to synthesize into something else that felt more natural to me. That dates from about 1958. I began to see the daylight at around then. So it's really an instinctual process, although I go back to what I said before — I hear certain kinds of phrases and gestures. Another important influence of the big band days has to do with instrumental coloration. I learned a lot in those days about combinations of mutes and so forth, and I became very interested in color.

As far as being able to directly analyze what is mine, I can't really, and in a sense don't care to do it. There are certain intervals you'll never find in my music, which naturally creates a particular aura. You can go from one piece to the next and almost never find a sixth, major or minor, and the same is true for a perfect fourth. That's a reaction, I think, to quartal harmony which I put myself through many years ago — you know, the Hindemith books and all. Well, I went through that and once you do and find out how facile it is, there's perhaps a reaction to it. I use things now, rather unabashedly, that I didn't before, such as triads and chromatic scales. I think it's hard to identify because style has more to do with rhythm than we realize. Viennese music is spotted by its rhythmic characteristics more than anything else. And I think that's true of my music, too. Also, perhaps, the treatment of form.

D.F.: There are chuckles and belly-laughs in your music. Where does the humor come from?

D.E.: I don't know. I didn't come from a background that had particularly humorous people in it. Humor, in a way, is something you do instead of crying; it's an alternative to feeling dejected. The dichotomy between the great clowns and how they really felt, and a tragicomic figure, like Charlie Chaplin, has been shown historically.

I don't think it's just humor. Humor is an emotion that is very profound, if it's right, and we have a tendency not to think of it that way, because we acquired our idea of what deep music is from a Germanic tradition, which was not very big on humor — *Till Eulenspiegel* is about as funny as it gets! Humor is very indigenous to this country, and I think we have expressed some very deeply felt things through humor. Certainly the sixties had a lot of that. You expressed your ideas about certain American institutions musically through humor, but the feelings that were being expressed were very intensely felt. That's deep in the nature of this country.

D.F.: It has been said that when one commissions you to write a piece, the result is that one purchases a couple of yards of Erb.

D.E.: Oh, God, that's a terrible statement. (Laughter)

D.F.: Is that necessarily a negative statement? Couldn't it be an indication that you do have a recognizable style?

D.E.: Well, it can be a negative statement. Was it meant that way? It can certainly have that connotation. Well, I think that statement is reflective, in part, of the attitude of commissioners. They have that attitude towards most things that they commission. They know that they're getting a typical kind of music from some composers and so they'll order some more of the same.

Actually, that statement represents one of the most common problems for a composer. You know, give-me-some-more-of-what-they-liked-last-year. That's a very common syndrome for artists in general and particularly for painters. "I sure would like a picture like the one that you did for so-and-so, which was so successful." So gimme some more of that, let's have some more of what worked. For a composer who's trying to move on to the next thing, the next thing might not be what is in demand. You can have a real conflict on your hands, sometimes an honest-to-God conflict over whether to earn a living or not. That's where people can get into trouble.

There's a saying attributed to Picasso, and I can't quote exactly, but it says, "When you steal from somebody else, that's okay, but when you steal from yourself, you're in trouble." I think that's true, and when you spool off another yard, you better be darn well careful that it's not the same fabric. When you start imitating your own successes, you're probably in trouble.

D.F.: You've mentioned that your own approach to form is primarily intuitive. Other composers tend to employ more systematic means. Are these methods of process incompatible?

D.E.: I don't know. I think that those items, whichever direction a young composer chooses, are things that a talented composer will work himself through. I think that sometimes those will represent obstacles to him, but I don't think that there's anything that could have stopped Berg, for example, from being a good composer. Whether he decided to write twelve-tone music, or non-twelve-tone music, wouldn't have made any difference. That he embraced that style of music is probably immaterial. So I think that differences in approach, let's say, the intellectual and the intuitive methods, probably don't mean too much.

I know people who think they're intuitive composers, and all they do is write second-rate facile music, and that can be mistaken for intuition. On the other hand, I know composers who consider themselves intellectuals who are not doing at all what they say they're doing. In that case, they're writing very good music, while if you listen to the words they like to say about their own music, you don't want to listen to it. You get both ends of the spectrum. But I think that eventually talent will out, regardless of the approach of the composer.

D.F.: One of the remarkable aspects of your career is the tremendous success you've achieved with large pieces; for example, fifteen orchestral works. That fact is rather phenomenal, especially in light of the difficulty of getting those works performed. Is working with large forces more comfortable for you?

D.E.: It's an old truism about music, that a good chamber piece is harder to write. I think that is probably right. I know that it's just an awful lot of fun to be able to write a piece for over a hundred musicians with all the palette available. If writing a trio is fun, why shouldn't it be fun to write a piece for a hundred people?

The business of the orchestral works stemmed from one or two that were successful with a lot of orchestras, so that there's been a whole succession of orchestral commissions, followed by something in a way that was even more intriguing — a whole series of concerti for some very intriguing soloists, people like Stu Dempster and Lynn Harrell; so that if I was about to be bored with the idea of writing for orchestra, it was very hard not to get excited again about writing a piece for Stuart or Lynn. That kept me moving.

I think it really is true, in some ways, that it is harder to write really tight music for six people, that really keeps working and moving and holding your interest. The orchestra gives you an expanded resource and, in some ways, that makes it a little easier.

D.F.: But a practical question: how did you manage to get those pieces played?

D.E.: Accidentally! The first piece was a work called *Symphony of Overtures*, which was, in point of truth, a graduate dissertation. It was picked in a contest by the Seattle Symphony, and one of the conditions was that I'd get a tape of the performance. With the tape of the Seattle performance in hand, I then managed to interest the Cleveland Orchestra. At that point, things began to take off. This eventually led to an invitation to be composer-in-residence with the Dallas Symphony.

I wrote *The Seventh Trumpet* and kind of the same things happened there: they played it, I received a tape, and off it went. That led to other pieces. Ever since that point, it's been self-perpetuating. The initial thing was by winning a contest! After that, it was serendipity; somebody would tell somebody, and so on. As you know, the classical music business is largely a word-of-mouth grapevine. It's such a small-potatoes world compared to the business of pop music, that that's how the pieces went around — conductors talking to other conductors.

D.F.: You've done a lot of work with tape, using both concrete and electronic means. But you seem to have stopped working in the studio. Why?

D.E.: I have stopped, because I didn't know where to go, artistically. I thought that with what I knew in the studio, I'd gone as far as I could at the moment. So I needed to back off and think about it.

D.F.: And what have you been thinking?

D.E.: I've been thinking that I still don't know what to do! (Laughter). But I think it might be interesting to go back with more of a musique concréte approach. I also would be interested in exploring the idea of using live performance instruments. I've done that a little bit, as you know, in some of the chamber pieces which use live electronic instruments of one kind or another, so I haven't totally left it behind. I've been using electric piano, small synthesizers, and the like. But I am interested in working my way through a more traditional approach to tape, if there is such a thing. And that's if I go back at all. I just became more interested in music without tape.

D.F.: That's interesting to me because that sort of reaction seems to have happened to a great number of composers working in electronic studios worldwide. They work for several years in a studio, and then they've done it and they leave.

D.E.: I spent about seven or eight years working fairly consistently in a studio. Yes, there was a kind of worldwide trend toward and away from it, and I think that a lot of people are kind of thinking it over now that they've made one big plunge. They're also thinking about where it's going and, also, some are waiting for the next developments.

You and I have already agreed that it's probably digital synthesis and computer studios. That might make things much more musical and a lot easier to accomplish. Of course, that's only a guess, but I think it's a pretty good guess, judging only by the few things I've heard. Some of the things from Stanford are so much more facile than anything you could ever do in a conventional electronic music studio. That seems to be the direction that things will go.

D.F.: What do you mean by "much more musical"?

D.E.: There's much more subtlety available. For instance, with a synthesizer you would set a registration and it would stay that way for note after note until you did something about it. So you were always stuck with the same kind of attack/decay patterns for a period of time and they're very hard to change, unless you want to splice every note. Particularly in the subtleties of attack and decay, where acoustic music still has the edge over electronic music by quite a bit. I think we'll be able to do something closer to acoustic music with computers.

D.F.: You've also done a lot of mixed-media works, but not too much recently.

D.E.: Well, that still interests me a lot — the only thing I haven't come up with is a good idea! I like the idea of theater. I grew up involved with that kind of thing, too. My parents, from the time I was a little boy, sent me downtown to the Higbee Department Store, where I had a job for many, many years as a child actor on radio, and I worked in their theater. I was on the air at 5:15 every Monday, Wednesday, and Friday in Cleveland. When my voice changed, I got fired. That doesn't have anything at all to do with music necessarily, except that theater always has interested me. The idea of theater pieces in the sixties I found very appealing. I didn't do very many of them, but one — *Souvenir* — is still performed. All I'm doing is waiting for another good visual idea to come along, but I haven't really come up with one.

I don't think you can force theater, and that was one of the problems in the sixties. A lot of theater pieces were sort of superimposed on a piece of music, and they seemed amateurish because of it. I think that theater and the music should come as a single idea, or even possibly having the theater grow from a convincing musical composition, and that isn't very easy to do. I've done about four theater pieces, two of which are still played. I've been working on an idea that has to do with hutches built out of balloons, but we'll see about that.

D.F.: With this amalgam of experience, you're also slowing down. The recent piano concerto took about a year. What comes next?

D.E.: I have a couple of chamber works to do and an orchestral commission in the not-too-near future — I don't know what it is — maybe at a certain point, and I'm certainly not a child anymore, and I've written a lot of music as you've mentioned: fifteen orchestral works. I guess all told, about eighty or ninety pieces.

D.F.: Not counting the ones that were torched.

D.E.: Right. And too, I've had a tendency, and maybe this is the beginning of the end, to look over my own shoulder a little bit. As I do that, I find that getting on to the next thing is getting harder. Maybe that's why a lot of composers at a certain age finally just slow down and stop; I don't know. I'll find out pretty soon, I guess. But I hope not. It is a much slower, harder process for me now than it was — much harder. Part of that has to do with the fact that as you hold down a job at a certain point in your life, there seem to be additional demands on your resources and time, too. Musical service organizations ask you to serve and help them. I don't think that one should turn them down, and they do take time. But it's important. If we're going to help the classical music in this country, I think you have to do your best to aid certain organizations.

D.F.: You've been really outspoken about the plight of the American composer and musicians in their own country. Could you expand on those ideas?

D.E.: The American composer is constantly fighting the snobbery of American management and the American symphony orchestras. On that level, the people who are management tend still to look to Europe for quality music. I don't just mean the concert managers. Many of the orchestras themselves have a tendency to look toward Europe. I think they do it unconsciously. It's an old habit that I'd like to see them break. They seem to just forget. Also, many of the music directors received their training by working in European opera houses. They have one foot in Europe. They have a tendency to look back in that direction more than I think they should.

There are a lot of good American composers around who would love to have a shot at writing an orchestral work. There's a lot of talent around, a lot of good, young talent. How can we expect this talent to develop if we don't give them a chance to grow? We have to give ourselves elbow room. When the Canadian orchestras go on tour, the government makes sure that they take a Canadian piece with them. We don't require any such thing and probably shouldn't. It should be a voluntary thing. But you can't learn how to write music unless people play it. The end result of composing is the presentation of the music, and at that stage the composer probably learns the most. If we don't constantly give him that opportunity, he's not going to learn from it. The only place where the composer is getting that kind of quick response to his creative efforts right now is on campuses. This is why so many composers have made homes on American campuses.

D.F.: Is that a healthy thing?

D.E.: It's a mixed bag. Obviously, it's providing the composer with a living and it's providing a limited laboratory, depending on who's on the performing faculty. Here, as well, many performing faculty are unsympathetic to their own composer-in-residence, but some people there are flexible, thus providing a limited experience. I think, though, that the composer really needs it on the professional level, too, and this is where we're not helping the American composer very much. I would think that now that we've gone through several generations, and found an Ives and Varèse and other people, we would know that there was good music written by composers who live here. So I don't see why people can't realize that, in this century, if we've produced several significant American composers, that's good enough.

D.F.: And what about Ives? He seems to have become a folk hero for American composers. Are there any specific, or general, ways in which he's influenced your work?

D.E.: I don't think he necessarily relates to my music. That's not where I came from. I have a couple of pieces that have quotes in them, but everyone's done that once or twice — you know, *Frère Jacques* in the Mahler, *Ach du lieber Augustine* in Schoenberg — so I don't think that part of it has much to do with me.

Actually, I have nothing but admiration for his music. I do honestly think that he's a significant composer. One of the interesting things about him is that I find that what makes his music communicate to me can't be analyzed. From any standpoint that I learned to analyze music, his music just doesn't quite make sense. But then, when you put it on and listen to it, you say, "Oh, yes!" I don't think this music is actually approachable from any of the old syntactical-analytical points of view. But you listen to it and it's dynamite. Not all of it, but there's enough of it that is. Remember, not all of Beethoven is wonderful either, so there you are. The Ives that's good is stunningly good, but it's very hard to know quite why.

D.F.: But what do you think he holds for American composers? He's held up as a kind of iconoclastic figurehead.

D.E.: In that sense, I think he's very American, you see, because we really do go through our lives setting up institutions and knocking them down as fast as we can. That's a very American thing to do. I mean, you set something up, get it running, then criticize it, and go tearing after it. And he did that with a lot of things.

I think the other thing he represents to a lot of us is an American composer who has really made it. In a way, you can look at Ives and say that there really may be some hope. Perhaps another American composer can receive proper attention one of these days. For me, it's nice to know that this country has produced a composer of this stature, although I hasten to add that Varèse represents the same thing. They represent people who lived here and made it. Ives, I suspect, is a lot better known to the general public, although Varèse is a composer's composer.

D.F.: How is your work at the National Endowment for the Arts geared toward helping some of these situations?

D.E.: The National Endowment is simply providing commission money for composers with very few strings attached. I think that's important. They ask for "x" amount of dollars to stay home and work on a piece for three months in the summer, and the Endowment tries to help them out.

D.F.: Rather than directly helping, why isn't money provided for orchestras to commission composers?

D.E.: That's very hard. Due to their lack of expertise, orchestras don't always do a good job of picking composers.

D.F.: From the point of view of your own lengthy experience with it, how would you characterize the American contemporary music scene right now?

D.E.: I think it's struggling, and struggling rather badly right now. Somebody back in the early seventies said, "If you liked the fifties, you're really going to love the seventies."

I think the country has taken a strange kind of turn, so that the country's almost split in half into, on the one hand, a leftover, fermentation-kind of decadence from the sixties, and a very conservative side on the other. It's the kind of split that's occurred in Britain, where the whole country is split very hard down the middle and there's very little middle ground. I think that's where we are here, too. On the one hand, we have some classic signs of decadence, and on the other hand we have a reaction to that decadence, a kind or arch-conservatism. This is a subject big enough for a whole separate day, of course. But it's a rather potent brew. In the thirties, it got us a Hitler.

I hasten to add that I don't think that will happen here, because first of all this is not a homogeneous society, but it is going to cause us difficulty and it is going to cause the arts difficulty, and already has. To me, this part of the seventies seems to be incredibly tasteless.

There's an awful lot of bad taste going on that's getting a lot of applause — more bad taste than I've seen in a long time, and maybe more than I've seen in my entire life. When whole questions of judgment about good and bad, truth and lies, and so on seem to be in an area of hazy ground, then we're dealing with one of those areas of decay. Strong words maybe, but I do think we're in a kind of decadent state at the moment. Those aren't just my words, a lot of people have expressed them and I tend to agree with them.

The solution may be that we should all tell the truth a little more often. That would be a good opener. I'm very concerned for the young composer in this country right now. In a way, my contemporaries and I were very fortunate in that we began working when there were opportunities. I think those opportunities have dried up somewhat. Many of us were on the scene when there were things to be done. There are still things for the middle-aged composer to do, but I'm very concerned about what there is to do if you're 25 or 30 years old. It's a very worrisome thing. We have to be concerned about the longevity of our profession and right at the moment it doesn't look as good as it once did.

One reason is the economic factor. I also happen to feel that the educational quality is slipping in the country. In other words, we're not training the young composers as well as we were. I have a gut feeling that it's just not as good. Education these days has become so fiscally sensitive; we cheapen the education in order to save a little money. We shorten the school year, we hire part-time people in place of full-time people — all as a way of saving money, but they're also changing the quality of the education. This has shown up sharply in some areas, such as musicianship training.

In summary, the promise of the sixties has not worked out for American composers in a way, and I'm sorry to see that. The sixties, although they were a little crazy, had all kinds of positive thrust, and the seventies have turned out to be really confusing times for a lot of composers in a lot of ways. The economic opportunities seem to be going down, the stylistic things have gotten very mixed up. Now we have some trends that I don't think are very relevant ones, or very interesting. These have been very hard times. I hope that the eighties will straighten out and go somewhere more positive.

10.

TÊTE-À-TÊTE
Heidi Von Gunden

I just had the strangest experience — someone was peering over my shoulder while I was looking at the score to my *Mass for Pentecost*. Not long ago I wrote it as a challenge to see if I could compose a contemporary Mass that was suitable for a litergical situation and not compromise my musical taste. What is this I hear?

VOICE — Hmm . . . is this an illuminated chant manuscript?

HEIDI — No, it's the magazine-collage score to my *Mass for Pentecost*.

VOICE — Oh, I see, you are experimenting with some new ideas. It was like that in my day. You should have heard my choir complain. No one was agreeing about modus, tempus, and prolation. We weren't coming out right at the cadences because they refused to follow a double tempus. Any prolation other than a three wasn't music to them. It was like directing a herd of mules. Finally I got them trained. We had quite a bit of trouble with the 'Amen' to both my Gloria and Credo. You know I really like those expressive hocket sections. I think of my *Mass* as a big motet. You should have felt the evil eye of my fellow clergymen when they heard it.

HEIDI — Could my wildest dream be happening? . . . You must be Guillaume Machaut and that is your *Messe de Notre Dame* you are talking about. Now I know why you are here. I like to imagine what composers of past centuries would say about today's music. Machaut, you don't seem as shocked at my score as some of these twentieth-century people. I think each age has its searchers of new sounds and ideas.

MACHAUT - Yes, I like to keep contemporary. We ghosts are aware of what is happening. I have been a member of the avant garde for many centuries. Tell me how does this strange looking score work?

HEIDI — There are seven poster boards for the different sections of the Mass ordinary. Each poster has a magazine-collage that shows an affective state. Distressed humanity represents the 'Lord, have mercy,' heaven space pictures are the 'Gloria,' trees depict the 'Holy, holy, holy,' desert scenes the 'Blessed is He,' and sheep are featured for the 'Lamb of God.' Directions tell the singers what pitches to use and the pictures influence the timbre and texture of their music. Taped environmental and language sounds accompany the Mass.

MACHAUT — What were these language sounds? I'm interested in them.

HEIDI — I had five of my friends say the text together in Spanish, German, French, Italian, and Chinese. That way I got a mixture of words and sounds. The choir was singing in English.

MACHAUT — It reminds me of some of the late thirteenth-century motets that use different texts and combine Latin and French.

HEIDI — I wasn't thinking about those.

MACHAUT — I like these pictures. Tell me, how did your choir react to the score? You know I was very careful about my scores and it made me angry when they wouldn't pay attention. My choir was accustomed to the old ways — chant, organum in two or three parts, plus occasional conductus style. At one time I thought there might be a rebellion.

HEIDI — You know, Guillaume, you don't mind if I call you by your first name, that's the custom today even among the clergy; I had the same experience. The group was so hyper and afraid of anything new that I felt I could show them only a little part at a time.

MACHAUT — Heidi, I'll imitate your mode of address, in my years of experience in an age that once was, I have found that choirs are odd collections of people. But mind you, they are sincere and if you can gain their confidence, they will try to go along, but of course, they find it difficult to listen.

I had a terrible time getting the choir to sing in four parts. I just love that full sound, especially when I included the third of the triad — such a rich, thick sound. I didn't have this texture all of the time, I alternated and had instruments play parts, but the band width was such a change from the single line of the chant Masses. I love that music, the chant I mean, and sometimes I think it is a mistake when choirs don't sing it. You know of course that the tenors of the 'Kyrie,' 'Sanctus,' and 'Agnus Dei' are cantus firmi from the chant masses.

HEIDI — Yes, I did the same thing for my *Pentecost Mass*. The sung pitch material and the organ part were from 'Lux et origo' and I based the time structure on how long the chant takes to perform it. In a sense it became a scaffold like your isorhythm. I certainly agree that the chant should be used. Its mystical sense reminds me of the Indian raga and the great spiritual power that group of people apply to music.

MACHAUT — It sounds like the Greek Doctrine of Ethos. I read those things in my seminary training, but people weren't so interested in aesthetics, writing motets and ballades were the things of my day. You know we really were experimenters.

HEIDI — I read that you even had a little trouble with Pope John XXII concerning the new style. Machaut, you are winking and what are those papers you are rattling?

MACHAUT — Did I ever have trouble. Wait — I think I've got it. Yes, let me read what the Pope said:

"Certain disciples of the new school, much occupying themselves with the measured dividing of time, display their method in notes rather than to continue singing in the old manner; the music, therefore, of the divine offices is now performed with semibreves and minims, and with these notes of small value every composition is pestered.

Moreover, they truncate the melodies with hockets, they deprave them with discantus, sometimes even they stuff them with upper parts made out of secular song . . .

Their voices are incessantly running to and fro, intoxicating the ear, not soothing it, while the men themselves endeavor to convey by their gestures the sentiment of the music which they utter . . . We now hasten therefore, to banish these methods . . . and to put them to flight more effectually than heretofore, far from the house of God. Wherefore . . . we straitly command that no one henceforward shall think of himself at liberty to attempt these methods, or methods like them, in the aforesaid offices, and especially the canonical hours or in the celebration of the Mass."

HEIDI — But that sounds like your Notre Dame Mass . . . "measured dividing of time, semibreves, minims, hockets, discantus voices running to and fro . . ." How did you ever have the courage to write your Mass?

MACHAUT — Sometimes in life one must take chances and let things slide like water off a duck's back. Where would art be today if there weren't a few daring souls? I hear you had some ecclesiastical trouble yourself!

HEIDI — Mine was bishop trouble. He wouldn't let me perform the Mass because "it seemed contrary to the nature of the Mass." I wanted to project my score behind the altar. It caused musical things to happen and I intended the pictures to be used for meditation purposes, too. And I am sure he thought my taped environmental and foreign language sounds were secular. What can you do? I gave an afternoon performance without the liturgy. I really noticed the lack. The liturgy was part of my score.

MACHAUT — You won't believe this, but I can't remember when my Mass was first performed. When you are as old as I am you forget such things. I do remember that it was for a grand occasion. I had nobility backing me so I wasn't quite as alone as you were. Some people found my Mass distracting. It reminded them of court music. Actually, I toned down my style and went conservative for the Mass. You should hear some of my motets and ballades!

HEIDI — I have. And to think that you wrote the texts, too. That music compared to the thirteenth century seems like worlds apart.

MACHAUT — Sure, instruments were improving. I think our literary activity was an important aspect. Philippe de Vitry's *Ars Nova* and Jean de Muris' *Ars novae musicae* influenced agreement on performing practices. Really the situation had gotten quite messy. No one knew whose system to use, how to divide tempus and prolation. Rehearsal time was spent arguing about notation. It seems you twentieth century people are having the same problems.

HEIDI — True, but I think we are going a different direction. Instead of going to standardization we are moving away from it. I know how precious rehearsal time is, and the notation must be absolutely clear. That's why I stressed simplicity. Before you leave, Guillaume, let me ask you one more question.

MACHAUT — Go ahead.

HEIDI — What do you think of the modern recordings of your Mass today?

MACHAUT — What a question. That's one of the pities of being a ghost, you hear everything but you can't talk back, except in extraordinary circumstances like this. I am most familiar with the Nonesuch, Archiv and Bach Guild recordings. The Nonesuch comes closest to the tempo I like, also, the choice of instruments for doubling the lines. But you just can't imagine the sound of our instruments. We didn't like a smooth blended texture. Our crumhorns made the most interesting sounds — many sounds at once — I think you call them multiphonics. That's what I don't like about the Archiv recording. It is too bland, a smooth four part vocal texture throughout. And they are too slow. Also, the acoustics of our cathedrals can't be recorded. I remember when they performed my *Mass* at Rheims and I was up at the high altar. No stereo set can match that. Now the Bach Guild recording is sensitive to my cadence points; they make the fifths pure and bring out what you would call my accented passing tones and parallel fifths. Those penultimate sounds were important to me and I like the overtones to resonate. It even helps if some of the chromatic notes on the crumhorns and partatives are what you would call out of tune. I like the spicy sounds. I have to laugh at the Nonesuch recording marking out my isorhythms with drum beats. Musicologists make such a big to-do over my isorhythmic structures. It was the sound that I was concerned about — structure was secondary.

HEIDI — Yes, sometimes I think we get hung up in the architecture and forget sound. I gather from what you said that you were interested in timbre and texture changes.

MACHAUT — Yes, the more the better.

HEIDI — Let me fumble around in this corner. I'm looking for some large grey tubes. Here they are. These are what I used for timbre changes in my Mass. You're laughing, Machaut, these dog-food-cans make resonating tubes and it enlarges the sound of the singer's voice. I guess as a ghost you can't try it, but you can feel the whole thing vibrate as you sing into it, that is if you are singing the pitch of the pipe. My people really liked using them.

MACHAUT — I guess it is not such a silly idea after all. You could use them to control pitch, and they look like one of those pipes from my portative organ.

HEIDI — Right on, Guillaume.

MACHAUT — Let me see the rest of your dog-food-can pipe collection. You have F, A, C, D, Bb and Eb. Is this *musica ficta* or the color of your *talea*?

HEIDI — Not exactly. I took them from the mode of the chant 'Lux et origio.' I wasn't thinking about isorhythm but I wanted the singers to create clusters about the chant.

MACHAUT — What are these clusters?

HEIDI — The best way to explain it is to take a dissonant sound from your Mass and have everybody sing their pitches without resolving them, or take the color and group all the pitches together vertically. I heard some potential tone clusters in your Mass.

MACHAUT — I know the spots you mean, the 'Crucifixus,' for example. I didn't always use perfect concords. It's more fun not to!

HEIDI — It is just like I thought. People haven't changed much since the 'Ars Nova.' There are always those souls who want to try new ideas.

MACHAUT — Speaking of souls, this old ghost is getting rather tired. I think I'll be returning to the atmosphere. Don't give up the fight, Heidi, there is still lots of music to be written and any time you want to talk to me just start listening to my Mass on your stereo. I must subconsciously tune in on the sound waves of my music when you earth people are listening to it. Just wait until you join my state, all your problems will be solved.

HEIDI — I hope so.

11.

AN INTERVIEW WITH HALSEY STEVENS
David Cope

D.C.: With all his experimental and technical writing, is the contemporary composer losing his audience?

H.S.: First of all, you have to decide what the "contemporary" composer is, and I think that's a very involved question which perhaps we could save until later. There is certainly a great deal of exploration going on, and much of it is objectionable to the conventional concert-going audience. I don't think that you will find many subscribers to the major symphony orchestras interested in the most recent music of Penderecki or Xenakis or comparable composers.

On the other hand, it seems to me that there is a growing audience whose primary interest lies in these or similar directions. We have had an audience of that kind for many years in Los Angeles, with the old "Evenings on the Roof" and the more recent "Monday Evening Concerts." How you evaluate the trend, I don't know. There is certainly something to be said on both sides.

D.C.: Is the so-called "avant-garde" composer's audience, the specialized audience you are speaking about, much like the audience that goes to hear, say, a Baroque music consort?

H.S.: There is a good deal of cross-over. I was afraid you were going to say, "Is it much like the audience that goes to hear Brahms, Beethoven, and Mozart," and I should think, in that case, no. But yes, a good many people who are interested in the latest manifestations of music seem to be equally interested in the early ones. Pre-Baroque, perhaps, rather than Baroque.

D.C.: Has the fascination in this century with experimentation relegated the composer more or less to treating composition as a hobby, rather than as a livelihood, due to his lack of audience? Or has it affected his being called exclusively a composer?

H.S.: I think that if you look at the history of music composition, once you get past the era of patronage, you will find that most composers have had to treat composition as a hobby. It's been a most intensive hobby in many cases, but not a large number of composers have derived their entire sustenance from the fruits of their composition. The composers who are involved in music of various "commercial" kinds (film music, television music, etc.) are able, of course, to do that, but most of what they write is never performed on the concert stage. It's quite a different kind of thing. It's different, too, from the more "avant-garde" artists, who seem to have been able always to sell, and at good fees, their paintings. But then, a painting is something you can hang on your wall and look at; nobody buys a composition to look at, and if you don't happen to have an orchestra or a chamber group at your disposal, then how are you going to hear the work that you have perhaps been generous enough to commission?

D.C.: There are numerous recordings now available, that weren't available forty years ago. Is this also diminishing the audience for the contemporary composer?

H.S.: No, as a matter of fact, I think that in some respects it's increasing it, because there is far more recent music available on records than anyone could ever have encountered in the concert hall — things, for example, like the five symphonies of Hans Werner Henze, which certainly you have not heard very often in performance, and that's only a very minor example. The music of any number of very forward-looking composers is available almost as soon as it is written.

D.C.: A number of universities and colleges throughout the country have given the composer an opportunity to make a living at something which is at least more closely related to his "hobby." Is this, do you think, giving more of an audience to the composer as well? The audiences at colleges and universities tend to be the audiences which would be interested in experimental music.

H.S.: In the sense that one would expect a university audience to be a cut above the intellectual level of the general public, one would expect, perhaps, a more interested attitude toward manifestation of this kind.

I should have to say, first of all, that this would not apply to European universities in general, because if there is a music department at all (and they're rare), it will consist of one or two professors, one professor and perhaps a reader or so, in musicology only; you would never find a music department comparable to a school of music or conservatory in a European university. Conservatories exist on a totally different level. Certainly the presence of many composers in the United States on university faculties could hardly fail to have some effect upon the availability, at least, of new music, and one would hope that, through their contacts with students and with their fellow faculty, they might generate a little enthusiasm for it as well.

D.C.: Has this association with the university been in some way responsible for the large amount of technical consideration by the composer of the twentieth century (seemingly more so than the composer of the eighteenth or nineteenth century), from the standpoint of electronics and various extremely technical philosophies?

H.S.: Well, that may be true. Certainly the acquisition of electronic studios by many universities has made it possible for composers connected with these universities, either as students or as faculty, to have some first-hand experience with them. In Europe, it has been mainly the radio stations (Radio Cologne, etc.) that have facilitated the exploration of electronic means. I don't know what they do about computers there.

D.C.: Could a computer composer exist today in America were it not for universities?

H.S.: It would be extremely unlikely, though possible.

D.C.: Getting back to recordings: possibly the ability to buy a recording, of even the newest piece, has created a rather lazy audience.

H.S.: Of course, that is true, and I suspect you might find a fairly substantial percentage of people who would classify themselves as music lovers who never set foot in a concert hall or opera house, simply because they have their walls lined with records and tapes, and they have everything they want to hear.

D.C.: What do you feel about the relationships between recordings and live performance? Is there, first of all, a big difference, and should composers, performers, and "music lovers" be interested in the concert hall?

H.S.: I think there is a good deal to be said for both. In the first place, if you lived a lifetime, you would not be able to hear a great deal of music that is available on records. But look at the programs week after week in the Los Angeles Times and the New York Times: there is a great deal of music being performed, but there is a great deal of music being overlooked. And much of that overlooked music turns up eventually, sometimes very soon, on records. Obviously there is a great deal of difference between a recorded performance and a live performance. The element of chance has been eliminated in the recorded performance, because if it has been engineered and recorded in the usual way, it is made into something like an ideal performance, by recording two bars at a time and cutting and pasting and having all the wrong notes and all the wrong inflections taken out; you may have a performance on tape which could never have occurred in a live concert.

On the other hand, I'd like to have some flexibility of performance; I don't like to have the same things happen in exactly the same way all the time. That doesn't make me a devotee of aleatoric music, but I do feel that some give and take, owing to the conditions of the performance, the acoustics of the hall, the condition of the instruments, the temperature, the size and constitution of the audience, and the way the performer or performers feel — all this, I believe, has something to do with what music is and how it works.

D.C.: Regarding aleatoric music: could I generally state that you believe that when one signs his name to a piece of music, he should be responsible for what happens in that piece of music, i.e., in aleatoric music the composer cannot attach his name in all integrity? Would that be an accurate statement?

H.S.: Well, not long ago, Los Angeles had three performances on one program of what was called *Piano Piece for David Tudor*, by Sylvano Bussotti. This was a graphic score which consisted of one single page with various designs on it intended to communicate something to the performer. The piece was played by three different performers, and I suspect that, if Mr. Bussotti had wandered into the hall and didn't know what was going on, he would not have had the remotest idea that those three performances, or any one of them, might have been his own piece.

They were so totally different in every respect that the only thing he could lay claim to was having designed the score, not to having composed the piece. Aleatoric music, it seems to me, as it is frequently pursued, is an amusing parlor game, the kind of thing you have when two people sit down at two pianos and say, "Let's play *Me and My Shadow*" without any previous rehearsal and not knowing even what key they are going to play it in.

Years ago, back in the Midwest, I knew a violinist and his brother, a pianist, who made a practice of improvising violin sonatas. This was my first experience with aleatoric music; it was in the early 1940's. They didn't know it was aleatoric music, and the improvisations were fairly convincing as improvisations, but if you had taped them, I'm sure you wouldn't want to hear them again. Organists, of course, have done this as a matter of course. They have to improvise to get from the key of the anthem to the key of the offertory response or something of that kind; but many organists have made a practice of improvising in concert on themes submitted by the audience, and these can be very exciting and even convincing in the process of performance. I've submitted a few in my time, but I think that in any of them you would become extremely weary of having more than the momentary performance. You would not want ever to hear them again. I can't see that there is much reason for aleatoric music where things are left up to the whim of the performer or the expediency of the moment, or that any lasting musical value is likely to result.

D.C.: There is a certain type of music today (statistical music) trying to tell the performer what his limits are. It can't be considered aleatoric, if anything really can be, or traditional, and certainly includes some improvisation. You have been quoted (by Wallace Berry in *Musical Quarterly, Vol. 54, No. 3, p. 303*) as saying: "As for aleatoric music, I am old-fashioned enough to think that if I sign my name to a composition I should stipulate as exactly as possible what notes are to be played . . ." The word I am interested in here is notes. Do you feel that there are valid ways, other than notes (as in a great deal of statistical music), to express to the performer your intentions without necessarily being aleatoric?

H.S.: You mean other notational systems.

D.C.: Yes.

H.S.: There is certainly the possibility of other notational systems; some of them can be devised very easily and learned very quickly. But it seems to me that if you have to learn a new notational system for each new piece you're going to have some difficulty in working up a repertoire. The aleatoric elements of the Lutoslawski *String Quartet*, for example, are notated almost exclusively in conventional notes. But it is the combination of those notes, the combination of those different parts (there is no score; there are four parts, one for each player), and how they fit together that is a matter of choice.

D.C.: A mobile structure?

H.S.: Yes.

D.C.: A number of composers have been using words rather than notes to describe to the performer their intentions. This, of course, would probably be less exact than notes.

H.S.: Notes are inexact enough.

D.C.: In music education, words have been used with success instead of more complex systems to convey musical ideas to those not yet versed in traditional notation.

H.S.: But I can't imagine that this would operate on a very high level of musical perspective. If the musician cannot read notes, then certainly he's not much of a musician. He hasn't had much training, he hasn't learned the first position on the strings or the five-finger position on the keyboard. I don't think we're talking about this kind of person at all, but a score which was written in words, it seems to me, could be only haphazardly specific when it came to application to actual musical phenomena.

D.C.: You feel, then, that notes are here to stay.

H.S.: I'm still using them and intend to continue in the foreseeable future.

D.C.: So, many composers today are avoiding the use of notes, feeling they are inadequate.

H.S.: Well, certainly they are inadequate. Leon Vallas, in his book called *Achille-Claude Debussy*, speaks of the ability of notation to register the most "subtle tremblings" of musical lines. But it isn't true at all. Those subtle tremblings, whatever they are, you cannot register with conventional notation; but you cannot register them either by any other kind of notation I've ever encountered. I saw in Zagreb, at the Biennale a few years ago, an enormous exhibition of graphic scores which were fascinating to look at, but I haven't the remotest idea what they meant musically. And I'm sure that any two or more performers looking at them would produce quite different results.

D.C.: Is there a city today, either in America or Europe, which, like Vienna or other cities in the past, represents the focal point of the musical life of the world? E.g., can we say now that New York is the place to be to get performances? Or Los Angeles?

H.S.: I think the place to get a performance is where you can get the performance. No, there is a great deal of decentralization, and every city would be likely to pride itself on its musical stature as it would on its theatrical and artistic stature and its standard of living.

Different things go on in different places, different kinds of things. You would not expect to find in Rome the same kind of musical activity you would find in London; you would not find in San Francisco what you would find in Savannah, Georgia. It's as simple as that.

D.C.: In the past there seemed to be a geographical route to take for a chance for success. By visiting a certain city or . . .

H.S.: If you were thinking of starting a career as a performer, then I think that New York is still the place to get the reviews. I don't see why it should be, particularly, but I've been connected with concert organization in various parts of the country that always looked to see what the New York critics said about the prospectively hired soprano or double-bass player or whatever it happened to be, without paying attention to what may have happened when that same singer or double-bass player performed out in the hinterland, which might be much more to the point.

D.C.: I know that there are a large number of American composers who, for one reason or another (survival, possibly), have left their "parent" educational institution to go out to the midwest, Canada, etc., and many of them have been 'lost' in the sense that they may have local performances, but because of their geographical location, may not have connections with publishers, record companies, or a performance by a large symphony orchestra. They grow old, die there with the bulk of their music yet unheard.

H.S.: Of course, it is quite likely that many of those would have been completely out of place in a large city and would still have had no more success than they had in their small towns. But I think that the spreading out of musical activity of all kinds, including composition, into all parts of the country, should be beneficial and, if a composer really has something to say, he can say it on the local scene and, if he is ingenious enough, can expand from that as a base as well as he can from 59th Street.

D.C.: Pierre Boulez has labeled Los Angeles, New York, and other large cities in the world "anthills," and has intimated that the best place he felt he could live as a creative artist was in a small town or "country" atmosphere. Do you feel that it could be taken to this extent?

H.S.: No, because I've had the experience of living in very small anthills as well as very large anthills. I've not found that geographical considerations have any real effect, any important effect, on how I feel or what I do. I've been able to write in many places, and been able to operate from many places, to about the same degree of efficiency.

D.C.: In other words, an unsuccessful composer in the midwest would probably be an unsuccessful composer in New York.

H.S.: He probably would be still less successful in New York; since he would probably be the only composer in his home town, he might be very successful there, despite a lack of talent.

D.C.: A composer, then, successful in a small town, would not be guaranteed success in a large metropolis.

H.S.: Certainly not. Would an insurance salesman in a small town be assured of a million-dollar clientele if he moved to New York? You don't know; he might. And you don't know about the composer. If the composer has something pertinent to say and knows how to say it, then his music should operate effectively in more than a local milieu. But if it doesn't, then chances are his friends are going to admire him anyway for doing it and applaud lustily at his performances, such as they are.

D.C.: Do you feel there is any political system in which the composer, or artist for that matter, operates more successfully?

H.S.: Not being particularly politically-minded myself, I haven't any idea. I would not want to try to practice the metier of the composer in a country where what I had to say and how I was to say it were established by decree. If I were instructed to write only within specified limits, I don't think I should be very happy about it. Actually, I might not want to go beyond those limits of my own free will, but I should resent being told so.

D.C.: You do not think, then, as some previous composers (Wagner, in particular), that the artist is "above the law."

H.S.: This, I think, is excessive.

D.C.: The artist, then, is like any other member of society.

H.S.: I think so. He's a very special member of society, but so far as his relation with society is concerned, I think the same principles apply.

D.C.: Is there really an "avant garde" and, if there is, what is it?

H.S.: You don't know whether there's an avant garde until you acquire some historical perspective. An avant garde is someone who paves the way for those who follow, and simple experimentation doesn't guarantee that anyone is going to follow or that this will be 'the way.' Unless the experimentation, the exploration, bears fruit in the guise of successors, then it proves not to be an avant garde at all, but only a diversion. Maybe a "derrière garde."

D.C.: Many composers seem to fear their being labeled "old fashioned" or being left behind, particularly by aleatoric and electronic music (the latter mostly due to impossible financial demands, too great for most composers to bear).

H.S.: Do they really mind? Do they resent it?

D.C.: I think one can many times resent immediate success of someone else, even though it's possible to laugh and say, "I know it's not going to last!"

H.S.: This is a "sour grapes" attitude which I don't share. It seems to me that if they are really concerned that somebody is going to "get there first," then the only thing left for them to do, logically and legitimately, is jump on the bandwagon themselves and become avant garde composers. This is something which has never interested me and something which I would not consider doing. I write the way I want to write, and it doesn't concern me that what I am doing now, and what I have always done, is considerably more traditionally oriented than most of what is performed in the little concerts of the avant garde.

D.C.: Is the avant garde (I don't want to use that term) . . .

H.S.: Like "neoclassic," there isn't a good substitute.

D.C.: Is the avant garde, then, a passing fancy, something that will soon die away?

H.S.: I'm not a prophet. I haven't the remotest idea. Judging by some things that have happened in the past (like the explorations that were taking place after the First World War: the microtonal composers Hàba, Carrillo, Vishnegradski, Georg Rimsky-Korsakov, Mildred Couper — those were very "avant garde" and have disappeared without a trace). But I would not want to assume that anything that is now happening would disappear equally permanently.

D.C.: Twelve-tone music, avant garde at least when it first arrived, seems to have lasted, with still many composers working with it. You seem not to have been too interested in it, at least in your own music.

H.S.: No, I've never used it (I should say almost never; I did write one twelve-tone piece and have done a lot of twelve-tone experimentation). But I have to disagree with you, David, when you suggest that twelve-tone procedures are as viable now as they have been, because it seems to me that in the last ten years or so, real twelve-tone composition has tended to disappear. Many things which are happening now are derived from it, or more specifically, from serial procedures which are not necessarily twelve-tone; but I don't think you'll find many composers nowadays who will admit they employ a twelve-tone "method."

D.C.: Boulez has said that "It is not deviltry, but only the most ordinary common sense, which makes one say that, since the discovery made by the Viennese, all composition other than twelve-tone is useless." He is referring here to the serialization of all elements of music.

H.S.: I'm surprised. He has written an article titled "Schoenberg Is Dead," meaning the whole procedure is dead. He can say that any composer who doesn't write within these specifications is no composer at all, but I could equally well say the composer who can't write a C major chord if he wants to is no composer. I don't write many C major chords; but if I want to, I shall do it.

D.C.: Do we now have a nationalistic (or American) music, as we did in the early twentieth century, or has it become international?

H.S.: I don't think we've ever had an "American" music. We've had individual composers who, for one reason or another, were hailed as American. Perhaps the outstanding example is Roy Harris, who has insisted upon the Americanness of his own music for years and years, and made people believe it. I suppose you could draw a rough parallel between the expansiveness of the American landscape and the expansiveness of Roy Harris' music, but it isn't particularly meaningful to do so.

The reason we have not had an American music is that we do not have in America the body of consistent folklore that has been true of the other countries where national music has been most successful: the Soviet Union, Hungary, Rumania, Spain, and to a certain extent, England. All these have had a very distinctive folk music which it has been possible to incorporate in one way or another into the language of art music.

It has not worked in the same way for Germany or France, except that the characteristics of French folk music are so diatonic and so "six-eight-ish" that perhaps you could say it has been present in French music for centuries and we didn't need a nationalist movement to make it so; and generally with German folk music, the chorales and the whole Lutheran literature, and certainly Bach, would be inconceivable without roots in Germanic folk culture.

D.C.: Is this folk tradition breaking down in Europe to the extent that we have a truly international style?

H.S.: I think this is perfectly true with the most prominent composers. There's still a strong emphasis upon nationalistic elements in eastern Europe; not Poland, but in Russia, Rumania, Hungary, Yugoslavia, and particularly in Czechoslovakia (these countries are still drawing from the resources of their own folk music). Ours is so diverse. We have the remains of English folk music in the Appalachians; we have a mixture of Protestant hymnody and African sources in the Negro spirituals; we have cowboy songs, and we have various northern European folklores in the midwest and Spanish-Mexican in the southwest. The only really indigenous folk music in America is, of course, the music of the American Indian, which has had no effect whatever on American art music; some composers have borrowed a theme or two (MacDowell's "Indian Suite", for example) with the idea of making an indigenous American music.

But it's no more indigenous than if they used the music of Bali, because they were not Indian themselves. They were just laying it on with a palette knife for purposes of local color. The only Indian composer I know doesn't write Indian music at all. He writes more like a combination of Wagner and Hollywood.

D.C.: Is there a vast amount of folk music available from the American Indian?

H.S.: There is an enormous collection of publications by the Smithsonian Institution that were issued in the latter years of the nineteenth century and in the first two or three decades of the twentieth. Frances Densmore did a great deal of research.

D.C.: No composers have taken advantage of this research?

H.S.: Composers have borrowed the tunes: Charles Sanford Skilton, Arthur Farwell . . .

D.C.: But in the sense of Bartók, that is, integrating them completely within their style?

H.S.: No. But you see, Bartók was a Hungarian. He was dealing with Hungarian music, primarily, though he exposed himself to the influence of other related musical cultures: Rumanian, Slovakian, Arabic, etc. But a New England composer of exclusively British ancestry trying to amalgamate Indian musical idioms in his own style would be as silly as MacDowell was, writing the Indian Suite.

D.C.: How about a non-Indian but southwestern United States composer?

H.S.: Well, I would doubt that he would know the music except for looking it up in the books or hearing the Folkways recordings of it.

D.C.: It must be more than a borrowing, then.

H.S.: Yes.

D.C.: As Rimsky-Korsakov did. Or Stravinsky.

H.S.: Well, Stravinsky borrowed from Rimsky-Korsakov's collection and other sources, but didn't do any investigation on his own.

D.C.: There has been for some years, and still exists, an idea of Ives as the "father of American music." Do you feel this to be correct?

H.S.: No, this is not correct for a very good reason. Charles Ives could not have been the "father" of American music because his music was unplayed and unknown during the years when American music was in its formative period. If there had been access to his music, as there was access to the music of Stravinsky, Hindemith, Schoenberg, Bartók, etc., he might very well have played an important part in the shaping of American music. As it was, he was in complete isolation. His manuscripts were in a barn in Danbury, Connecticut. He was selling insurance in New York; he had resources which would have made it possible for him to subsidize performances of his music, but he refused to do that. I admire him for that, but it's a little short-sighted.

D.C.: Some composers have suggested that the "international style" is so complete that there is no contradiction of styles or different direction in music between the continent and here.

H.S.: I think it's a shame. There should be some difference. I don't like it when everybody's music sounds like everybody else's.

D.C.: I didn't mean to suggest that.

H.S.: But it does.

D.C.: Why do so many composers seem to dislike each other? Even factions of the avant garde are "killing each other off!"

H.S.: Well, in the first place, if you are a creative artist of any kind, you must be committed to what you are doing, and if you are doing it, you're doing it right; then everybody else must be doing it wrong. The composer who is generous about his colleagues is a rarity; I think I'm practically alone. I do happen to like a few other composers' music, but there is a great deal of music I don't like. Some of it is by people I like very much. As a matter of fact, I've made a kind of cliche of saying that, generally speaking, I dislike the music of my friends! That isn't completely true, fortunately.

D.C.: Is the so-called "post-Webern school" still thriving and, if so, is it more prevalent in Europe than in America? Is it dying out?

H.S.: It's one of those convenient titles that cover a multitude of various things.

D.C.: Pointillism, then.

H.S.: Pointillism is a term borrowed from the painting of Seurat; it applies rather inaccurately to music, I think. Is it dying out? No, I don't think so. There's a great deal of post-Webern "pointillist" activity. At least the pieces I hear seem to deal in these terms about as much as they deal in any others.

D.C.: Aside from Stravinsky, what composers of our time have the position of a Brahms, a Beethoven?

H.S.: After Stravinsky there's no one — and I have doubts about Stravinsky.

D.C.: Is this an interim period, or will someone now withstanding the test of time be discovered later?

H.S.: I don't imagine that anyone now active will be so considered in later years.

D.C.: Is there a particular reason for this, or just happenstance?

H.S.: Well, it seems to me that, to have a Brahms or a Beethoven, you must have some widespread recognition of worth at the time. They were both highly respected as composers (Brahms particularly) in spite of the antagonism they aroused in many quarters. But I think they were still recognized as very significant composers in the important places.

D.C.: The world was much smaller then.

H.S.: The world was much smaller and there were fewer composers, and the sifting process now has to be much more extensive. When you have a composer-in-residence in every public school in the country, it's going to be still harder. I can't think of anyone that can begin to approach the stature of Beethoven or Brahms.

D.C.: Do we have composers, then, reaching the status of . . . a little less status?

H.S.: A César Franck?

D.C.: Yes.

H.S.: Dozens. Dozens of better composers than César Franck.

D.C.: What is the motivation which drives a composer like, say, Carl Ruggles to spend years on one work? Certainly not money, not fame, little success? Not stature . . .

H.S.: With Ruggles, of course, it's a puzzle, but with most people it is . . . at least with me it is . . . mostly the pleasure I get out of the process of putting the notes together, of seeing the most unprepossessing ideas take shape and assume significance in relation to each other, and leaving the composer at least with the feeling, after the piece is done, that he has had an adventure, that he has begun somewhere and gone meaningfully from there to somewhere else.

D.C.: Do you mean that you compose for yourself?

H.S.: I compose for myself first of all as every composer does, I think. Every composer who is worth his salt composes for himself first of all. But I would not want to leave you with the impression that I compose exclusively for myself. Most of the time I don't think in terms of a specific audience, but I should be disappointed if I failed to reach anybody in a performance of something I have written.

D.C.: What do you feel about film music, rock-and-roll, and "Muzak?" Do they not, with their financial success, represent a threat to the serious composer?

H.S.: You are equating success as a composer with money. I think that if most of us were concerned with the financial rewards, we should have turned to something else. There are some composers, I assume, who go into composition because they have hopes that they can make a lot of money doing it. They're mostly mistaken, because the financial rewards for composition come generally from things which are not so much concerned with composition as they are with the commercial values of music, which is fine: I have no objection to that, but it is an area of music which doesn't interest me at all. I am not interested in film music. I am more than not interested in rock.

D.C.: What is the reason for this?

H.S.: I think it's a bore: dull, repetitious, noisy, and vulgar.

D.C.: What about jazz? There seems to be a closer tie here with serious music.

H.S.: Since I've been out of college I've not had much interest in jazz. I played in bands when I was in school, but I did that for financial reasons and I have no particular interest in it (or flair for it). The thing that bores me about jazz is its entire lack of rhythm. It seems to me that that is the one thing which it is credited for and the one thing it doesn't have. Everything is tied down to a monotonous beat of guitar, bass, and drums, and the most wayward inflections of melodic lines are lost rhythmically (that is, the rhythmic sense is lost) because of this steady pulsation; if you could just weed that out, you might have something very subtle and very imaginative and, perhaps, even very beautiful.

D.C.: Has jazz been given credit for affecting "serious" contemporary American music when, in fact, it has really not been an influence?

H.S.: No. As a matter of fact, it must certainly have affected it. Anybody who grows up surrounded by it could hardly fail to have absorbed some of its qualities, some of its attitudes, and I would certainly not want to maintain that I am entirely uncontaminated by jazz in my own music. I don't think about jazz, I've never thought about jazz or the possibility of incorporating it into my music, but I grew up surrounded by it, and it's quite natural to suppose that musicologists might find traces in this or that score or perhaps all of them.

D.C.: You would not, then, place jazz in the same classification as rock? Or film music?

H.S.: No. They are three separate categories. They touch, of course; they may even cross from time to time. But I don't set myself up as an authority on any one of the three, simply because I have not had the kind of interest that would lead to a study of any of them.

D.C.: I have been told that I, as a composer, am not fulfilling a need: that society and life are based on "supply and demand" and that film music, jazz, etc. are fulfilling a need. They are wanted.

H.S.: It seems to me there are a good many products that are in demand that don't have any particular aesthetic justification. I don't think that you can judge the value of a production of any kind exclusively from that standpoint.

D.C.: What projects do you have under way at the moment?

H.S. I seem to be involved in a series of commissioned works just now. The first of these is a *Double Concerto* for violin, cello, and string orchestra, to be premiered in November 1973 at the Music Center, Los Angeles. Beyond this, I have a commission for a major work for violin and piano, and one for a choral work (perhaps with orchestra); this is scheduled for first performance at a large Long Island high school. As for compositions "on my own" (that is, not commissioned), having completed works for each of the conventional orchestral instruments — beginning with a *Sonatina* for flute and piano in 1943 and ending with a *Sonata* for oboe and piano in 1972 — I am now interested in writing for the less conventional instruments, still in solo or duo works. Last year I wrote a *Dittico* for alto saxophone and piano; I have another composition for bass clarinet and piano, and am thinking in the direction of English horn, alto flute, and perhaps even contrabassoon.

D.C.: Wallace Berry has noted that you seem to have avoided dramatic works.

H.S.: No, it isn't a matter of avoidance. I've done one incidental score for the Yale Drama School's production of *The Rivals* and, years ago, I did some incidental music for a play of Thornton Wilder. I have considered opera from time to time; as a matter of fact, I even started work on one at one time, but at this point I don't imagine I shall ever write an opera. I'm much interested in the possibilities, but I can't quite see affording the amount of time that would be necessary to do such a work.

D.C.: Do you write almost exclusively from commissions?

H.S.: No. I write what I want to write. If I wrote exclusively from commissions my output would be much smaller. I've had a good many commissions over the past twenty years, but very much of what I write is something I want to write.

D.C.: Any further literary projects under way?

H.S.: Usually, I have something of the kind in hand: reviews; articles for encyclopedias or periodicals. I have recently written an article on Bartók for the new edition of the Britannica; I'm involved with a long-term study of twentieth-century symphonies which I hope will be completed before too long, and a volume of studies in Hungarian music. If time permits, I should like to edit a volume of profiles of American composers, but this is in a very nebulous state so far.

D.C.: Is music publication as important as it once was?

H.S.: No, not really. With present-day processes of music reproduction, distribution of new scores is not so dependent upon engraving and printing as it was even twenty years ago. Now there is little necessity of publishing large works, since they may be readily duplicated and held on rental. There is a disadvantage, perhaps, if you have a recording of a new work and want to study it with the score; but the only music that really requires publication is that which is needed in large quantities: choral music, for example.

D.C.: Distribution, though, is still important.

H.S.: Yes, of course. Most composers are not able to handle distribution of their own music, with all the complications of duplication, wrapping, shipping, insurance, billing, and so on. That is why certain distributory projects are so important, and why composers who undertake their own publication (as I have done with Editio Helios) must generally contract with an established firm to handle their distribution.

D.C.: Are there advantages to self-publication, then, other than that of making available music that would otherwise gather dust on the shelf?

H.S.: There have certainly been advantages for me. From the purely practical point of view, returns on sales may amount to 35% or even 50%, as compared with the standard 10% royalty paid by most commercial publishers. The self-publishing composer, too, may be able to push this or that work through circulation of review or examination copies, where the commercial publisher with too many composers in his catalog has to scatter his fire. And if he does that, naturally he will concentrate on the music that will bring the most immediate and profitable return.

D.C.: Are you generally optimistic about the future of music?

H.S.: I have mixed feelings. Much of the new music I hear says little to me, and I have observed little change in the last decade or so. The use of an international style I think is disadvantageous, yet I do not believe there is much viability in the restrictive, nationalistic viewpoint that sometimes seems the only alternative. I should like to come back in fifty or a hundred years and see whether today's music has proved prophetic, or only a temporary aberration. That being impossible, I believe each composer should pursue his own paths without too much regard for the procedures of his contemporaries.

12.

SHORT ANSWERS TO DIFFICULT QUESTIONS
John Cage, Lukas Foss, Iannis Xenakis

The Buffalo Festival of the Arts Today was the occasion for a panel discussion which included three composers: John Cage, Lukas Foss, and Iannis Xenakis. Foss suggested a game: all three composers are on trial; each trying the two others. The questions had to be difficult, the answers short, well under a minute. An unidentified voice asked a final question.

CAGE: Lukas, what is an idea?

FOSS: A connection of parallels suddenly revealed.

CAGE: What is a musical idea?

FOSS: It would be a musical parallel which hadn't occurred to me before; something that makes things fit where before there appeared to be no connection.

CAGE: The French speak of an idée fixe — can we now conceive of an idée non-fixe?

FOSS: Well, an idée fixe is an obsession; an idée non-fixe would then be a free preoccupation, a non obsessed, a non fanatic, a non single-minded one; that's what we work with most of the time.

CAGE: Marcel Duchamp says that a work of art is not art until it becomes such in an observer or listener. What do you think about that?

FOSS: Beauty in the eye of the beholder? An accepted truism. "je ne suis pas contre."

CAGE: Music is a form of government; a composer essentially tells others what to do. Thoreau says the best government would be no government at all; would the best form of music be no music at all?

FOSS: I think there is an error here in the analogy. If we didn't need government we would, indeed, be better off, but if we didn't need music, why would we be better off? Put that way the analogy between government and music no longer works.

XENAKIS: Lukas, do you think that the public is necessary?

FOSS: The public as such, no. Other people in the same boat, yes.

XENAKIS: Are you interested in ancient, pre-medieval music?

FOSS: Not yet.

XENAKIS: How do you feel the influence of the future on you? Let me clarify my question. You say that we are influenced by the music of the past; I think that we are influenced by the future. How can you answer this?

FOSS: There is a future and I don't know it. This not knowing something feels like an ominous presence; we can't quite see it but we know it's there — the only thing we know is that eventually we'll die. I think that if I didn't know that death is my ultimate future my work would be entirely different.

CAGE: Mr. Xenakis, what compositions are you working on currently?

XENAKIS: 'Currently' means 'now'?

CAGE: Yes. What is the nature of your present work in composition?

XENAKIS: For orchestra instruments and for technological means, computer, etc.

CAGE: What do you think is wrong with the United States?

XENAKIS: Too much power.

CAGE: Is your music related to your political views?

XENAKIS: I think my music was related to my political views, now less maybe. It was once like a reconversion of political things into music and there were events in my youth, sound events and form events which have influenced my music.

CAGE: What do you think of the work of Buckminster Fuller?

XENAKIS: I don't think that he can cover the earth.

CAGE: I asked a Spanish lady scientist what she thought about the human mind in a world of computers. She said, "Computers are always right but life isn't about being right." What do you say to that?

XENAKIS: The opposite-life has reason and computers are often wrong.

CAGE: You have been an architect and now you are a musician. Are you going to go on to some other activity?

XENAKIS: I'd like to but it is difficult.

FOSS: Iannis, all the music of yours that I know is built on mathematical premise, mostly probability. Is there any aspect to chance that is not mathematical, that is, not probability theory?

XENAKIS: All my music is not based on mathematics — there are parts of it which use mathematics. As to chance, it is not like dice or tossing a coin, this is ignorance, as if there were impossibility of predicting. What does chance mean to you?

FOSS: Anything I cannot control. You left architecture for music — why?

XENAKIS: Mostly because architecture was a business and music is less business.

FOSS: In order to compose you need time, solitude — what else?

XENAKIS: To live in a big city.

FOSS: If someone imitates you (I know of an instance) does it flatter you or make you angry or both?

XENAKIS: I am angry — angry and depressed.

FOSS: What did you want to be when you were a child?

XENAKIS: An elephant.

FOSS: Has your native Greece shown interest in your music, and if not, why?

XENAKIS: My people have but it is very difficult for them to hear my works because of the tyrannic grip of the actual government; they are practically never played in Greece. John, how do you consider the faculty of thought in respect to the whole full way of life that we have?

CAGE: I think that if the activity of the mind, that is to say thinking, could flow from that point to any other point and could go out in the sense of sense perceptions, or could go out in the sense of dreams, then there is no real distinction or disconnection between those things.

XENAKIS: What is your relationship to your own past and, in general, to the past of the rest of humanity?

CAGE: My feeling about the past changes according to what I do; what I do is to bring to my attention things which I had not noticed in the past.

XENAKIS: Do you think that a new era of mysticism is going to come for humanity? Christianity was a kind of era of mysticism which came at a period which was so much like ours now today (Alexandrian times). When science and all ways of life were so rich Christianity came like a sponge.

CAGE: Comics, no?

XENAKIS: Razor, no? As a sponge to erase fantastic ways of rich life and bring to humanity a certain degree of thought which was very, very different.

CAGE: I believe that we are living in a period of change from competition; we're moving to a situation of overlap, interplay, where things which have seemed opposite and contradictory become part of a general cooperation; and I think that in that situation an attitude of mysticism could be entertained by individuals but that it would not be required — a period, in other words, of multiplicity of ways, all of which will manage to interpenetrate and not obstruct one another.

XENAKIS: What sense do you make out of working with computers — what does it mean to you?

CAGE: Well, I'm in the process of doing it and discovering what it does mean. It brings about the possibility of realization of projects so complex that I could not have approached the projects without the aid of the computer. I am heartened and delighted with the fact that there are no secrets in this field; that programs that are already available are shared; that what seems to be resulting is not music made by one person but rather music made by men, or many people.

FOSS: John, what do you do with a composition of yours which you don't like — withdraw it?

CAGE: No, I keep it.

FOSS: Could you conceivably dislike a piece by someone else written totally in accordance with your own orientation, your own parti-pris? What would have to be wrong with it for you to dislike such a piece?

CAGE: Some defect of it that would indicate that it was not done from belief.

FOSS: Could you conceivably like a new piece of music totally opposite to your own music? If so, name one. And what would have to be right with it?

CAGE: I think the work of La Monte Young is virtually opposite to mine, and I like it very much for the reason that it changes the way I hear.

FOSS: Some years ago Stravinsky visited Pope John and the Pope said, 'My son, is anything bothering you?', and Stravinsky said, 'Yes, I cannot take criticism.' The Pope said, 'Neither can I.' John, can you take criticism?

CAGE: I pay very little attention to it.

FOSS: My last question: Is it possible to ask a colleague a non-general, that is, a non-technical question which is not idiotic?

CAGE: Yes.

TAPE (Unidentified voice): As precisely as memory permits, retrace the history of music from 1900 to 1990; just the highlights, please.

XENAKIS: I think that during the next ten years we will have a crazy mixture of music in everyday life. Then a kind of feedback will come in about 15 to 20 years. It will probably be a decay if another world war does not happen.

FOSS: Erickson says that there will be two kinds of people — those who know what they're doing (the technologists) and those who mean what they say. I suppose I belong to the latter group because I mean what I say and I don't know what I'm doing — I certainly don't know the music of the future. If I knew it, I would write it.

CAGE: I think we can expect in the future finer performances of classical music than we have now since societies will gather together to preserve things which we have the feeling might disappear if they didn't . . . just as we now have pro musica 'Orchestra.' I think we have yet to be surprised by further technological possibilities. At the same time there will be a greater and larger influence of cultures which have formerly been separated. I think that music will not swing back to something with which we are familiar — that it will include, not exclude, the past.

13.

AN INTERVIEW WITH KRZYSZTOF PENDERECKI
David Felder/Mark Schneider

(The following interview took place in Cincinnati's Music Hall, March 31, 1977, following a rehearsal for a forthcoming concert of the composer's music).

David Felder: You've experienced an extensive compositional career. Would you trace the development of your style as it exists now, through the various changes and evolutions that you've undergone.

Krzysztof Penderecki: I think the first period of my development, I would say, would be from the first compositions written in my style, *Anaklasis* and *Threnody*. I finished the two pieces in the fall of 1959 and the spring of 1960. As a student I wrote many, many pieces, but they were in a style like Bartók, a little like Stravinsky. They were actually not lessons, though maybe the earliest ones were. Afterwards, in 1957 or 1958, I wrote a piece called *Psalms of David*, in which I think there are some elements you will find in the *St. Luke Passion* later, as in the second a cappella piece. The a cappella sound in *Psalms of David* and *St. Luke* is really the same — I used the same technique. Anyway, I used orthodox twelve-tone technique in the a cappella sections. I used the same technique in the *St. Luke Passion*.

Then I wrote a work for two string orchestras which is influenced more by post-Webern style — *Emanations*. That also contains elements of my later style.

The third piece I wrote is the *Strophes* for soprano, which was influenced by Boulez and maybe Luigi Nono.

So the first pieces I wrote, really, are *Anaklasis* and *Threnody*; and that was the beginning of my music. It was something new for me at that time. Afterwards I wrote *Dimensions of Time and Silence*, in which I used the same techniques for chorus that I had used previously with strings.

So it was the first piece, really, that used all types of sound that the chorus can produce. The date was 1960. Then, the *First String Quartet*, then *Polymorphia*, which is a very important piece for me, I think. Then, *Flourescences* and *Canon*. I think I wrote the *Canon* before 1961. That's all. I think that in those pieces I tried to explore all possibilities — not only to find my own style because, of course, that was the foremost thought I had in mind, but also to try to find new techniques, for chorus, strings and all instruments.

I think after I finished *Flourescences*, I would say that the first period ends, because I couldn't go and explore anymore. I didn't see any more possibility for developing the things I was doing at that time. So, in 1962, I backtracked a little and wrote *Stabat Mater*. I didn't know which way to go at that time, and I wasn't sure that what I was doing was really right. Maybe I had gone too far and there was no way back. So, I studied counterpoint — specifically, the Netherlands School counterpoint of the sixteenth century. *Stabat Mater* is written using some of the same techniques as Ockeghem and Obrecht — also incorporating, of course, some twelve-tone elements. As a matter of fact, I used an advanced polyphonic technique in that piece, so the *Stabat Mater* is the beginning of the second period, I would say.

The second period lasted until 1973, because that is when I finished the *Symphony*. During that time, I just used my own language. I found some new possibilities in Netherlands polyphony. As a matter of fact, in the *St. Luke Passion* you will find both complicated polyphonic writing and also my experience with diverse compositional materials. Also, I should add that in the late 1950's I spent four years in the electronic studio. It helped me develop my hearing a great deal. Without having had experience in the studio, I would never have written *Threnody*, because the studio was something which opened my mind and ears for something new — unlimited possibilities as far as sound is concerned. During the second period in my music I used mostly what I had discovered before. I wrote six pieces like the *Passion*. The second big piece was *Utrenja*.

Utrenja is like a continuation of the *St. Luke Passion*, using the same techniques, though more advanced, perhaps. Something happened after *Utrenja*, because the polyphonic technique which I developed in *Utrenja* is so extreme — and so difficult. The same thing that had happened to me after *Flourescences* happened once again.

After I finished *Utrenja*, what more could I do? I don't like to repeat myself. Of course, I could have written many, many pieces in the same style, but I didn't want to. So after *Utrenja*, I wrote some pieces that I think were important for me; for example, *De Natura Sonoris #2*, in which I used some new techniques. Another piece that I think was very important for me was *Partita*. In *Partita*, I used some rock elements, like electric guitars. As a matter of fact, I started by writing a piano concerto, for which I had been commissioned. After a week or two, I decided that I couldn't write for piano because it doesn't sound, really. I cannot use piano with other instruments because it's out-of-tune. So I never really wrote the piece for piano — instead I found a combination of five instruments which are very similar: harpsichord, two electric guitars, harp, and double bass. I used this group of instruments as soloists, as in a concerto grosso.

After that, I wrote a symphony, which is important for me because it is the first large piece I wrote for orchestra. I think the third period begins with the *Awakening of Jacob* and the *Magnificat*, and maybe *Ecloga*. In 1972 and 1973 there are some changes in my thinking, in my music, which I developed after *Ecloga* and *Magnificat*.

D.F.: Specifically what changes would you be talking about?

K.P.: First of all, I've returned to using the normal sound of an orchestra which I missed for so many years while trying to develop new playing techniques for all the instruments. I am no longer using a great deal of percussion, nor am I using special effects. I think I've written enough pieces which utilize all that. I don't think I need it now. Also, I think that pitch is becoming more important now. Pitch is an element that I didn't care too much about in my early music (excepting, of course, the *St. Luke Passion*). In some of my pieces, pitch is not very important — what is important is the relation between clusters, between registers, between groups of instruments.

The best example of this would be the *Symphony*, using groups of instruments, in this case brass and woodwinds. A similar idea is used in *Partita*. I used only groups of instruments, specifically the group of five soloists against all the string instruments, and then against woodwinds, and then percussion, and then brass, and then combined, and so forth. I don't really use this technique anymore.

As far as orchestration is concerned, I think I use more or less traditional orchestration, I would say. Also, I've employed harmony more than I had previously as in the *Awakening of Jacob*. Before, my music was more polyphonic. I was more interested in setting line, more involved with the horizontal than the vertical. In *Utrenja*, each line is very important — if you pick out the fortieth or thirty-seventh voice, the line is very interesting, and it has a logic. Now, I care more about intervals, as in the *Magnificat*, where the minor third is a very important interval. I start with D, and then the choir starts with F, and all this is combined. In the fugue, the first subject is a combination of seven voices using only minor thirds. The first voice uses only C-A, and the second, F-Ab, and so forth. So I have fourteen different pitches, but the listener will remember the interval. Also, I am repeating things more, which is new for me. You will recognize the same chord in *The Awakening of Jacob* both in the beginning and at the end. I used the same idea — it is also a minor third. I also repeat the harmony more. I am building form by repetition, which is the old way, nothing new.

D.F.: You've discussed three stylistic divisions or groupings. Would you consider the first period to be one in which you were trying to expand your vocabulary in different directions, through the use of texture and various other parameters, and then, perhaps, the second period to be one in which you were more concerned with dramatic implications?

K.P.: Yes, because in the second period I was just using the language I had discovered, using my own compositional language. During the first period I was always concerned about finding something new and being different — finding a different music. I was obsessed that my music must be completely different from any I had ever heard. It was! You know, in 1959, in 1960, with *Threnody*, a completely new style occurred. Maybe there was no path for me to follow after that, because I thought I had done everything.

D.F.: Would you consider the third period to be a kind of synthesis of what you tried to accomplish in the first two periods?

K.P.: It's too early to say yet. I think it began in 1974, and I am still looking. I've completed a violin concerto recently, using a technique similar to that of *The Awakening of Jacob*. Other works include the *Symphony* and the Opera for Chicago. It's a very hard piece, because it's a very lyrical opera. The subject is lyric. It's not dramatic at all, except at some moments, but it's very sophisticated and lyric.

It has a very beautiful text between Adam and Eve, and Satan and God. The music is very lyric and I couldn't just use the same technique writing the piece. I couldn't do it right using the language from *Utrenja*, or even *Magnificat*. Remember, *Magnificat* is more dramatic. Therefore I had to find something new, maybe something a little like the techniques used in *The Awakening of Jacob*.

M.S.: Something a little more specific — you mentioned earlier the influence of Boulez on some or your music. Could you elaborate?

K.P.: In my study. It was before I really started to compose what I consider my music.

M.S.: Do you still use any 12-tone or serial techniques? Of course this isn't a very recent example, but in the *St. Luke Passion* you used three rows . . .

K.P.: Oh, yes; sure. I did use some serial techniques. For example, I used some in *Psalms of David*, *St. Luke Passion* and, not as strictly, my instrumental music. On the other hand, the middle section of *Threnody* is written very strictly. *Canon* is not only 12-tone, but also dynamics are controlled — everything is very strictly written. But I don't use these techniques any more.

M.S.: Your orchestrational technique using groups of instruments and pitch class registers reminds me of, say, a band pass filter on an electronic instrument. Do you see that analogy?

K.P.: The work in the electronic studio influenced me very much, and opened for me, really, the possibility to hear many things I hadn't heard before, because I was trained in school very traditionally. I studied harmony, counterpoint, etc. My professor was against 12-tone technique so I never wrote any 12-tone music. Also, Poland was closed to the West until 1956, you know — new music wasn't allowed to be played.

We didn't have any possibility of traveling — it wasn't allowed. We didn't even have scores! For the first time, in 1957, Luigi Nono came to Poland, to visit. He brought some scores with him, and he gave me some. I remember the *Five Pieces* of Webern. I was already writing my own music at that time (1957 or 1958). He gave me some of his music also. I think it was *Il Canto di Spezzo*, *Varianti* for violin and orchestra, *Cori di de Doni*, the piece for chorus, then Improvisation *sur Mallarme*, by Boulez. All this was very new for me, and I tried to incorporate these techniques in a very short time. This was in 1958, till the middle of 1959. And then I decided to go my way.

D.F.: Exactly where did you work? In which studio?

K.P.: In Warsaw.

D.F.: The Warsaw radio?

K.P.: Yes, the studio was established in 1956. It was well noted — the third studio in the world, I think; after Paris and Cologne.

D.F.: Excepting a couple of isolated works (for example, Canon for the two string groups) you don't employ too much electronic music . . .

K.P.: No, I don't really like to combine electronics and live. I don't think it works.

D.F.: Why?

K.P.: I don't know — it's just a feeling. I don't like piano, because I don't like the sound. I will never, or rarely, use organ with orchestra. In the *St. Luke Passion*, I used it a little bit in the Christ aria. In addition, I use clusters only two or three times — not too much. I think there are some instruments you cannot use in the orchestra. I don't like the sound of the piano. It doesn't mix together for me. I will never write a piece for piano and a string instrument, Never! It's the same with electronics. I'm allergic to the combination.

D.F.: How did you arrive at your notational system — it's a very unique system, and, of course, it's been extremely influential.

K.P.: I discovered this system for the music I wanted to write. This system was very simple. As a matter of fact, the technique in *Threnody* was very easy after I discovered it, you know. It looks fairly easy — just a few clusters going down and up, and different densities, and so on. I think the technique is very clear, and also, it's similar to writing in shorthand. I think I remember writing the piece — you know, thinking about the cluster between C and G, and how the cluster will come between F and C (or something like that). I had to write in shorthand — something for me to remember, because my style of composing at that time was just to draw a piece first and then look for pitch; even more than now I think I was interested in pitch. I just wanted to write music that would have an impact, a density, powerful expression, a different expression.

At that time I still played violin, so I tried to find some effects, some new possibilities: playing behind the bridge, on the bass — playing on the tailpiece, or directly on the bridge, etc. I tried to use an instrument as an entire body with which I could make music. So, this way I found out what works. For example, striking the strings with the hand — of course, it's a much better effect if you use it with 'cello or bass, which are larger instruments. So I experimented a while using this whole process, and then I wrote a piece.

I think this notation was for me, in the beginning, like shorthand, really, coming from drawing the piece. I used to see the whole piece in front of me — *Threnody* is very easy to draw. First you have just the high note, then you have this repeating section, then you have this cluster going, coming — different directions from the one note, twelve, and back — using different shapes. Then there is a louder section; then there's another section, then there is the section which is strictly written in 12-tone technique. Then it goes back to the same cluster technique again, and the end of the piece is a big cluster, which you can draw like a square and write behind it fortississimo. Then, to remember, just write "between G and the two octave lower G," and then divide it for instruments. So, it was shorthand. And then I discovered that it works. I didn't need to write a big score — fifty-two different voices. Also, I discovered new symbols for behind the bridge, for highest pitch — I had to do that, because these didn't exist! It was necessary to do it. I didn't want to write in bars, because this music doesn't work if you put it in bars.

M.S.: Do you consider your notational system where it stands now as indeterminate, to a degree; or, if it is indeterminate, for what purpose?

K.P.: I think what I said was that this notation was discovered for the music I wrote, and now, even now, writing different music, sometimes I discover something which helps me notate my ideas. But I think this kind of notation is only for this kind of music. You cannot use the same kind of notation and compose in neo-classical, neo-Bartók, or neo-something idioms. It works only for this music, I think. So it is not a universal notation for everything.

M.S.: Are you worried about how another conductor might interpret some of the notational symbols? For example, in many pieces there are no exact timings marked out for the proportional notation.

K.P.: Yes, sometimes. Usually I put 'circa' 12" or 24", like in *Threnody* and other pieces. You don't have it in the *St. Luke Passion*, because I think the music has something like its own pulse and tempo. If not, it doesn't really work. It doesn't help if you put in bar lines and write metronome '72. I didn't want to write very clear tempos. The idea behind writing the *St. Luke Passion* is similar to Gregorian Chant, really. There is no measure at all; just at the beginning. You know, it was very hard for me to find this kind of notation, I couldn't put it in bars. Sometimes, of course, a conductor who doesn't feel this music will do it differently. Of course it can happen. But today you can have tape, or recordings. I think these help a lot.

D.F.: In some of your music you ask almost the impossible of certain performers. I can think of one specific example — the part of Phillippe in *Devils of Loudon* has that astronomically high C and, of course, that immediately limits the number of performers who can accomplish it. What purpose does this serve?

K.P.: If you had asked a musician to play or try something which seems to be impossible — first of all, he tries and sometimes it happens — he can do it. Sometimes when writing a group of notes together in a very fast tempo, like in *Capriccio* for example, I know it is impossible to play all of them. But I did it because then I had achieved a tension in the sound. If I would have written only four or five notes, he would just do it, you know, so you would lose all the tension I have in the piece. I know this exactly.

Performers ask me all the time: "Please, this is impossible." I reply that ". . . it is absolutely possible — you will do it." Maybe the player will miss two or three of them, but there is a tension there. I used to do it, for example, using the human voice, writing very, very high for sopranos. You have something which you would never have otherwise — a kind of tension — because two or three sopranos can sing it, maybe. The others try. Of course, some of them cry a little bit.

D.F.: Do you think it's the responsibility of the composer to expand the vocabulary with new works?

K.P.: Tchaikowsky wrote a violin concerto and the performers at that time said: "It's impossible, it's an unplayable piece, it's too difficult." Now, the student in the conservatory can play it. The technique of the instrument has developed so much. In *Magnificat*, I employ very high D trumpets, really E and Eb. It's very high, almost impossible, but they tried and they did it. Some didn't, of course. But I like this kind of sound which is produced — being impossible.

D.F.: There is something that really intrigues me. While a lot of composers are avoiding large forms, in that they feel they can't sustain interest with the vocabulary, you tackle these large works with a 'passion.' Could you relate your feelings regarding the large work, considering that some of your earlier works were, indeed, shorter?

K.P.: I was afraid to write large works early in my career. Now I can compose large forms because, first of all, I spend a long time writing a piece. I live with a piece longer. Every day I get up and think a bit, or write a little bit, edit a little bit, and throw away a little bit. There is something which grows for a long time. Of course, I never start from the beginning and go through the piece — never. In the *St. Luke Passion*, I wrote the a cappella sections first, then the arias, then the orchestral parts, then the beginning, then the end.

Then there was something which I wasn't sure of in the middle section, and so on. I think that in writing the piece, you have to be aware of everything — what is after, what is before — like playing chess, you have to think exactly ten moves ahead. If you can do it, you will win; if not, well . . . So, in writing the big piece, you just have to know and be aware of what's going on, how it will be, and how its impact will be, and what technique to use. Also, I feel that when I started to write the *St. Luke Passion*, I had been a composer for many, many years. I didn't want to be an old composer just writing short pieces. I wanted to continue the tradition of the large work as in the 17th and 18th centuries. I think it's necessary.

M.S.: Many of your larger pieces seem to have religious themes or liturgical texts. Could you elaborate on the use of these subjects in your music?

K.P.: I believe, first of all, it's something which is important for me. My background is very religious. I grew up in a very small community, and went to church almost every day. This atmosphere, this kind of music I grew up with — I think it was so important for me, and still is. I believe we miss this something — the mystery of the liturgy. My music is not liturgical at all. But you know, we are living in a very technical time. You have Coca-Cola, plastic flowers, and things like that. It's not enough. I think I feel that life is so short, really. What happens after? I don't know if there is something after, but I'll try to do something which is not only for me, but for other people. It was upsetting living in a communist country, in which the government doesn't agree with, or allow, religious works.

I think I wrote the *St. Luke Passion* because religious music wasn't allowed at that time – absolutely not allowed. The first performance was in Germany. They didn't want to give me a passport to go. They didn't want to do the piece, of course, in Poland. It was commissioned by the German radio and they performed it at the cathedral in Muenster — Poland didn't even want to give me a passport. Later on something happened, and they did the piece in Poland. I think it was very important for the people to have something like this. Afterwards, they felt they had something more than only Marxism, which you can understand, whether you agree with it or not.

D.F.: In the *St. Luke Passion*, which is a conscious attempt at being eclectic, what gave you the idea of using antiphonal chori, as in *San Marco*. Was that a conscious reference?

K.P.: Not really. I didn't have *San Marco* in mind. Of course, I knew about it and the old technique because I studied Renaissance polyphony. I don't care whether you say eclectic or not. It doesn't matter — because in music it exists. It's behind the time a little bit. I believe music is a language which is more universal. I am aware that what I did was a very important development, maybe, developing musical language and technique. But I always only wanted to write music. I think the *Threnody* is still a piece of music for me, not only experimentation. It is experimental, of course, but this kind of expression is still fresh now, I think. It's different and it's mine — I wanted just to express myself, my feelings.

D.F.: In comparison with your early works, a listener would find increasing usage of tonality in more recent pieces. For instance, the *St. Luke Passion* ends on a huge, wonderfully scored E major triad.

K.P.: Yes, but it has nothing to do with tonality, really. It is more like tension and release. I used the major chord for the first time in *Polymorphia*. The form of *Polymorphia* is like an evolution from the very low basses at the beginning, then a sustained note, and then it grows. Next comes a section in which that idea is developed and in which I use more percussion effects. Then it grows into clusters, but in different directions, with a line similar to an encephalograph graph. At the end of the piece a section with a very dense cluster occurs — using quarter tones and scratching. But actually, the start of the piece was the major chord. I was thinking what to do with the major chord. At that time, of course, it was sacrilege writing a major chord (in 1961). Can you imagine that after the Darmstadt school?! You cannot discard something which worked better, I mean purer, more elemental like catharsis.

So I was thinking about incorporating the major chord in a piece. The beginning was, I think, that middle section. And then I decided to repeat it in the end, like catharsis, really. After there's a tension, this whole dissonance, really very tense and unpleasant dissonance, then suddenly you have this release. And this has nothing to do with tonality. It is not tonality, because with tonality you will have dominanta and tonica.

But notice — the same thing happened in the Gloria in *Stabat Mater*. I have eleven pitches going and repeating in the end section, the last twenty bars. I repeat all the pitches except F# — to have it as the top of the D major chord. I was looking for something that would be adequate for "gloria." What can you do? Cluster, no — there is tension, but there is not release. Unison — it doesn't sound so well. Octave, no. It's only the chord — the major chord. Also the same thing occurs in the last bar of the *St. Luke Passion*. If you know the score, several times I repeat "domine," but the only resolution of the "domine" is at the end of the piece. The children are singing "domine, Deus" at a fast rate, which is the only resolution of the chord. Release! The whole piece is preparing this chord.

D.F.: Then, you work primarily with harmonic-vertical sonority?

K.P.: Yes and no. Tension-release. And also, something which I am very concerned about in most of my music, consonance and dissonance — I think it is still very important for me. Sometimes the dissonance is a tension, and consonance is release, as in *The Awakening of Jacob*. You have the E in the last bars and you have D-F in the horns. There is a very beautiful consonance there, together with a cluster in the occarinas. So, it's a very pure sound in this case. I think the relationship between consonance and dissonance is very important for me.

M.S.: To cite another specific example, in *Utrenja* there are sections in which there is a triadic harmony. It occurs to me that perhaps you've employed quotation there.

K.P.: They are not quotes. I just wasn't using the same style. Preparing the piece, I was traveling in Russia and Eastern Poland and Bulgaria, and discovering — being in the service and the old cloisters. Sometimes I wrote down what I heard, sometimes I just listened to the chords. But I didn't use any quotation, except in the Resurrection — it is not quite a quotation, but it is very close. This is almost a quotation of a hymn in the Eastern Service.

D.F.: Obviously you haven't done much work with media, lighting and other effects. What are your feelings regarding these effects? Why don't you use them, and how do you feel about those composers that do?

K.P.: As a matter of fact, I am a traditionalist more and more I would say, because, after so many years writing music, I feel like I would like to concentrate on a very narrow type of thinking. I think I would like to continue with my operas. I have three or four in mind, and I have three or four more big oratorio-like pieces in mind. I would like to write a Requiem. I would like to write a Christmas oratorio, and a Byzantine Mass using a Greek text. I am very fascinated by this music now, really. I have been to Greece, and I am going next year to spend two or three months there; to listen to music, and I think I will write a piece using the text. So, I am not really interested in what you've referred to. I think I was aware ten years ago of what I was going to do.

I would like to concentrate and just write a few pieces, really, but go my own way. And I don't really care what's going on in the musical world now. I think I have my way to go, because how long do I have? Maybe twenty or thirty years to write music. I would like just to go my way. I don't like to use effects, because everything which is more than music for me, you know, even tape, is a little more effect than deep or necessary. So, I think I would like to concentrate on writing my music.

M.S.: Recently, you've conducted a great number of concerts of your music. What problems does this pose for you?

K.P.: Oh, I have no time to compose. For example, between now and June I have something like 20 concerts to do. Of course, I'm doing this for my music. In Europe I am performing mostly my own music, however in Berlin I'm doing Stravinsky's *Symphony of Psalms* and in Stuttgart Bruckner's First. I don't have enough time to spend with my own music and in the future would like to conduct just those concerts that are very important for me and spend the rest of my time writing music.

D.F.: What advantages do you see in conducting your music?

K.P.: I learn a lot by conducting. For example, my notation is clearer now — I write very careful cues for the conductor. I think my music changed after I started to conduct in '72 or '73. Perhaps the change is due to my experience as a conductor.

D.F.: Will you return to usage of the bar as an organizational device?

K.P.: Oh, sometimes, if necessary. In *The Awakening of Jacob* there are many, many bars. On occasion I write bars 'senza misura' — freely. I don't really like to put my music in bars, but sometimes it's necessary. I think the composer has to have experience with the orchestra, it's very important.

D.F.: You've spoken about current and future projects. The "Bicentennial Opera" is noteworthy. Would you elaborate on the state of that work?

K.P.: You know, it's an important piece for me. I chose the piece, found the text, and it's similar in nature to what I've done before. The *Paradise Lost* is a very beautiful Biblical story and in an important language. It's a continuation of what I've been doing, because what I had in mind was to compose a 'creation' and a 'last judgment.' Both possibilities are there to use in *Paradise Lost*. There is a beautiful description of creation and there is a kind of last judgment in which Michael shows the future of Adam. This is similar to Dies Irae, thus it has my interest. As I mentioned to you before, it is a very difficult piece because it is so lyrical, except for the last section. So I have to have a lyrical language especially for use in the many long duets — duos between Adam and Eve, Satan, and so on. I think I have found the language because I've already finished the sections that were very complicated for me — the lyrical ones. More than half of the opera is completed.

D.F.: How long is the entire work?

K.P.: More than three hours. It's a very long piece, large choirs and extensive choral sections. I call it a 'rappresentatione' rather than an opera. I will do it in Europe after its premiere in Chicago. I'll do it in a church, as it should be. I'm going to perform it in a church in La Scala.

D.F.: Would you describe the performing forces required?

K.P.: Yes, it's not too big. It employs a normal sized orchestra, as in *The Awakening of Jacob*, a large chorus — I would like to have a hundred voices, children's chorus for two sections, and about fifteen soloists.

M.S.: As you probably know, there has been a good deal of 'discussion' regarding the fact that a Polish composer received the American Bicentennial commission.

K.P.: I know, I know! At the opening of the Suez Canal, Egypt asked an Italian composer for a work, not an Egyptian, and *Aida* resulted. It doesn't matter — they asked just a composer to write an opera and I'm not the only one to receive a commission. Perhaps over 50 others got them. There were many, many works written.

D.F.: Do you work entirely on commission?

K.P.: Yes, because I don't write too many works, you know, I haven't finished a piece since '74 except the *Violin Concerto*. So I've spent about three years for one piece and I'll need a few more months to finish the opera. I have several commissions after that. I just write what I want to write and if someone is interested in doing what I want to do, then fine. In the case of the opera, I was asked to write about an American subject. However, I wasn't interested in the American Revolution or something like that. So I said I would like to write a piece, but *Paradise Lost* was it, because of its importance to the English Culture.

M.S.: Are there any other compositional projects which are currently interesting you?

K.P.: I would like to write a big oratorio and the subject of Ivan the Terrible is my obsession. I think I'll do this in Russian. I'm currently looking for text. I've read several books and plays about Ivan, but I'm not satisfied with these. I would like to find someone who would write a libretto for me. It is a very powerful story, very dramatic and beautiful, too. I think that I would like to do it very much.

14.

AN INTERVIEW WITH ALVIN LUCIER
Loren Means

Loren Means: What brings you to Mills?

Alvin Lucier: I was one of the recipients of a Ford Foundation grant whereby sixteen composers have been asked to come out here and tape record or compose any piece that they are interested in, and they have access to the studios here. There are a lot of them — there's a studio for electronic processing, a studio for tape recording, all kinds of things — and it gives one a tremendous chance to work without any other problems, without having to teach, without having to go to meetings, or any other kind of thing. It gives one a terrific chance to really concentrate and tape record or compose anything.

I've spent a lot of time tape recording sound effects that I've wanted to do for a long time. I'm also here doing a tour with the Viola Farber Dance Company, and we've got concerts in San Diego, Los Angeles, and Eugene, Oregon.

L.M.: And you're doing a concert at Mills soon?

A.L.: Yes, since I'm around they asked me to do something, I'll do a big piece that I've been concentrating on for about a year, which uses the phenomenon of standing waves. In a space with very simple sine wave oscillators, I set up geographies of standing waves which the audience can perceive. Now a standing wave is a physical phenomenon where a simple sound wave bounces off an object, for example a wall and — I won't try to explain it all, because it gets a little complex — but if certain acoustical conditions are right, you can feel pockets or lines where the sound accentuates itself. The wave bounces off a wall and as it returns to you it's in sync with itself.

And at spots in the room where this doesn't occur, where the opposite occurs, where it's out of sync, it tends to create pockets where there isn't any sound at all, or theoretically in any event. Now that interests me a lot, because it's a real physical dealing with an audio phenomenon. And I've learned to control that, that is, I can predict where those lines are going to be in a space, and I've learned by untuning — I won't go into that, it would take me an hour to explain it — by untuning two oscillators just a teeny, teeny bit, I can send those lines or pockets around the space — they actually travel. They don't travel from speaker to speaker, it's not panning, it's not turning a dial . . .

L.M.: The room is doing it?

A.L.: Well, it's the phenomenon on beating, the sound waves beat, and as they do the phase situation comes into play, and you can actually feel the sounds going around the space. And I can control that speed. So the piece involves that, and then it involves instrumentalists who come into the piece and act as another oscillator, and in acting as other oscillators the players can play with the oscillators that are there, and can attempt the task of creating these standing waves. Now this means that the player has to regard his or her instrument in a different way than one generally does. In order to make the standing wave phenomenon as clear as possible, you have to produce the purest kind of tone. Therefore the player has to make a sound on his or her instrument that most precisely resembles the pure sine tone.

Now the sine tone is just a simple fundamental, without any other components in it. So it's very hard for a player to do, because what distinguishes the sound of one instrument from another is in fact those other sounds that occur above the fundamental. So the player has to oppose, go right against, the way he or she was taught to play, but by doing that they can try to do the standing wave thing, which they couldn't do if they played in the way that they ordinarily do.

When these standing waves beat around a space, they beat toward the lowest tone. If you have one oscillator tuned at such-and-such a pitch and the other tuned slightly below it, the standing waves are going to move in the room to the low direction, the low speaker. So that what we can do is if I am beating a standing wave in one direction, the other player can be doing it in the opposite direction, so you have two beatings going on.

L.M.: This piece sounds similar to your *I Am Sitting in a Room*.

A.L.: Yes, well, one of the features of avant-garde music, if you want to use that term, is that we think we write different pieces each time. Like in the eighteenth century, when a composer would write six quartets, they would be pretty much the same — there was a general style that they would follow, and they could write six quartets in a month. Whereas in this electronic field that we're in, where we're pioneering, pieces used to hardly get played because things were so complex. In our early performances we didn't have the technology that you have now — even the cables weren't right.

But now when I look back on that period — *I Am Sitting in a Room* was written in 1968 — my pieces seem all to be about the same thing. And that is how sound acts in spaces that we find ourselves in. Do you know what I mean?

L.M.: You're concerned about the shapes of the spaces, and how that affects you and other people . . .

A.L.: Yeah, I mean you notice when you talk to somebody in a room, certain feelings you get about communication. And sometimes you think it's psychological, or it's the other person, or you're in such-and-such a mood, but I'm sure that quite a bit of it has to do with the way your voice carries in that space. And when you think of it in those terms, then every space is like an instrument. When you talk about the bell on a brass instrument and what it does to the timbre of the sound — after all, it's just a column of air- the shape and consistency and quality of the metal has everything to do with the timbre.

Now if you talk in a room, and you generally always do, the essence of that room — the size, the shape, the acoustical qualities, the materials on the walls — all make a specific instrument on which our voice is played. And I discovered this through a friend of mine who is a physicist: you see, every pitch has a particular wavelength. The note B in a certain octave has a wavelength so many inches long. And that sound goes out into the space in that wavelength. Now if you play a note very low, it's got a long wavelength, and if you play a note way up high, the wavelength could be an inch or so.

Now if you're in a space — this is very complex, I can't even explain it — and you play a pitch of say a ten-foot wavelength in a room let's say twenty feet long, or a room that has a simple physical relationship to the wavelength, it may reinforce that sound in the same way that I said the standing waves were. If you have a ten-foot sound and it bounces off a wall exactly ten feet away, it'll come back in sync with itself, thereby amplifying itself. Now a sound that's eight feet, or six, or anything that doesn't correspond to the distance of the wall, won't be amplified at all.

So you know when you speak in a room certain components of your voice sound strong. That's because those pitches that are in those components reflect off the surfaces of the room and get amplified. The pitches that don't correspond don't get amplified.

L.M.: So the room is selecting in a way . . .

A.L.: Yeah, according to what the room is. Now you're unable to perceive that under ordinary circumstances, but if you could amplify that in some way, then you could perceive that. The way I amplify it is by recycling the sounds into the room again, again, again, and again, until through the doing it again and again those pitches that do correspond to the resonances get amplified and those that don't go away. So I employ tape, that's what I use tape for in that piece.

I decided to use speech instead of using a musical instrument, because speech is one of the most interesting sounds you can imagine. Nobody talks like any other person. Every person has a very peculiar original speech. And I knew that speech was complex enough to give me a wide variety of sounds. There are a lot of low sounds, unvoiced sounds — oo, ee, ah, mn — there's a lot of noise in sounds like sh, p, t, k. So before I start I've got a very complex input. Then I decided to choose a text, it could be anything, and sit in a room — any room, it didn't matter which — and tape record my voice, in the room, onto a tape.

Then what I did is play the tape back into the room again. Now, people think I just dubbed from one tape recorder to another one, but no, I played it back into the room, and tape recorded that.

L.M.: The important thing was playing the tape into the room, not just how many generations were undergone . . .

A.L.: Yeah, because you could do a degeneration of tape easily, just re-record from tape to tape. I wasn't interested in that. Every time the speech goes back into the room, it picks up whatever characteristics the room has. And by repeating it again and again and again, you amplify those that do reinforce and you eliminate those that don't.

Now I had to make a composer's choice, and I gave it a lot of thought. I decided to use the simplest speech I could find, like I could imagine some other composer thinking, "The material has to be interesting," and reading poetry or Joyce or something where the voice would rise and fall, stop and start. I decided against that, because I didn't want the input to be so composed as to take away from the idea of the piece.

L.M.: So the sound is the content?

A.L.: What the room does is the content. Now, I didn't want to read a spectacular poem, I didn't want anything dramatic, because that has nothing to do with the phenomenon. I just wanted to expose that phenomenon in the clearest way. And if I'd done anything complicated it would detract from that. So I invented a text that simply described what I was doing.

And I thought for a while what speed it ought to go at, I just tried to intuitively sense the room. I tried really to tune into the room, and just think, "What speed should my voice go at to try to do this as optimally as possible?" So I just paced myself, and I chose a sort of quiet, moderately slow speed — "I am sitting in a room, different than the one you are in now . . ."

You know, if we had a couple of tape machines now, we could do the piece. The piece has to do with carrying nonverbal — well, it destroys the speech. And that really affects people. I've had people come up and say, "It's like somebody's dying."

L.M.: I experienced the piece as your annihilation of yourself.

A.L.: I was in England, and I have some very political people over there that I know quite well, and they say it's a pessimistic piece, in the Marxist term. They say you shouldn't make pieces that destroy speech, pieces should be optimistic. And in a sense they're correct, because so much of what we do in America is pessimistic — the films, the TV, it's all pessimistic.

The news is always bad. If you hear every day bad news, bad news — inflation, energy crises, Viet Nam — you get lulled into a very pessimistic state — what can you do, you can't do anything. In that sense, they're right, the Marxists are right. On the other hand, my piece does annihilate the content of my speech — the text — however, it makes perceptible these particular frequencies that are implied in the room. And if we're going to survive in a modern electronic age, it's to our advantage to perceive those things. I can see it would be a great feat to know about frequencies. It might help astronauts, for example — it might help people build better places to live. If you figured out that certain frequencies were beneficial to you, you might design particular rooms that would help people feel that. So, in that sense I don't think it's a pessimistic piece.

L.M.: When Peter Gordon played the Source magazine recording (#7, Jan. 1970) of this piece on KPOO in San Francisco, people phoned in and told him his needle was stuck.

A.L.: That's because they don't hear the change, it doesn't happen with enough speed. It's funny, engineers don't enjoy that, because they know the phenomenon, and they say to me, "I could do that in two passes." They don't realize that I love to hear the slow change. There's no joy for me in doing that piece fast — I like to hear each slow change, because at every point you're in an area where you don't know if it's changed, or it's changed a little bit, and there's a point in that piece for everybody, a different place in the piece, where they no longer hear the speech. And each person has a different point. So it's a piece that has a particular structure in that way, but it makes its own — I didn't determine that point.

There's another piece from that period, written in 1969, that's similar to *I Am Sitting in a Room*. It's called *Quasimodo, the Great Lover*. It's simply a piece where you send sounds over a long space. You produce any kind of sound, and you send it physically over a long geographical space — in through rooms, down across fields — through pieces of metal — anything that sound can travel in. And you send it far enough so that at the end you don't know the origin of the sound — that is, the sounds have picked up the acoustic qualities of the environments through which they go.

If it goes through a room that has a reverberation situation, the sounds pick that up. If it goes through other spaces that add different things, it picks that up, so by the end of the space — it could be a mile, and the sounds could be amplified along the way — the sounds change according to the environment.

Then there's a computer-controlled piece, called *RMSM 1*. Once again, it's about spaces. I was on a ferryboat once from Belgium to Amsterdam, and to interest myself I had a cassette tape recorder with earphones. And just to enjoy myself, I walked around the boat with the earphones on and the microphone on so that I could hear everything amplified. It was like having super-ears, because I had the volume turned up on the cassette recorder. And I was very struck by the differences in spaces that you go through. For instance, if you're in a large room, you hear the room tone — a very large, ambient sort of room tone. If you go into a small room, the whole ambience changes.

Now, if you've ever acted in a film, or done sound for a film, you know that if the director wants to splice in some quiet in a scene, for instance during a pan to a picture on a wall, you just can't put in empty tape, because it's obvious that the ambience of the room gets cut. So what the sound man does is call for a minute of quiet on the set, and he simply records the room tone, which is recording the general ambience of the room. It could be air conditioning or just the echo-reverberation qualities.

And I was struck by this when I was walking from room to room of this boat. It struck me that large rooms sound as if you're in a band-pass filter. Whereas when I went into a small room, the room tone changed a lot. So I got the idea to make a computer-controlled environment, which is a very simple idea. I took a microphone and I put it in a room. I didn't care whether there were people in the room or whether the room was empty. The microphone comes out and goes through a very simple configuration of electronic devices — a reverberation chamber, two amplifiers, and a filter.

Now, I tried to figure out what made rooms sound the way they do, with reference to how big rooms are, and of course if a room is very reverberant, it can either be a big room or a room that has very bright surfaces on it, so that the room sounds bright, or sounds reverberant. If there's no reverberation, it means that the room is very dry, that is it could have things on the walls like drapes that would cut down any reverberation.

So I set up a configuration of electronic equipment that the computer could control. In other words, the live sounds are going into the equipment, but the computer is opening and closing that equipment in such a way as to simulate that the room that the microphone is in is getting smaller or changing size.

The room that the mike is in is a specific size, but by processing it, through reverberation chambers, amplifiers, and filters, I simulated making the room change to any particular size. And because it was controlled by a PDP 10, I could do that at very fast speeds, and very accurately.

The decisions upon which I based the changes have to do with a visual image, and that was a bird. I designed an artificial bird that would fly through the computer program — it was designed into the program. So that at a given moment, the wings of the bird would flap at a certain speed, which was the sampling rate, and if you caught the bird at a certain instant, the span of the wings would give you the width of the room that the bird was in. And I set up dimensions — the room could be a thousand feet wide, a thousand feet tall, by the way the wings were. If the wings were in vertical position, that would give me the dimensions of the width and the height, but the particular length of the room was generated in the computer itself, and could be anything at any given instant. But the maximum dimension was sixteen thousand.

So depending on the physical situation of the bird, the dimensions of the room can be told, and the computer calculates that and carries out the calculations that I put in, and will give four channels of output voltages into the electronics in a attempt to simulate the change of room size. Do you understand that?

L.M.: I don't understand how you get the bird into the computer.

A.L.: There's a sub-program in FORTRAN that deals with the mathematical function sine. So I used that sine curve as the abstract wing of a bird. You know when you drew birds when you were little, you could just draw one line and it looks like a gull? Two lines, actually. I just visualized that as the wing of a bird, as these sine waves would open up.

The idea was you could do it as a live environmental control piece. You could set up a microphone in a space, have your electronic equipment in another space, and have your program control that, so that you could control over a long period of time, changing the size of the room that you're in.

15.

FIVE QUESTIONS: 40 ANSWERS
Newel Kay Brown, Barney Childs, Sydney Hodkinson, Don Martino, Richard Moryl, Pauline Oliveros, Elie Siegmeister, John Watts.

These questions, originated and sent by Thomas Everett (editorial staff, THE COMPOSER) to the above-named composers, are presented here with the responses of each of these composers. The listing is alphabetical, and no composer was aware of the answers given by any other.   - Ed.

 # Have you composed and/or worked with any type of electronic music? What advantages or interest does electronic music hold for you? What disadvantages?

Brown: This past summer I enjoyed an introduction workshop in electronic music and plan to continue working in the field, seeing the greatest possibility with combination of instruments and prepared tape. Another advantage is that of exploring the mixed media field. The only disadvantage is that it requires TIME. Lots of time!

Childs: Yes. Occasional ways to deal with familiar sounds. Usually too much work to produce sounds I don't much care for.

Hodkinson: a) Yes. Early works were produced in an educational FM radio station in Charlottesville, Virginia with a colleague, David Davis. We "used" everything from a boiling coffee pot and our own vocal chords to pure sine tones and often did incidental music for the Drama Dept. A film score for *Scissors* by Kee Dewdney was written at the well-equipped studio at the University of Michigan in 1967. Since I have been away from Ann Arbor, recent works employing tape have involved simply the pre-recording of live instrumental sounds.

b) Many (advantages), the same ones as are held by most of my colleagues — those often quoted in Music History books, I suppose (That's not intended as a snotty answer). c) My own ignorance and lethargy (are disadvantages). The field itself grows overnight so who can say where we'll be and what we'll have to work with even two or three years from now? The all-too-common ugly toilet-flushings, belches, beeps, etc., hold little interest for me, however, and if the sounds don't interest you, baby, it's all downhill.

Martino: I have not as yet composed an electronic piece, nor have I had an overwhelming desire to do so. Up to now, in spite of an oppressive preponderance of poor performances, I have not been driven to electronic resources because there have always been a sufficient number of skillful, even brilliant, performances and enough modest commissions (though never as many as I might hope for) to incline me toward writing performer-required works. Moreover, neither a file cabinet full of bad reviews nor the knowledge that I am not generally regarded as being "in," has sufficiently motivated me to leap to 'lectric music (or any other kind) because I spend more time composing, after all, than listening to my compositions in performance or reading what other people think about them. And I have found that greater-amount-of-time very enjoyably spent the way I now use it.

It is probably my habit of endlessly tinkering and toying with my little musical games in the solitude and comfort of my study that most prevents me from using electronic resources. For I could not bear to work away from home, to forsake my study for a room I have not made and to which I must agonizingly commute, only to find my composing time restricted by others' needs. And the same factor that prevents me from owning an adequate piano or tape recorder prevents me from owning even the most modest electronic equipment.

Finally, the sense that there still remains so much to explore with non-electronic instruments and so very little time in which to do it has thus far kept my nose very close to Passantino. I guess that of all the obvious and often-cited lures of electronic music, to me the most seductive is the possibility of almost completely controlling the total music-work — that is, of performing again.

But I still regard myself as a performer, although I have not played in public for many years. And I know that if I live long enough I shall again concertize as I shall also come quite naturally to confront electronic media.

Moryl: I have, since 1965, composed a number of works for instruments and various electronic sounds. I feel that this new medium, in both studio and performance capabilities, offers endless possibilities in the combination of sounds which have never before been available to the composer. The advantage lies in the immensely wider musical perspective, which requires a greater musical imagination than ever before.

The disadvantages, for most, have been the mechanics of the studio itself, and the amount of time needed to control what finally comes out. There are relatively few composers who have developed enough skill to be the master of the machine, rather than its victim.

I feel that its greatest contribution so far has been its effect on instrumental writing, as it relates to textures and more abstract musical shapes.

What electronic music needs now is some good composers who will realize its great potential, without limiting its execution to the instrumental concepts of today.

Oliveros: Yes. Advantages for the use of any musical medium, electronic, acoustic or what have you?, accrue when a balance or mutual dependence exists between the medium and the message. The medium serves the message and vice versa or the situation is natural. Since the quality of nature must be infinite, all of the advantages cannot be known simultaneously. Time must pass. Repetitions must occur. As certain advantages are discovered others may be hidden by the discovery. More advantages of a musical medium surface as the context changes, or as conditions change, or both change. As contextual and conditional changes occur, even the medium and message may change. More advantages surface when conditions, context, or both are held constant during repeated use.

Disadvantages for the use of any musical medium accrue when balance or mutual dependence does not exist between the medium and the message. The medium does not serve the message and vice versa. The situation is not natural. It is likely parasitic. Disadvantages are discovered in the same way as advantages: during repeated use of a medium with constant or changing elements.

Advantages and disadvantages exist on many different levels. For certain kinds of music (message), the band is an excellent medium where the orchestra or another kind of ensemble is not. A condition might be playing out-of-doors in the context of a football game. On a very windy day, a poor out-of-doors condition might be improved by some sort of acoustic shell to keep the sound from blowing away from the intended audience. The message (music) has a better chance (serving the medium) of fulfilling its intended function (spurring the rooting section for the team, generating excitement during lulls, etc.) if the medium (band) serves the message: Instruments or elements of the band chosen for their ability to project sound out-of-doors then are advantageous. An ensemble of guitars, though rousing or exciting in a small indoor space (condition) for entertainment of perhaps a different kind (context), would be disadvantageous at a football game because of far less ability to project sound out-of-doors. The medium is then parasitic or out of balance in such a context and does not serve the message.

What are the characteristics of the medium? What are the characteristics of the message? What is the context? What are the conditions? The answers (a continuous process which must involve any composer) to these questions yield more and more and less and less of the advantages and disadvantages. However, what is advantageous in one context or with one kind of condition may be or become disadvantageous in another context or with the change of any condition or vice versa. With the above considerations in mind, I choose the electronic medium when it suits my purposes and my purposes suit the medium.

Siegmeister: No; no advantages. Disadvantages: ugly sound, disorganized, formless arrangements of primitive material.

Watts: Yes. The advantages can be summed up in two words, "accessibility" and "immediacy." Disadvantages include quickened friendships with technicians, repair men, and bankers, jealous wives, and girlfriends, and ever-present reminders that we've done little more than scratch the surface of the medium so far.

 # Some music being created for records or tapes lessens the importance of the performer: with the aid of electronics, the composer creates the work without outside assistance. Other music depends on the performer to complete the music (e.g. aleatoric and improvisational techniques). What role do you see the live performer playing in the future?

Brown: The performer of the future has to travel with a larger bag. Beethoven concertos will always be with us (I hope) but some performers will desire to add to their abilities. New ideas and performance techniques are coming on so fast it's enough to scare old dogs like me. Don't worry — the tape deck will never replace him!

Childs: Much the same role he has played so far.

Hodkinson: The same as in the past. I can't see the importance of the performer being "lessened" by electronics. Aleatoric and improvisational techniques in the hands of knowledgeable, gifted players, often produce groovy results, but isn't that true of Bach and Bacharach also?

I like tubas, violins, slide whistles, and so on and performers are still investing the good part of a life in trying to play them well. My personal interest as a woodwind player tends more toward live-electronics and I hope to learn what little I can about this in the future.

Martino: The fundamental role of the performer, essentially unchanged throughout the history of notated music, is to transform the symbols of music notation into sound. The magnitude of that role and the propriety with which it is executed have less to do with the composer's philosophy or its attendant notational idiosyncrasies than with the performer's interpretive genius. To admit that a performer played musically is not to admit that he played music. Which music he chooses to interpret often has less to do with the intrinsic value of the music-work than with fads and fancies whose transientness is thankfully guaranteed. But as there will always be composers, there will always be those among them who, despite the very considerable lure of electronics, will remain dedicated to live performance simply because there will always be performers of genius to inspire them.

Moryl: It would seem that the relationship between the composer and the performer has become more as one. The dichotomy between the two has narrowed into a more dualistic relationship, which I feel can create a kind of total involvement, and thus improve the final results.

The performer can now contribute as never before to the overall shape of a piece, not only as interpreter of symbols, but as an individual with greater creative potential.

Oliveros: This question is based on wrong assumptions. For example, the Beatles (both composers and performers) became more and more studio-oriented (created music for records and tapes). Studio technique expanded their performance means. Their role as performers was emphasized in importance, not lessened. The range of aleatoric and improvisation techniques is pitted against a narrow view of electronic music (the composer working alone in a studio without the aid or collaboration of a performer). In this case the composer is the performer and the role of the composer has been expanded. Music for records and tapes is still being performed. It could not be otherwise. There is more performance and composing today than ever before in history. There is no reason to believe that the performer and composer will ever not have the same or expanded roles in music now or in the future.

Siegmeister: He will continue to be the mainstay of musical life. After a time, people will become bored with mechanical sounds.

Watts: One of my persistent fantasies takes this form: One day (soon?), all composers everywhere will go on strike and refuse to release anything to performers or the public for at least ten years. Wouldn't that be something? Among the first to squirm would be those musicians and listeners alike who think their service to music ends somewhere around 1910. (That alone would make a strike worthwhile!) While it would be somewhat unfair to that small, dedicated minority group of musicians who performs contemporary scores, at first glance, this interregnum might even make their positions more secure in the long run by allowing the public a catching-up period (If there isn't a public, then it's folly to talk about the "live" performer). More and more composers (the ones I know at least) are writing less and less for the "generalist" (the grand opera, the symphony, the concerto, etc.), but, rather, zeroing in on the "specifist" situations (an experimental work for amplified accordion, soprano sax, and tuba? why not?). I see two things happening, then, in the near future: more and more tailoring of works for the individual performer; and more direct and personal collaborations between composer and performer, to the extent perhaps that, in time, works may have collective "composers" and so noted.

 # Who comes first: the performer that interests composers in new techniques for his instrument; or the composer who forces a performer to learn new techniques in order to play his music?

Brown: In the past it has always been the composer pushing the performer to explore his instrument beyond the status quo and I believe it will continue to be the case. In the past fifteen years or so, however, there have been more interested performers — interested in exploring their "thing" with an eye towards interesting a composer (or commissioning a new work). This trend is healthy but certainly not widespread. I'm not pushing the composition of musical or instrumental effects!

Childs: Chickens? Eggs?

Hodkinson: What difference does it make? The latter is more common, of course, but the former is not at all unheard of. What is important is that some rapport between the two be attempted. What is it anyway, a race? Who wins? Does one get a prize?

Martino: I have experienced this phenomenon in both ways. That is, on some occasions I have "expanded" the performer, on other occasions he has "expanded" me. It really doesn't matter "who comes first" as long as the dialogue continues.

Moryl: There is no question that the performer himself is the composer's best guide to new performance techniques. Pieces are usually written for particular performers who are willing to experiment and become part of the new sounds. The composer may know what he wants, but it is up to the performer to develop the new techniques needed for the execution of his ideas. Just as Brahms worked with a famous violinist when writing his concerto, most composers depend upon the performer to show them the way.

Oliveros: I don't care.

Siegmeister: The composer.

Watts: This is one of those chicken-or-the-egg and/or indeed, tertium quid questions; obviously, it happens both ways. As for any kind of implied moral ascendancy in one order or the other, toss a coin.

Is there an "American" style of music?

Brown: Eclectic is the style. Jazz is the most original contribution.

Childs: No, not like the Amerikanische musik of the '30s and early '40s. But there is an increasing New World way of thinking in the arts, a breakaway from the whole historical-critical Western European evaluative and careerist business: I find it shown by a delight in sound, a refusal to be conned by the masterpiece racket and by process-mongering, an immediacy. Two citations from D. G. Jones, the Canadian poet and critic (he's writing about poetry here, but the stance is throughout the arts): . . . the crude actuality of place, the isolated moment of experience that the speaker refuses to gloss or distort by referring it to some social or moral or metaphysical idea. The meaning is all in the tone of the talk and the gathering up of detail, not in the ending, not in a conclusion. (Butterfly on Rock, 171)

Hodkinson: My job as conductor of the Contemporary Directions Ensemble in Ann Arbor necessitates perusing a large number of American scores each year, and I think I can safely answer "certainly not"; a few provincial similarities, yes. I know it may be reactionary to say so and certainly a little pompous, but the "styles" that matter to me are still categorized like my kids' report cards.

Martino: The New York Times (along with a number of other rags) has done its damnedest to push the notion of an International Style. Now, if you prefer reading about music to listening to it, then perhaps this phony journalistic slogan may be convincing. But if occasionally you have the wax cleaned out of your ears, you tend to hear not so much differences between nations (although they exist) but between men. And these are the differences that really count.

Moryl: There appears to be no specific style of music that one can call "American," yet Americans are responsible for most of the innovations in all Art today. We have many young people of extraordinary imagination who are searching for and, I believe, will find new modes of expression. As with Charles Ives, we are becoming not imitators of European tradition, but the leaders in the new esthetic.

Oliveros: Is there a Venusian style of music? Of course there is if there is music on Venus. The question should be "what are the characteristics of the American style of music?" but it isn't, so I am not going to answer that question.

Siegmeister: Yes.

Watts: Yes, if only residually. If we had a panel of composers put to the blindfold test, listening, say, to twenty works from all over the world, I have no doubt that American works would be selected unerringly most of the time. Just as Esperanto hasn't become a widespread lingua franca, neither has an international common practice become a language we speak (or even want to) convincingly; and — let's face it — we're not Poles, Nigerians, Polynesians, or Swedes, however much we have in common.

Every period of music has had an outstanding composer who functioned as a leader and model for other composers, and whom history has considered as being characteristic of those times. Do you feel we have such a composer representing the second half of the twentieth century?

Brown: This sounds like an easy way out of the question, but I feel it's much too early to tell. With electronic music still experiencing birth pains, who can say — And if all the composers decide to live as long as Stravinsky, the historians will be in an even greater mess.

Childs: I surely hope not.

Hodkinson: Who cares? Of course there will be such figures; talent will out and time will tell: the everlasting bromides. Each cat ought to function as well as he is able with the equipment he has been granted. One just muddles on, surely without worrying about which man will "represent the second half of the twentieth century." One attempts to produce what one's ears say as competently and professionally as one can. It might be the job of historians and theorists to determine your "characteristic models and leaders," but I think I've got better things to do. There's too much model-mongering going on anyhoo. A passage from the English playwright N. F. Simpson of which I am particularly fond, offers me a decent way of closing this questionnaire: "I lay claim to no special vision, and my own notions as to what I have in mind here may well fall pitifully short of your own far better notions. No. I am the dwarf in the circus — I give what scope I can to such deficiencies as I have."

Martino: If it is true that "every period of music has had an outstanding composers who functioned as a leader and model for other composers, and whom history has considered as being characteristic of those times," and if the second half of the twentieth century is such a "period," then the question must be answered affirmatively.

Moryl: The name of John Cage comes immediately to mind, perhaps less as a composer of music than as a person of ideas. He has, almost single-handedly, turned Western music around, and made us conscious of an entirely new set of expectations. There are other psychological shapes which are as valid as the great crescendo, which has engulfed Western Art for centuries. Western man himself, and Western Art have always considered themselves unique, but have much to learn from other civilizations and attitudes.

Oliveros: Yes, one from the many and many from the one.

Siegmeister: Bartók and Ives.

Watts: Fifty years is a long time, and we're a long way from the end of that "second half." I earnestly believe that the outstanding composer model-leader has yet to emerge, and maybe won't. "Characteristic of those (our) times?" Well, let's make Varèse Chairman of the Board Emeritus; Stockhausen, Alchemist-at-Large; Babbitt and Xenakis might want to fight it out (old IBM cards at ten paces) to see which is to be the resident bookkeeper. If you're taking nominations from the floor, Brown, Crumb, and Penderecki are as good a troika as any.

16.

A MUSICIAN SEDUCED INTO CARPENTRY
Rodney Oakes

Since his death in September, 1974, I have come in contact with more of the music of Harry Partch through the media than I ever did when he was alive. I have witnessed during the past year two television specials on Partch, a number of newspaper articles attempting to place him and his music in perspective, and a late night television news commentator announcing an up-coming concert with a superficial look at Partch's beautiful, but baffling to newsmen, instruments. I am still waiting patiently for one of his associates to publish an in-depth book about his music. Perhaps it is not necessary as Partch probably said it all in his *Genesis of a Music* (2nd edition, Da Capo Press, N.Y., 1974).

I am writing this while on vacation at a small beach town north of San Diego called Solano Beach. We do not come here very often, in fact this is the first time in seven or eight years. The last time I remember being here for any length of time was on New Years Day, 1968. Harry Partch had invited my wife Jeannie and me over to his house in Solona Beach for an afternoon chat.

At that time my sister had been working in a bank where Partch opened an account, and when she waited on him, she happened to ask if he was a composer. He was amazed at being recognized by a bank teller, and started an informal friendship with her. This New Years Day visit had been arranged through my sister.

At that time, Partch was living in a small, two room bungalow, about two blocks from the beach. We were surprised by the lack of space, the amount of clutter, and the sense of either simplicity or poverty. Partch's kitchen was overflowing with dishes, boxes of different brands of soaps, and enough small utensils to supply a large sized restaurant. The tiny living room had one chair, one combination sofa and bed, and a table. A number of scores were lying around, haphazardly, among all sorts of small items that cluttered the area.

Strategically placed on the small table were wood-working tools, pipe and tobacco, and a bottle of brandy. Partch offered us brandy, graciously claiming that it was not the best brandy in the world, but neither was it the worst.

So we talked with this man. His fingers ran continuously through his hair. He was wearing what I have since discovered to be his usual apparel; beach clothes, an old hat, and sun glasses. In this relaxed environment, Partch offered some views on the music world and his own participation.

Jeannie and I wondered about his earliest musical experiences. Partch was born in Benson, Arizona, where he lived until he was twelve. His formal education ended after the fifth grade. His parents loved music, but were not musicians. They ordered all the instruments that were available through the Sears and Roebuck and Montgomery Ward catalogs.

Where did early professional support come for his music? We were quite surprised to find out that Howard Hanson had been very encouraging to Partch during the 1920s. Partch had written a string quartet for either three violas and one cello, or three celli and one viola, he could not remember which combination for sure, that utilized an unusual tuning. A performance of this work had been rather unsuccessful in San Francisco, but Howard Hanson heard it, liked it, and gave Partch encouragement. Encouragement from other composers during the time came from Otto Luening and Varèse. Partch considered Varèse to be an especially good friend.

We were especially curious about Partch's impressions of the avant-garde music of the time of our visit. Partch grabbed a copy of Source magazine, and we examined some of the scores published there by John Cage, Lukas Foss, and Barney Childs. Partch was reluctant to comment on the aural effects of the music and was much more concerned with the visual organization of the printed music itself.

Partch always wrote his music on a five line staff because that is what musicians are used to reading. He wanted to communicate the fastest way possible the pitches he wanted the players to perform. He did not want to develop his own notational system. Examining the notation of Foss and Childs, Partch wondered out loud if they used draftsmen. Partch was especially unmoved by the music of Childs, and felt that this music had no momentum for him.

At the time I was a student at the University of Southern California and Partch's comments on USC were quite interesting to me. He was not fond of USC. He stated that the faculty paid lip service to knowing him and promoting his music, but the fact was that they had never done anything for him.

Partch discussed the present state of his own music. He was quite pessimistic. He had never been happy with his experiences in the academic world. One of his major complaints was that he never had access to use wood shops on college or university campuses to build instruments. At that time he was teaching at the University of California at San Diego and that campus did not have a shop, which to him was a crisis. His ideal was the Renaissance, and his model was Vincentino.

Partch did not feel that his music would last after him, primarily because very few people understood his instruments, the tuning of them, and the care of them. He really felt that Dan lee Mitchell was the only person who knew how to maintain and tune all of his instruments. As for himself and his music, it was too late.

Partch had always been mystified by foundations, grants, and academic politics. He did not know how he had received a Guggenheim Fellowship. He felt that he did not have enough energy or the health to write another work or prepare for another performance.

In the midst of our conversation the phone rang. Partch did not own a record player, tape recorder, or so far as we could tell a television or radio. Yet his phone rang not with the usual buzz, but with a chime! Apparently it was worth the added expense for a less irritating telephone ring. The call was from Dan lee Mitchell, who besides conducting his music and caring for his instruments, periodically checked on Partch's well-being.

Partch was pessimistic about the future of his music and the future of music in general. I have talked with others who have known him well, and I gather that he was usually pessimistic. He did have a number of successes after our visit. Capitol Records released an excellent album of his music. We heard an outstanding performance of his *Delusion the Fury* at UCLA a year later, and the audience loved every moment of it.

I cannot be as pessimistic as he was. Granted, Partch placed barriers between his music and traditionally trained musicians and audiences. But his uniqueness, his inventiveness, have an appeal for a rather large audience. I think that he has reached a larger audience then he ever realized. Partch wanted people to discover their own music and disregard the artificial exercises of the virtuosity that is so much a part of music of the Western World. Consequently, the music of Partch is based on a very personal aesthetic; his own melodies and harmonic invention played his own instruments. Such music is not designed for a broadly based audience. Yet, it so delightfully pleases the ear (and the eye when it is perceived in its purest form, danced on the concert stage) that it demands to be shared with many. Partch's philosophy, that each of us discover our own music as he has done for himself, is an important message to the composer and the lover of the art of music. It is imperative that the music of Partch should live.

17.

INTERVIEW WITH HENRY BRANT
Tom Everett

TOM EVERETT: What is your reaction to the fact that Polish composer Krzysztof Penderecki was commissioned to write an opera for the American Bicentennial?

HENRY BRANT: I can imagine two possibilities. One of them is that our U.S. view of musical creation is so highly democratic, that we make no distinction between American and foreign composers, but choose the one who's most gifted whether he's American or not, a citizen or not, a visitor or not. Another possibility which, I fear may be the actual one, is that there's still an American tendency to look with some contempt on our domestic products in concert music and opera and to assume that a native-born American trained here, is automatically inferior to a top flight European. I'm afraid that may be the more serious possibility although I do hope not. What do you think?

T.E.: Possibly, they feel there is not an American composer that would bring in publicity, or world-wide acceptance of a new work.

H.B.: Well, in that case the assumption seems to be that an opera by a European is superior to one by an American in terms of the publicity it can generate. Suppose that the situation were reversed, with the Polish government considering an opera to commemorate the 20th Anniversary of the New Polish Revolution; does it seem likely that their democratic principles would extend so far as to find that a gifted American possesses musical powers so superlative as to out weigh the talents of the best Polish composers?

T.E.: Have you written in the opera medium?

H.B.: Yes, I've written one. I expect to begin work on another in the very near future. My "first" opera, *Grand Universal Circus,* is an effort to introduce into use in my concert music, which means not only different kinds of music heard simultaneously from specific different places in the theatre, but also highly contrasted dramatic situations similarly spaced out. One advantage of this is that plot can be dispensed with to some extent, and replaced by the simultaneous contrasted or contradictory subject matter. I would not attempt this spatial montage method if story-line or logical dramatic sequence were present, but I'm much less interested in story-line than in a kind of theatre ritual. I'm sure that the spatial montage procedures will be carried much further in my next opera.

T.E.: When you write a large work does it help you to know what hall it is going to be performed in? Wouldn't that affect what you can do and how you conceive the piece?

H.B.: Yes, always. I begin by checking out the first hall where the projected new work is going to be performed.

T.E.: Then do you adapt a work for another setting?

H.B.: It has to be workable in almost any hall, and without major alterations in my basic spatial plan for the location of the performers. In my initial plans I always think of possible adaptions of the spatial arrangements and it's been very rare that any hall has been spatially unadaptable to my music. Avery Fisher Hall in New York, for example, would be a very difficult place for any spatial piece of mine because of the throw from back to front is so vast that sounds proceeding from different parts of the hall reach the audience at different times. My *Voyage 4* was written for Woolsey Hall at Yale University and requires deep balconies running the entire length of the side walls plus a large rear balcony. This layout does not exist everywhere, which limits the performances of this piece. Some of the fine old halls and churches in Boston, with their deep continuous balconies, would be ideally suited to my space music.

T.E.: Are you interested in having your works published, made available in print?

H.B.: Some are.

T.E.: I'm just thinking of the problem you would have if you're constantly reworking or revising a work to the situation; publishers would be reluctant to put it in a final print.

H.B. All my musical material is fully notated and in final form. That isn't to be changed. It's only the location of the performing forces and the separation between them where adapt ions must be made, and occasionally in dynamics. If for instance, something for a few instruments with low dynamic markings is played in a vast space it would be only realistic in performing it to use higher dynamic levels. That's occasionally necessary, but as a rule not. There are very few occasions where I have had to do it.

T.E.: Many of your pieces are concerned with spatial location, and so forth, of the players and music comes from many directions. How did you develop this sense; was it through trial and error? Did you study acoustics and do you experiment with every piece you write? Just how did you become interested in this and find certain solutions to problems you had?

H.B.: About 1950, I was writing a kind of music that was polyphonically as complex as I could make it. I wanted to have a lot going on, with much simultaneous and highly contrasted material, and it seemed that I couldn't pile on much more without producing a confused amalgam, impossible to keep track of in its details, where separate linear constituents would collide over the same octave and get in each other's way. I didn't know how to make such polyphonic complexity intelligible and was unwilling to accept a less dense polyphony as a solution. About this time, when I was teaching at Juilliard, I heard for the first time some Gabriel i canzonas with the choirs properly spaced at the back and front of the hall, and then I performed Ives' *Unanswered Question*, spacing the three elements as far apart as possible.

Shortly afterward in Paris, I heard the Berlioz *Requiem* at the Invalids with the spacings that he intended. All these experiences together pointed to a clear solution for my dense polyphony namely, a controlled use of spatial resources. I didn't write the first multi-spatial piece, it was composed in 1952 by a former student of mine, Teo Macero. He heard the same spatial music that I had and he suggested to me a piece for five jazz groups, all spaced widely apart in the hall, to include improvisation as well as written material. It's a remarkable piece and quite neglected. He composed this work, *Areas*, in early 1952, before I wrote my first spatial piece *Antiphony I* later the same year. In *Antiphony I* I worked out the main spatial procedures which have guided my subsequent work, and the acoustical assumptions underlying *Antiphony I* have since been confirmed by repeated experiment. The first is that the wider the distance between the performing groups, the less influence they have on each other, especially in terms of harmony.

This should be obvious, something any musician can try for himself, but what musicians find workable by trial and error under practical conditions later proves to be scientifically accountable in acoustical terms. Such discoveries can also be codified in theoretical form, and that is the usual history of all musical discoveries. First, musicians try them and find out practically how they work, then acousticians account for this workability in scientific terms and theorists codify procedures. What I'm doing spatially is now in the stage of practical trial to find out what works easily and unmistakably; if it doesn't work I t m not interested in the theory, the acoustics or anything else.

My assumptions are simple and obvious, perhaps so much so that many musicians would consider them too infantile to bother with. For example, if you want two instruments to sound in the closest possible relationships, you must place the two performers as close together as possible. They can then play more exactly in rhythm together if that's your intention, and more exactly in tune, and more closely in harmonic relationship. If you want them unrelated in these respects, then separate them as much as possible.

The separation device led to a surprising conclusion, many times verified, which is that the influence that the separated constituents have over each other is so much cancelled out that the result, for practical purposes, is as though each were playing in a different octave range. You can write, then, highly contrasted textures freely over the same octave and they will appear to "pass" each other without harmonic collision, just as though they were written in different octave registers. This means that the amount of polyphonic or heterophonic material you can crowd into the seven octaves that are available to us is immensely more if the participating constituents are physically widely separated than if all were situated in the same location, such as the stage area. This phenomenon is out of the speculation stage; anyone may try it and will be sure to get a similar result.

Another spatial device originates, I believe, in Ives' *Unanswered Question*. He assigns not only particular tone quality, but also a specific, highly contrasted kind of music, to each particular location in the hall, permitting no change in the character of the music proceeding from any given location. This procedure is the opposite of Renaissance antiphony, where groups were likewise stationed in different locations, but all stated the same or similar material, usually one group at a time, and sometimes two or more simultaneously. Each group by itself usually presents four-, five-, or six—part polyphony.

The combining of two groups will thus result in eight or more polyphonic parts, and twelve or more when three groups combine. When the groups are widely separated, as they should be, the time-lag which exists in many halls and churches makes it almost impossible to get exact rhythmic coordination between two, three, or four separated groups, and the result is frequently an unintended montage of diatonic near-polytonality.

In this connection, Leopold Stokowski told me that some years ago he obtained permission, after much difficulty, to perform Gabrieli's Canzonas at St. Mark's Church in Venice (the church where Gabrieli worked), and that immediately the most complicated passages for the separated groups in combination became acoustically perfectly easy and clear, the ensembles coordinating perfectly without any special effort.

I find this a convincing indication that these Gabrieli canzonas must have been specially written for the specific spaces of St. Mark's Church. It would accordingly have been entirely practical for Gabrieli to have written his twelve-part polyphony for combined separated groups if they could thus be so easily and clearly coordinated.

But nowadays one finds very few places where this is possible. This problem was brilliantly solved by Ives, with his conception of separated groups, each in itself rhythmically controlled, but so planned as to dispense with overall rhythmic coordination. In 1950, when I began work along these lines, if you were to write for two groups that didn't keep together rhythmically, it was looked upon as a rather bold and dangerous idea. (This was before the word "aleatoric" was known.)

But aleatoric is not the right term here, because there is scarcely any element of chance involved and no improvisation at all. It is simply that a certain amount of leeway, within well-defined limits, is permitted in the rhythmic relationships between the separated groups. Thus time-lag present in many halls can become an advantage, if several simultaneous tempos are set up, each accurate in itself, but uncoordinated in the aggregate. Rhythmic relationships, of course, can be controlled in lots of other ways, but the first thing is to give up the idea of absolute *all-over* rhythmic coordination between all the separated groups.

Some of my contemporaries take the spatial dimension into account, but consider its use optional, and prescribe only minimal distances between the groups. Some supply directions to separate the groups "if convenient." That to me is like saying "play C if convenient, if not, play C# or some other pitch." If the separation is really necessary for musical reasons, then it is mandatory and it must be emphatic, with maximum distances prescribed.

Separations between soloists or small groups placed at opposite sides of the stage are not emphatically perceived (aurally) by the audience unless the stage is very wide, at least 60 feet across, and then only if there are no other performers in the middle of the stage between the separated groups on each side.

But for real spatial impact on the audience, the distances between groups must be maximal, as for instance between the stage and the back of the hall. Maximum vertical separations, as between the ceiling area and the floor level of the lowest seats, are likewise emphatic in their spatial impact, and should be used to enhance spatial effect whenever available.

In the matter of vertical spacing, one of my favorite questions is this: you have written a duet for piccolo and bass tuba, the lines entirely unrelated, and requiring no rhythmic coordination. You are to position one instrument in the ceiling and the other in the basement. What is your choice? To me it's obvious that the piccolo goes in the ceiling where it will appear to be even higher in pitch than its actual notes, and the tuba in the basement will seem even lower-pitched than it actually is.

But often the first reaction of colleagues, before making the experiment, has been, "wouldn't it be interesting to place the piccolo low and the tuba high?" For me that would be comparable to whatever interest might result from playing a wind instrument standing on your head or singing in that position, but I find this sort of speculation a mere interesting caprice. It's not the kind of thing that I'm looking for, which is a norm for everyday practice; like the length and attack of a note. In other words, I am seeking new but normal and natural procedures.

T.E. Do you find that often musicians are reluctant to go through the physical movement that your music requires? Are they reluctant to actually move to another part of the auditorium, or that they have been rehearsing the piece without the proper spatial dimensions?

H.B.: Occasionally, what happens is that conductors make the mistake of doing the first reading with all the groups rehearsing at once and sometimes they go so far as to say "Let's have it together on the stage just so we can get an idea of how the thing goes, and then spread out." That's absolutely disastrous because music which is written with specifically planned spatial arrangements becomes total chaos when played from a single location.

The most efficient, time-and-energy-saving procedure is to rehearse each group first in a separate room, then combine them in the hall in exactly the locations to which they will be assigned at the concert. As far as the individual musicians are concerned, they are sometimes initially disconcerted by the distances between groups, since in accordance with their traditional training they strain to hear all the parts.

Once they understand that precision in their individual efforts is as important as in any music, and that the spaces between groups actually increases the distinctness in the projection of what they are playing, the musicians are most often quick to assist and cooperate in the spatial procedures prescribed.

T.E.: That's right. But the reasoning is sound from a conductor's standpoint, to possibly want to rehearse that way. It shows they don't have a true understanding of the music. For ensemble purposes, that sounds reasonable to pull everyone together so that you don't have the problem of these spatial effects.

H.B.: The way my pieces are written, any group can be easily rehearsed by itself because it doesn't depend on the other ones at all either for musical completeness or for coordination. Seldom more than an hour is necessary for the rehearsal of any one group. At that point, everything will generally go without difficulty when all are assembled in their proper locations in the large hall, usually with no more than one or two run-throughs with perhaps a few stops now and then. In large halls a P.A. system is a practical aid at the full rehearsals, so that the conductor can communicate easily with distant musicians or sub-conductors. Sometimes performers ask me whether accurate intonation and precise rhythm are important, or whether approximate playing will sound just as well in spatial music. When assured that fine detail makes just as much difference in spatial music as in any other kind, because in spatial setups distance and position will more intensely identify what is coming from each direction, musicians are nearly always ready to do their best.

T.E.: Do you write music with the intention of relating to and being accepted by the general public (and not just music students and fellow composers and performers)?

H.B.: In the last part of your question do you mean music that colleagues and students might appreciate and enjoy?

T.E.: Well, particularly in a college situation, people will appreciate a certain type of technique and so, a composer will write for that appreciation as opposed to writing music that, hopefully, everyone can respond to immediately.

H.B.: Well if you're thinking of a concert (of which there are a great many in New York) in which there are about 8-10 musicians playing 'far out' pieces in the whole rather complicated to perform and needing many rehearsals — I've never noticed that the audiences were large or their responses violently enthusiastic. Have you ever heard such a piece really bring down the house — everyone present becoming rapturously ecstatic? That's not the kind of response I've witnessed. It's hard for me to imagine that music could be written principally for the enjoyment of a small group of other composers unless the ones I've seen at concerts are unusually restrained in their enthusiasm.

T.E.: Well, it seems that other composers are doing that, and I think if someone like Elliott Schwartz, who seems to be writing pieces with the intent that anyone can appreciate them on their level, will write pieces to be performed on campus, under a tree, while people are walking to and from classes , and so forth, it's almost as if he is making an attempt to bring music to all the people? Do you understand what I mean?

H.B.: I've heard the view expressed, but I confess that it's not clear to me. I always write for a client and the client's fee makes possible the time I can devote to the work. I will go to any length to oblige the client who says "these are the instruments and voices available, this is the amount of rehearsal time, this is the hall where it is to be played, this is the deadline, and this is the length of the piece. I respect these things and that's all I 'm concerned with. (It is unusual these days for a client to specify style, character, or subject matter.)

As to the audience which will assemble to hear the work, I don't see that there is much I can do about anticipating their wishes . All I can do is to adhere strictly to agreed upon practical limitations that 's the agreed contract and write what interests me at the moment. If it genuinely interests me, I flatter myself that others may be interested. I haven't really had any trouble with audiences although what I expect is nothing less than riotous applause, even if the piece ends quietly (of course it's more difficult to achieve an unmistakeable reaction in such cases, as every composer knows).

T.E.: You have been particularly affected when that reaction happens after a subtle ending?

H.B.: It seems to point to a kind of communication along humane lines, rather than one achieved by violent assaults on the nervous systems of those present. But I must admit that the violent end is much safer   it leaves the audience in no doubt that the piece is over.

T.E.: Do you compose everyday (as Stravinsky did) or do you write only when you receive a commission (or request)? How does inspiration enter into this?

H.B.: Do you think Stravinsky really wrote everyday?

T. E. I was under the impression that he had certain hours in the morning in which he would do sketches and work things out every day he spent some time composing.

H.B.: I can see that, and it seems very likely he had more commissions than he could keep track of, In that case, the way he worked would apply more to the second half of your question he wrote when he had a commission (which was all the time) setting aside what time he wished to.

Now, composers whose ' 'serious" music is not sufficiently in demand to enable them to compose music full time can't always choose to set aside the morning hours. They can only set aside whatever hours are available when they aren r t doing something else for a living, such as teaching, performing or assignments in commercial music.

The inspiration thing is simple. Any professional composer can write substantial music at any time why not? That is an essential occupational adaptation. If there is a commission, then the ability to meet deadlines is an indispensable technique.

You asked whether I compose only when I have a commission that is so without a commission I don't pick up my pen. It is dangerous to do otherwise and I would counsel all composers against it. Without a written commitment for each first performance your music may not get played at all. To have, something in your desk that makes no noise and hasn't made any for two or three or four or five years is not a •good thing for your-ego, psyche or professional expertise.

The first steps in writing any piece should be to settle whether there is money involved or not, then a firm written understanding as to when and where it will first be played and by whom.

T.E.: Didn't Ives write a vocal piece that he did not expect to be performed? A piece for soprano and piano?

H.B.: Yes, I think so.

T.E.: What are your definitions or descriptions of the following terms: aleatoric, instant composition, improvisation, interpretation, realization and composing?

H.B.: At one time I thought "aleatoric" meant music where accident is a substantial factor. If that's what it means , it's useful as a term. It doesn't, however, apply in my own music. What do you believe most musicians mean by "aleatoric."

T.E.: Well, that's the point. Every composer and performer gives a different definition and there is no single, accepted source. Most people respond as leaving some interpretation or choice of rhythm or notes on the performer's behalf, allowing that performer more freedom than normally permitted.

H.B.: Since these devices don't appear in my own work, I don't think I have much authority in adding to the definition of t 'aleatoric". As to your next term, "instant composition," 1 would define it as planned improvisation without notation.

T.E.: Could improvisation ever be developed to such a high degree that it could be called composition?

H.B.: Undoubtedly it can, if produced under the direction of a composer-conductor, and equally successful when controlled by the participating groups themselves. Personally, I believe it a mistake to begin with pitches in prescribing improvisatory devices. Pitches should rather be the last thing or else unspecified altogether. If, instead of pitches, you prescribe exact specifications for register, tone quality, volume and articulation, the result becomes both more spontaneous and at the same time more controlled. The test should be whether the "instant composition" can be performed twice in succession with such substantial similarity that no one would have any hesitation in saying, "Sure, that's the same piece", and not "It sounds sort of like a variation of what they played first."

Improvisation, I suppose, is any music not notated and not memorized. But these are hairsplitting terms, and I found out at Bennington College that my first year beginner t s class could make philosophical and semantic mincemeat out of the definition of any musical term I could offer. Now, I thought I had an iron-clad definition for "music," something general enough to include anything which anyone might wish to term "music." In this definition music was identified as any arrangement of sounds and silences, devised on purpose to be listened to, and for no other reason.

Well, my beginner students beat that one logically to death - so I no longer believe that even the most precise definitions in music are irrefutable. Improvisation suggests to me something that is only minimally planned in advance, and where the improvisors for the most part proceed spontaneously intensifying dynamics Interpretation - that to mind is an admirable term. Interpretation ought to consist in not altering anything printed on the composer's original page, and in not removing anything that's there, but rather what is already present.

I think intensified dynamics, contrasts, and at times (not always) additional small fluctuations of rhythm, are all proper concerns of interpretation that need to be supplied. Likewise super accents, extra-short staccato, and separations between slurs.

It is often the duty of the interpreter to see that these details are in a controlled way exaggerated, if necessary, for audibility and distinctness. What I have just said applies mostly to music since 1750; the interpreter's problem in Baroque, Renaissance and Medieval music is of course much more complex and responsible. Realization — you mean in Baroque music?

T.E.: Yes, and also of a composition for tape in which the performer realizes the tape part. The performer plays on tape and then plays along with his taped performance. You create the accompaniment yourself.

H.B.: There again, if the term "realization" expresses that clearly and is understood by enough people, it is useful and functional. (It doesn't apply to anything in my own music). I do, however, see the undesirable possibility of confusion if a single term such as "realization" is permitted to have one connotation in Baroque music and an entirely different One in 20th century music. Composing is the entire process of conceiving and planning music by whatever means. It may or may not include improvisatory devices. If someone throws a brick through a window and says: "I've composed a piece of music," I have no wish to dispute his use of the term. To be useful and functional, the term composing should be broad enough to include anything anyone wishes to consider pertinent in the conception, notating, planning or improvisation of music.

T.E.: Thank you very much for your responses and time .

N.B. Mr. Brant has just received a commission from the International Trombone Association to write a large trombone choir work in 1978.

18.

TEN QUESTIONS: 270 ANSWERS
Tom Everett

#1: Do you view any of the techniques or materials that you use currently as innovative? What role does being unique and/or taking risks take in your music? If no or none answers these, do you view the compositional process as a synthesis (integration) of many known techniques or an extension of one approach and how?

T. J. ANDERSON: The term innovative is somewhat misleading when used in relationship to composers and their music. All changes or variances represent re-arrangements of existing orders and, therefore, appear to be new; however, they are mutations of the old. The synthesis concept is only understood in terms of tradition, while an integrated approach, representing great diversities, is often thought of as an extension of the art form.

LESLIE BASSETT: Techniques that are innovative one year become current, even standard, a few years later. I once thought that invention of a "non-meter time signature" was an innovation, but it has been so useful to composers that it is now quite widespread. We all want to be unique. No one wants to write a piece that is a re-hash of someone else's music. It would be difficult to compose if we did not feel we were breaking new ground (at least for us) in some respect. On the other hand, each of our oval scores has many similarities to our other music (known as 'consistency of style and language,' if you wish).

WARREN BENSON: No. I take risks in everything I write, or I don't find the writing interesting. To assure that this has a 'role' in my music suggests that risk taking is a special element to be added to or taken away without particular effect or affect. Even so, whether or not one risks anything in the music provides no criterion for estimating its value, any more than does being unique have anything to do with fundamental musical value.

I view the compositional process as an invention of the new and also a selection from the past to suit the particular needs of the current work. This suggests synthesis for integration which may well be what happens in a given case. It bypasses the issue of 'my style' in favor of specific selectivity within an inclusive frame.

WILLIAM BOLCOM: No. I take risks all the time, but they are risks with musical language. I simply use more vocabulary in musical language than many composers, so I suppose my process is synthetic.

EARLE BROWN: Most of the techniques that I use were innovative when I first used them in 1952 and 1953: 'open form,' 'graphic notation' (as well as what is now called 'proportional notation.' When I first used it in 1952 I called it 'time notation' to distinguish it from 'metric notation.' (see introduction to *Music for 'cello and Piano*, 1954) new performance attitudes and techniques, solo and collective improvisation (subject to various controls and definitions), statistical generation of textures and densities, etc. Although all of my work does not necessarily utilize all or any of these techniques, I have continued to develop and extend them in many of my works since 1952. 'Being unique' has never been a conscious goal but 'being like everyone else' is certainly less than interesting, creatively. Unless one has a naturally unique thing to contribute to composing it is merely a craft. Most of the above techniques were decidedly 'risky' when I first used them, but I had very solid reasons and justifications for needing those potentials in my work. Every artist (vs. craftsman) risks his 'poetics' being rejected but risk is not interesting merely for its compositional process as an extension of my personal approach and 'poetics' as well as a synthesis of everything I have known in art and life.

JOHN CAGE: I always want to start from zero and make, if I can, a discovery. Some works, of course, fall together in a group as, for instance, the *Sonatas and Interludes* or, recently, the *Quartets* for concert band and amplified voices and for orchestras which *Hymns and Variations* for 12 amplified voices from a group. So that a new piece is one more in a field of possibilities, the field itself already having been discovered.

Sometimes this discovery is of material (plant materials as in *Child of Tree* and *Branches*, water-filled conches as in *Inlets*, or, earlier, radios as in *Imaginary Landscape No. IV*) and sometimes it is of compositional means as in the *Music of Changes* or, currently, the *Freeman Etudes* for unaccompanied violln and *Roaratorio* for folk musicians, speech and tape. I do not know what to start from zero plays in my music except that father was an inventor and in work I have tried to follow in his footsteps though he was an electrical engineer and not a musician.

ROBERT CEELY: Rather than techniques I use being innovative, I would hope my music is innovative. There is very little new under the sun, and most of that is burned out. Since most of us are unique without trying, the unique role is not too important to me; on the other hand, taking risks is extremely important. Risk-taking is good for the mind as well as the music. The compositional process is whatever the composer makes of it in whatever piece he is engaged in writing at moment in time.

BARNEY CHILDS: No, I don't ever think about innovation as such. Each piece anyone writes is presumably new, unique, and special for him while he's writing it, whether he's exploring process or approaches or stances that he's never tried before or whether he's making familiar elements do familiar things successfully. As for risk, how can this be present in non-commercial music? All you can fail are your own expectations, and I don't know any composers who, if something isn't coming out right, won't rework it or alter it until it does come out right. I suppose the compositional process is "a synthesis of many known techniques" if you look at it one way, I presume we each draw on whatever 'techniques' we may feel will do the particular job at the moment, will work right (America, after all, invented pragmatism). The compositional process may equally well be 'an extension of one approach,' that approach being simply to 'make your best choice.'

NORMAN DELLO JOIO: I make no conscious effort to be innovative or unique, since I find so much of today's music insufferably dull that is based on the premise that to be different is a mark of quality. In my own music, I incorporate whatever process my intuition dictates. Rigidity to a system produces perhaps interesting paper designs but seldom, in the hands of a mediocre composer, anything in sound that gratifies the ear of one's inner being.

DAVID DIAMOND: Innovation by rote is what goes on today among the last survivors of the Cage-Berio-Crumb-Feldman tribe. How innovative can any one artist be in any given generation? Aesthetic inquiry and creative impulse are totally different aspects of musical composition.

Yes, the 'compositional process' is integration of many concatanated procedures from the Past. Any composer who assumes he's found something new, wholly new, is fooling himself. The difference today is that money is handed out to help fool oneself; and in a Yes and anti No generation of Transition, fooling oneself is both naive and successful. Up to a point.

ED DIEMENTE: I don't *think* about innovation. I have practical problems to solve in communicating to performers what I want them to do. I try to solve these problems.

DAVID EPSTEIN: The thought came to mind, as I read this question, of a distinguished scholar in a recent article on scientific theory-making: 'Ideas are cheap,' he said. What counts (in science) is the systematic construction of a world-view through ideas. It's striking how much this applies to music. Here, too, 'ideas' in the sense of techniques, innovations, materials, can be sort of easy-come, today's innovations are tomorrow's old-hat clichés. In music, too, what really counts is the constructive use of ideas within the specific context of a musical work. And context for me inescapably means, in part at least, a structural context. This may be old-hat, but music without construct, structure, contextual meaning is for me music not worth taking seriously. I'm struck also by the fact that most of the composers in history whose music we regard as innovative in the best sense — Beethoven, Monteverdi, Schoenberg — achieved the unique cast of their music by integrating innovative ideas in the way we've just discussed.

ROSS LEE FINNEY: I have always viewed the techniques and materials that I use as innovative. Being a composer is a gamble and being unique is inevitable but not always interesting. The only security is in mastery of craft and a personal honesty as to what one wants to accomplish as an artist.

The crafts that a composer uses today are somewhat different than they were a century ago largely because of electronic and technological discoveries. We are right now on the threshold of new developments such as video that will augment a composer's expressive language. New developments never erase the crafts of the past; they only add to them.

LUKAS FOSS: Innovative techniques? Yes — both — in vision and in organization, since every work I compose attempts to solve a particular problem. A work of art is good only if it is *unique*. The *risk* we take is that of being misunderstood.

JAMES FULKERSON: I tour a great deal as trombone soloist playing music and music by other contemporary composers. Consequently, I appear in widely varying countries and musical contexts. Stated simply: sometimes I am the radical fringe, other times a conservative (isn't virtuosity old fashioned?), sometimes I'm told I've sold out. What matters to me is my own self-critical evaluation *plus* a steady-working process involving composing daily, practicing daily, and performing quite often. I took the attitude about 10 years ago that it was important to play at moderate fees a lot rather than perhaps one third as much at 3-4 times the fee. These three situations provide me with my own truths and the basis for continuing to work. I feel that the results of this process will result in work which is most likely of interest to others, but I have no doubt that the artistic process stems outward from the individual and that this individual needs to be 'centered' in her/his living working — or else totally 'off the wall.' Thus my answer to parts 2 and 3 is that while those 'values' used to be important, the qualities are so relative that I no longer find them too important. The emotional feel of a sound does seem important to me, however.

GEORGE HEUSSENSTAMM: Technical innovation used to be a subject of considerable concern to me. It no longer is, although I am surely interested in new contributions to this area. But being unique and taking risks has only a small connection with technical devices, but rather refer to the far subtler and inexpressible aspects of composition such as the nature of change, of contrast, of interplay, timing, opposition, etc.

Technical devices represent a somewhat superficial portion of the total musical fabric. They tell one very little as to how to proceed daringly with an idea. Whether a more general synthesis of many known techniques or a pursuit along more restricted lines will apply and depend upon the individual composer. Indeed, this may vary from work to work with a given composer.

KAREL HUSA: Yes, some of the free, aleatory passages, extensions of ranges and pitches, difficult virtuoso treatment of instruments and ensembles, expansion of percussion sounds, unusual combinations of existing sounds. The risk is that some performers do not take the time to learn some of the new devices as well as techniques (yet, the difficulty existed in practically all works of the past and only by tradition and knowledge of how to learn them do they become performable). In my music I do use synthesis of many present and past techniques, and hope that the *ideas* and *personality* will make my music unusual.

JEAN EICHELBERGER IVEY: I can best answer this, I believe, by an excerpt from the program notes I wrote when my *Testament of Eve* (a monodrama for mezzo, orchestra, and tape, with my own text) was premiered in 1976 by the Baltimore Symphony: 'The synthesis of many elements, many diversified influences, in a unified, coherent, and expressive whole, strikes me as the prevailing historical task of composers now at the end of this innovative century. I aim at combining tonal and atonal elements, and I consider all the musical resources of the past and present as being at the composer's disposal, but always in the service of the effective communication of humanistic ideas and intuitive emotion.'

KARL KORTE: I'm not sure that I can answer the first part of this question objectively. I've lived long enough to have become highly suspicious of terms that suggest 'progress' when applied to Art. Was it always so difficult to tell the difference between uniqueness and gimmickry; true originality and what is only a passing fad? So much of what has been loudly touted as new and 'important' in music during the past 25 years should now be re-evaluated in terms of Huizinga's statement from *The Waning of the Middle Ages*: "In history, as in nature, birth and the decay of overripe forms of civilization is as suggestive a spectacle as the growth of new ones. And it occasionally happens that a period in which one had, hitherto, been mainly looking for the coming of the birth of new things, suddenly reveals itself as an epoch of fading and decay." As to taking risks, every composer takes a risk every time he has a piece played in public.

ANDREAS MAKRIS: I think that my music is innovative. If I didn't think I was composing something which was contributing in finding new ideas of expression, I would not compose. Naturally, I use new 'techniques and materials' which can be explained through very long articles or simply by listening to my musics. But if you call 'new techniques and materials' hitting the violin and bowing the drums, my answer is 'no.'

I do not use these techniques. If I don't like the sound of a drum, I try to find different percussion sounds. Hitting the violin is a rather theatrical effect with visual interest, but one can accomplish better percussion results from the proper instruments. I realize that in the past, as well as the present, composers did and do combine the acoustical and visual arts. At times, this idea provided an extra dimension to the music, while at other times, it was self evident that the music was simply lacking substance and needed to borrow material from other sources.

I have used these techniques when I was much younger; presently, I do not; who knows, in the future I may use them again. Concerning the possible risks I take with my music, the only thing I can think of is that because of the intricate rhythms which I write, the music becomes rather difficult and therefore can only be performed really well with a high calibre orchestra. While this is rather sad, a composer must always take the consequences of his writing.

BART MCLEAN: For me, my works are always innovative. For others, the question of innovation is a function of the listener's experience. I don't believe in an absolute definition of avant garde or of innovation. These are personal directions, not absolute quantities. Personally, as style (or accumulated idiosyncrasies, as the case may be) develops, I move away from integration and toward the extension of one approach (a different one for each work). The problem of most new music for me today (and it was far worse a few years ago) is with the 'synthesists.'

I do not believe that a common language existed since the demise of functional harmony. Yet the synthesists continue to act as if there were, not realizing in my opinion, that ideas are created, and structures are formed COMPLETELY FROM CONTEXT ALONE in most of today's styles.

Furthermore, since the context is the sole determinant of the power of a particular idea, when that same idea or one similar to it surfaces in a different context in another work, there is no underlying structural functional harmonic framework to undergird it, and so it merely becomes part of the dull gray mass of material that has been, up to very recently, the bulwark of the sort-of-post-Webern-neoclassical-you-know -what style. The only solution, as I see it, is to adopt a completely different set of materials for each work. Since the demise of functional harmony, the truly great works of this century have been essentially extensions of a unique approach. The mediocre works have been attempts to imitate these extensions by utilizing the same approach, an approach that was only good for one or two first-class works.

PRISCILLA MCLEAN: Most of the techniques and materials I use in music are innovative, but not original in the sense that I was the first to use them. From electronic techniques to using whale sounds in my tuba and whale ensemble pieces entitled *Beneath the Horizon*, I enjoy using new sounds and ways of writing. I take risks all the time musically, but if the risks don't work in performance, they end up in the wastebasket!

VINCENT PERSICHETTI: Composers are beginning to amalgamate the materials of the 20th Century. From this practice will come the valid music of the future.

ELLIOTT SCHWARTZ: I think you really have two questions here. As far as 'taking risks' is concerned, I'd like to think that I (and most of the composers work I admire) go out on a limb all the time, trying new ideas, situations, materials, and techniques.

Being 'unique' or 'innovative' is another matter entirely. Even though something may be new for me, or my audience, I'm realistic enough to recognize that nothing is unique anymore. After our experience with several waves of avant-gardes and the discovery of non-Western music, anything that anybody tries can be allied with some respectable 'tradition' or other. (Or synthesized from a number of traditions.) There's really no point in trying to be unique. But — given the vast number of options in our century — why not try as many unfamiliar stylistic paths as we can. In that sense, by all means take risks.

ROBERT STARER: Of late I have been primarily interested in the human voice and human gesture, the development of situations between people. Most, though not all, of recent writing has been for the musical theatre. I am lucky to have found a collaborator whose style and ideas agree with mine and whose verbal rhythms are much to my liking.

HALSEY STEVENS: My techniques and materials cannot be viewed as 'innovative,' nor is my music concerned more than fortuitously with risk-taking or uniqueness. I believe its roots are firmly anchored in tradition; it acknowledges strong tonal allegiances without insisting upon traditional harmonic functionality. Of course, I have assimilated many of the techniques that have shaped 20th-century music; mine, however, has the clearest affinity to that of Bartók, although its vocabulary was well established before I knew of his music.

FRED TILLIS: I view the compositional process as a synthesis.

#2. Is the academic situation for the composer in America today merely a refuge for the weaker composers, a bastion of non-competitive music, intellectual and uninspired, referenced to an uninterested general public? Or is it, as many have suggested, a replacement for the 18th-century courts, and the Renaissance Church, a center for musical activity; indeed where innovations and inspiration are released? What would you imagine to be the best location for the composer in the future?

T. J. ANDERSON: Colleges, universities, and conservatories have become the patrons of the composer at this juncture of 20th-century music. It has placed us in an intellectual environment, has made available time to compose, and in some cases has given us the mediums by which we can express our artistic talents. The price we have paid for this alliance, which may or may not be beneficial to all artists, has caused us to become intellectually a part of the University's community. I would only hope that this particular format would prove to be one of several-ways composers might exist within the society.

LESLIE BASSETT: Academia is often a refuge for the weak composer, of course, and many have stagnated or disappeared in it. It is also a home for the strong composer, giving him a sense of belonging and comradeship with other musicians, and freeing him from serious concern about finance and survival. I doubt that pressures on a composer to conform are any stronger within the academic than without. The chief dangers within academia can be overloading in teaching and disinterest among the composer's colleagues — non-support of his efforts and aspirations.

WARREN BENSON: The academic situation is no more a refuge for the weaker composers today than teaching (private or institutional) has ever been a refuge for the composers of the past. The few composers managed to survive in a comfortable way without teaching include only *some* of the better composers of the day.

The academic situation today includes only some of the weaker composers. It also includes some of the very best. The phrasing of the question ('merely a refuge for the weaker composers, a bastion of non-competitive music, intellectual, and uninspired reference') and the negative fog surrounding "intellectual and uninspired reference," not to mention the lovely linkage, suggests that the academic situation is all of these.

It may be none of these without being a replacement for the 18th century court, or without being a replacement for the Renaissance church. It is indeed a center of musical activity, although not always at the highest performance level or critical level.

Innovations and inspirations are indeed released in these centers, though it is not very often that they are seriously discussed and/or considered by either performers or critics to any significant degree. Never having seen a 'competitive' piece of music, the issue is hard to imagine, but as for being 'non-competitive,' the living artist's work, if he resides 'there' is not considered appropriate material for *serious* scholarship, though it may well be thought so in the University.

So, I would imagine that the best location for a composer of the future would be the same as it has always been, wherever he finds himself. Composers have always had to make their way, either by marrying a rich companion, an angel, a choirmaster-organist job (teaching Latin on the side), devoting sufficient time to secretarial service to go the grand router, or teaching. All of these are perfectly valid, I suppose, if they are satisfactory for the composer involved. It is interesting that today, when major authors, poets, painters, musical performers and composers, great scientists, historians, etc., reside in the university that it should be put down as a second rate refuge! Many are, but being outside is just as poor an environment — given the individual talent.

WILLIAM BOLCUM: (I like the "bastion" of non-competitive music; since Women's Lib we also need a 'bastionne'.) Most university composers are boring, that is true, but then so were most of the 18th century Kapellmeister. I've freelanced, and I still do; I concertize, and not only new "serious" music, but also in American popular music; I play ragtime; I write on subjects. My solution was to *diversify*, in order to get in contact with the world around me. I don't know whether being in a university has any good or bad effect on an artist. You have to eat.

In an age of patronage — there were people with their heads in the sand too. In the future: what will develop will develop. There aren't many jobs for composers in the universities anymore, and there will be fewer of them, so that more composers will have to diversify as I have. That may make their music more attractive all around, by sheer force of circumstance: commercial music will improve, and 'non-commercial' may be more communicative.

EARLE BROWN: The academic situation is a kind of subsidy for the composer to be able to live and work. I have never been permanently connected to an academic institution because I feel that it tends to isolate one and deaden one's initiative and ingenuity relative to the real musical community with which one must ultimately deal. It is too easy to fall into patterns of thinking and being content with the currently acceptable style and habits of one's colleagues .

In general, I find that there is great pressure (and desire) to conform in order to keep the job rather than to 'follow one's nose' wherever it may lead, and the latter is essential to real creativity. I don't find that innovations and inspiration are released (generally speaking) in the academic environment; it basically follows (usually at considerable distance) these conditions, as it very well might be expected to.

None of the techniques that I mention in my first answer were 'innovated' in an academic situation; nor were 12-tone techniques, 'musique concrète', electronic music, 'live electronics', etc. This is certainly not to degenerate the academic situation or to imply that there is not a great deal of talent and creativity therein, but to point out that it does not have a history of being fertile ground for 'innovations' of an inspired nature.

JOHN CAGE: The university in America is, as has been suggested, the center of musical activity as in Europe now the national radios are (in Germany particularly). Even if, as in my case, a composer is not directly connected with an institution, he is nevertheless dependent, for performances and income, on universities in our country and on radios or festivals abroad. The best location for a composer in the future is certainly at home wherever he chooses to make his home.

ROBERT CEELY: The academic situation is all of these, but at its worst it is the most terrible home for a composer. At its best, academia is tolerable. A composer, like a trombonist, must feel needed. University life is not a life in which a composer will feel needed; used, yes; needed, no. The university must decide whether the composer is necessary to them and if so they must be supported in a real way; if, on the other hand, the university decides to be honest with itself and the composer, the university will decide that they do not need composers and will throw them out. This will lead to (perhaps) marches on Washington, BMI, ASUC, and the NEA, or else maybe all the composers will join CETA or else they will take up the banner and go into early music; but what is certain is that the present state of the composer and the university benefits only the university, since the university gets a teacher who loves his subject: MUSIC, whereas the composer gets immersed in a pool which is slowly draining. The best location for the composer is at his desk (which may be the piano, the console, the terminal, the accordion) writing his tunes. Upon occasion the composer should rise from his desk to eat, make love, drink, or retrieve the money which has slid silently under his door.

BARNEY CHILDS: The language of this question assumes an acceptance of the inherited/brainwashed careerist value — judgment — centered view of musical composition, and as so is discouragingly loaded. What is a 'weaker' composer? Is this a way of saying a non-popular composer? Someone who doesn't write 'masterpieces' (whatever they are)? What is 'competitive' music? and what's it competing for? Who are the officials in this competition? Is it possible to foul out? The academic situation is just another job. I find it pleasant to be paid in a situation with colleagues who play music and think about it and talk about it, rather than an endless discussion of current events, a la *My Weekly Reader*.

I suppose each person tries to be, in Cecil Rhodes' phrase, the best man for the world's fight, settles eventually for giving through what best means he can; I presume therefore that this is his voluntary choice and, although perhaps not always that option pleasing him most, maybe likely to be that displeasing him least. Why do some university-based composers assume a public posture of some kind of grumbling or shame or guilt about it? If it is a position one does not care for, there are still opportunities for other sorts of employment. The best location for a composer, future or past, is that where he most wishes to be (although I'm charmed by an answer to this question provided by a friend, that the best location for the composer in the future is to work as a bag boy at Von's Market).

NORMAN DELLO JOIO: Unfortunately the academic world today unwittingly fosters too many composers who have little or no contact with the world of professionalism. To exploit students who are in a sense captive has become an intellectual racket.

The best location for a composer is his private studio and the arena of the public outlets which he can serve, if he has the will to do so. To adopt the pose of misunderstood genius is to fly in the face of the history of the composers who met the demands of their time.

DAVID DIAMOND: The composer in the future should stay away from Music Departments in Universities, try to work privately with qualified teachers, be prepared to starve, stop reading esoterica and looking for words for titles in Mrs. Byrnes' Dictionary. Rhythm, of impulse and articulation, is an almost lost art among the avant-garde speculators. And so their notes and sounds and diagrams produce boredom when not plain apathy. The 'best' location for a composer in the future will be in his own domicile with the challenge of empty score paper to be filled with communicative, mysterious language of the Spirit guided by Craft, not gimmickry.

ED DIEMENTE: *Some* composers in universities are weak and uninspired. Some are as gifted as any, at any time, anywhere. The university community is not like the court or the church. The conversion is not a good one. The best place for a composer to be is Nice, France (with an orchestra and chorus at his disposal and an eager audience awaiting his next work).

DAVID EPSTEIN: Your question is stated so fully that I think you have answered it as well as asked it — and answered it fully also! Obviously the academic situation for composers in America today is all of the things you have outlined — for different composers in different academies. It is also clear that academic life is the only realistic solution for the majority of composers. The facts confirm this; few composers have 'made it,' on economic terms alone, not to mention artistic ones, in the competitive marketplace.

Nor do I think many more will in the future. Our society at present is just not set up to support the kind of artistic product offered by serious composers — certainly not to the extent that it can accommodate much or most of this profession.

The advantages of academia are those that you point out — time to do one's work (though less of this than many people think), opportunity through teaching and contact with colleagues to explore musical ideas and literature, an atmosphere conducive to the intellectual task of facing the issues and challenges of serious composing. It is also clear that for some, the university has become a haven of escape. (It has also in some cases, through a kind of academic inertia, tolerated the mediocre.) But all this, as I see it, is part of a larger process of 'natural selection,' if you will. In other words, there are only so many composers in any generation who will 'succeed' in terms of artistic stature and contact with an audience. The qualities that make for this success are of a complex and subtle mix, and indeed, many of us are called but few are chosen. Whether those few are living and working in the academy seems to me incidental rather than determinative — they would have succeeded in any case.

ROSS LEE FINNEY: There is something pejorative in the manner in which you ask this question. The university is neither 'a refuge for the weaker composers, nor a replacement for the 18th-century court.' It is a remarkable institution that gives opportunity for intellectual and creative development of the young and is an environment in creative minds in all fields have an opportunity to flourish.

The composer in this environment should be judged just as the creative mathematician or historian. Is he or she a constantly productive composer, a serious and conscientious teacher, active in the local environment, and contributive to the administrative welfare of the institution. It is true that while most universities have come to understand the creative needs of scholars and scientists, they have not yet come to understand the needs and functions of the creative artist. Some of the fault comes from musicians themselves who seek to increase their power by over-enrollments and proliferations of course offerings.

LUKAS FOSS: It can be either, depending on the particular job and particular composer. There is no 'best location.'

JAMES FULKERSON: Having basically nothing to do with the academic situation for the past ten years, it's a fairly irrelevant question for me. If you think about those applied music teachers in the American universities, most of them couldn't make it as professional players or as independent private teachers.

So what? I don't think we learn to play or compose in the university per se — and how to make a living (especially doing what you want to do) certainly seems to start *after* graduation. Yet, without doubt, most of America's finest composers are — or have been at some time — associated with the university system. I find it interesting that composers or artists make good situations around them wherever they happen to be. Getting doctorates seems to be another question — the process either excludes creative people or kills their creativity in the end.

Kenneth Gaburo is the only exception to this that I know, in fact. What you don't acknowledge in your question is that the music business operates quite differently in the USA than it does in Europe and in the Soviet bloc countries. In those countries, the government is very actively involved in the music industry. By charging a tax on all of the radios and televisions, the governments are able to maintain an orchestra, jazz group, chamber orchestra, etc. at each radio station. This creates a lot of work for musicians *and* composers. If your traditional views composing as another job in the music industry which must be supported along with the others, then classical composers not only have an alternative to the university, but they have ensembles and performance opportunities effectively at their disposal. The fact that this is all at a professional level gives them a greater status in the eyes of composers, musicians, and the concert going public. They don't realize that these composers have been effectively promoted by their government subsidized industries — support not really available to American composers.

GEORGE HEUSSENSTAMM: It is both — why not? Wherever you look for composers, you will find those who are weak and those that are strong. Academia is big enough and flexible enough to accommodate a homing ground for either. As for the future, the composer should be situated wherever his audience is most aware, most plentiful, most interested, most enthusiastic. At present, audiences for new music are sparse no matter where you go — on campus or off campus — and I am unable to foresee how this is to be changed. Accordingly, many of us have adapted our expectations to the reality of small audiences and do not sink into despair when confronted with row upon row of empty seats.

KAREL HUSA: I do not think that only weaker composers live in the academic situation in America today. There is no question that teaching is a source of income for many composers, weaker and stronger, but much is going on in research for new possibilities, instruments, and much performance of new music too.

Chamber music and solo works dominate, but universities today have first class Wind Ensembles, excellent Choral organizations, and often Orchestras too. I do not know the statistics, but would think that more than half of all performances of new music are given on the campuses. Let us not forget, that composing is not a profession, for only a few composers can live from the income of their music. Universities have the resources also for the needs of a composer: laboratories, scores, records, tapes, halls, etc. On the other hand it does not seem yet, that the academic situation replaces the 18th century courts and the renaissance church, for the *contemporary* music represents only a very small fraction of what is cultivated in music today. Many schools still profess the cult of 'the past,' similar to the proportions of some museums, i.e. 95% old and 5% new, not at all the proportions of the 18th century courts or renaissance church. Probably some 'Modern Art Centers' will be the locations for music together with other arts. As for myself, I do not see anything wrong with teaching; as provided by universities it is very enjoyable work, leaving the composer time for his own work, assures him financially, and helps him in his further development with laboratories, libraries, but most of all, gives him the chance to be with young people, from whom he can also learn (not only teach them).

JEAN EICHELBERGER IVEY:. A composer has to earn a living at something! It would certainly be better for the American composer if, like his colleagues in many other countries, he could earn his living from commissions and performance fees. The academic milieu differs a good deal from place to place, and works well for some composers, but it is *not* comparable to the support of a patron, institutional or personal.

Seldom is the composer on the academic faculty being paid to compose. He is paid to teach or administer, and he does his composing in his (all-to-often meagre) spare time. Doubtless my feelings are influenced by the fact that my academic career of some 25 years has been marked by low salaries, heavy teaching loads, and no sabbaticals. However, I must say I have enjoyed the stimulating contact with many fine colleagues and students.

KARL KORTE: This question also begs for objectivity. It is difficult the way you have phrased it. You use the term 'non-competitive music.' Who are the competitors? Are the values of the Artist the same as those of the market place or the football field? Before our time, no Artist had to deal with the phenomena of mass culture, the 'democratization of the arts,' 'instant' hits, 'platinum' records, and the plethora of media-hype that constitutes the American Entertainment Industry.

For most it is impossible to keep artistic integrity intact in the face of the billions of dollars and incredible power that inevitably accompanies them. In this sense, at least, the 'academic situation' does offer a 'haven' for the uncompromising. The problem is, at what point does integrity become self-indulgence or preciousness? Your analogy between the present academic situation and the Renaissance Church or the 18th century courts also poses problems. I doubt that obtaining a church or court appointment in the past involved any less in the way of luck, politics, and talent (in that order) than does obtaining a staff position for CBS or tenure at Yale today. As to 'the best location for a composer in the future,' probably, as in the immediate past, in the insurance business.

ANDREAS MAKRIS: Tie academic situation for the composer in America is as good as ever. Some of the finest universities, music schools, and conservatories are here. Of course, as in the past, so it is presently, the academic circles include the very best knowledgeable and sincere composers as well as the 'weaker, intellectual and uninspired' ones. This is nothing to fear. It is a historic reality (to the point that one could call it absolutely normal) that there will always be people who do things and there will always be people who know how this should be done if just the rest of the world would understand them.

The world, as well as the music academic circles, need them both. In answer to the question of 'is' the best location for a composer, I would say that the composer is such a unique germ that he can survive in the best cultural centers in Europe or in the severest conditions some place say in Bulgaria; maybe not successful, but creative. At any rate, I strongly feel that the United States is as good a place for a composer to develop as any other place in the world.

BARTON MCLFAN: The academic situation today is all of these things, as are government institutions in Europe. There are always composers who will take refuge under umbrellas of mediocrity, and those who will prevail despite the odds. At present, the action still seems to favor the university in America, for those who are not commercially oriented.

PRISCILLA MCLFAN: I conducted a similar informal question survey this year when producing the ASUC Radiofest: New American Music radio series (ASUC: American Society of University Composers), as I interviewed over 35 composers from all over the country. From first-hand information while listening to hundreds of pieces by the composers in the society, I can say that most of the exciting and excellent music is being written today by composers located either full-time or part-time at universities. How many composers of serious music can one name who are *not* somehow connected to a university? And the consensus of opinion was that the universities are patrons in as much as they supply performers, space, and materials, as opposed to a more personal and economic fostering of new compositions as in the patronage of past centuries, and that teaching or conducting at a university is a job apart from patronage, and not to be confused with it.

VINCENT PERSICHETTI: The composer should have a simple room where he can write what he is moved to write, accepting commissions only when they coincide with his creative plans.

ELLIOTT SCHWARTZ: I'm not sure there is a 'general public.' There are, rather, many fragmented mini-publics, each with highly selective tastes: opera-goers, symphony audiences, early music freaks, jazz, rock, country, whatever. They hardly speak to each other. College and university students form a substantial sub-culture of their own (with a few hardy faculty members thrown in); that's a 'public' as legitimate as any other. Apart from their value as a collective audience, college kids also make great *performers*.

They're sympathetic to new ideas, and they play either fantastically well or with no traditional skill at all (depending upon the sort of college), both levels providing exciting challenges for a composer. The dull, cerebral music that gets labeled 'academic' usually results from faculty composers writing for other faculty colleagues, rather than for students. But what the hell — they're a legitimate 'public' too, and entitled to the music they enjoy. As for the future, I'd like to see more music commissioned by big industry, commerce, and government — to celebrate occasions, to enhance large public spaces (parks, lobbies), to reach mass audiences on videotape/television in a way that expands the potential of that medium. There may be more free-lance composers making their way, but I'd guess that a majority will still be attached to institutions (colleges, radio stations, dance companies, newspapers, magazines), supporting their creative activities by performing, conducting, writing, teaching, talking.

ROBERT STARER: I do teach. I like to and it leaves me free to write what I want. I have written music for documentary films and dance works. This is often interesting and technically challenging, but there is only so much music I can write. Teaching seems to draw on a different source of energy within me and thus does not drain or diminish anything vital.

HALSEY STEVENS: By 'academic situation' I assume reference is made to the large number of American composers who teach in colleges and universities? The best location for a composer is where he can function most effectively: one which will provide mental stimulation, time for creative activity, and an outlet for his work. For some, the academic aegis is appropriate, for others whatever the present day equivalent for Church and Court may be. Subsidy is not necessarily the solution for every problem. I believe that the real composer will compose, no matter "what his situation."

FRED TILLIS: A replacement for the 18th century courts. Some in universities, others as free-lance composers.

#3. Advancements in computer technology, digital-to-analog converters, software, etc. have made this instrument viable and somewhat available to at least some contemporary composers. What role do you see it playing in your music, if any, and what future might it have in music in general?

T. J. ANDERSON: Since I have not personally participated in the area of computer technology, I believe my answers would be extremely superficial on this particular question.

LESLIE BASSET: At the moment, computer technology does not play a part in my music. I have been impressed by its possibilities and am aware of several fine works for computer. Perhaps, some day I'll get back to electronic music and computers.

WARREN BENSON: I don't see computer technology playing any particular role in my own music from my present stance. I think it will probably have an important place to play in electronic music of the future and in music that chooses to employ electronic means to produce some, if not all, of the sound needed.

WILLIAM BOLCOM: I'm interested in performers, in theater, in people performing, and people watching. Some composers use computer-related activity in their work; I don't, and I note that fewer and fewer students seem to be interested right now. That may reverse, and I hope we don't stop buying equipment in case there are younger people who develop an interest.

EARLE BROWN: Computer technology is, to a large degree, an 'innovation' of academia by financial necessity, although the concept goes back to Varèse, and others, I believe. I have been invited to partake of it and I probably will, but I'm in no hurry. It's future in music is certain but, as I felt about 'electronic music,' it is simply another medium that a composer can work in, not something that will put the orchestra or anything else out of business.

An orchestra (the instruments *and* the humans involved) is still the most intricate (controlled yet variable) sound producer we have. To paraphrase Varèse, the 'art' that results from the use of a machine is no better than the 'artist' that activates it. The newness of a machine can make you *think* that you're being original and creative but it is dangerously seductive to eager opportunists.

JOHN CAGE: Computer technology is here to stay. I do not know whether I will be able to make any discovery in this field. I intend to study what has been done and to make if I can a new departure.

ROBERT CEELY: I would imagine a fairly large role, but that will depend upon it and me, and it will, of course, depend upon them: the orchestras, the instrumentalists, the foundations, the government.

If they/them convince me they want real music for real instruments, then that is that they will get. I do not think technology will save us. If we can have the minis in our houses rather than going to the sterile institutions which house the maxis then things will brighten up.

The pianist must own a piano; he does not wish to walk to the conservatory every time he wants to play. The role of technology is more serious and more interesting. At best now we are (all) writing Electronic Music or Computer Music. The music is not Electronic or Computerly. By this I simply mean that we are using the machines to simulate performed music — on the one hand — and instrumental compositional forms — on the other hand. Nothing too wrong with this, but what about using the machines to inspire the music and the forms.

Certainly the new 'smart' sequencers (to use a small example) are capable of inspiring permutational procedures which are inherent to them rather than from outside. Finally, the future of all music as well as computer music will depend upon the talent and worth of the blokes using them, it.

BARNEY CHILDS: I don't see the computer playing much of a role in my music, although I can't call the future. So far I'm not much impressed by many of the computer-electronic music sounds I've heard, but if I had the time and skill to learn to work fluently with this potential, I wouldn't mind giving it a try. I suspect it will become an increasingly popular vehicle for composition but, as any other special compositional resource, restricted largely to those people who prefer it.

NORMAN DELLO JOIO: Computer technology is as yet no source that can intrinsically add to the texture and shape of my own music. I am reluctant to spend time on what I see as merely coloristic experiments. This is not to say I would not incorporate some sounds if I were convinced they had structural validity. But sounds for their own sake do not attract me.

DAVID DIAMOND: Computer technology? For me? You may as well ask me to deal with robots. If they resemble and sound like Donald Duck, fine. Of course, computers will have some function unless they become obsolete by their own ability to talk to themselves. That will be the day. Music produced by them already does; talk to itself, that is.

ED DIEMENTE: Computer-generated sound is a valuable addition to other methods of sound production. The problem is for the composer to gain access to computer facilities.

DAVID EPSTEIN: At present, computer technology has not played a role in my music, which is not to rule out a future role. I confess to a tremendous attachment to instruments; having worked with them for so long, as conductor, performer, composer, I am enamored of their sounds, their wide expressive range, their flexibility in shaping and modifying nuance. I like as well the human role of performers, especially I can work with them in shaping my music (most often in first performances, some of which — I have been fortunate — have subsequently been recorded).

That has discouraged my interest in computer technology from this synthetic-composition perspective, is the reverse side of the picture: the great amount of time and technical manipulation often required to do with sound or nuance what a flick of a finger may achieve with a performer. Obviously, the potential range of sonorities, effects, nuances with the new technology, is immense; limited time and, to be honest, a comfort and fondness for the rich older medium have kept me from contact with the new technology — to date.

ROSS LEE FINNEY: The university is an ideal place for the development of technological advances of all sorts. (You have not mentioned video, though it is perhaps the most important.) I have tried to open up such opportunities for my students at The University of Michigan. How such innovations have influenced my music has never interested me very much though I am often distressed when a composer thinks of himself more as an engineer than an artist. I was once given a music typewriter (without asking for it) when what I really wanted was a good grand piano. Administrations find it easier to allocate funds for mechanical gadgets than for musical instruments.

LUKAS FOSS: I am not exactly an electronic composer, but the electronic climate has changed our music and has shaken 'live' music. I welcome the challenge. The combination of live music with electronics can only be fruitful.

JAMES FULKERSON: I've used systems in my compositional work since the last half of the 1960's and find it conceptually very useful. The soft-ware available today is incredibly flexible and therefore useful. Do you remember these types of questions about synthesizers? Funny, isn't it?

GEORGE HEUSSENSTAMM: As powerful as computers are, I do not envision myself becoming involved with them in the composition process, either as an adjunct to composing for standard instruments or as a means of creating purely electronic music, simply because I happen to be obsessed with the notion that a tremendous amount needs to be done with the instruments we now have, and because I am quite satisfied that the means I currently employ are more than adequate to my needs. But this stance is in no way intended to denigrate computer technology and its relation to musical creation, for I firmly believe that computers in music have a healthy and potent future, and I eagerly look forward to experiencing the music so generated.

KAREL HUSA: I may use them in my music, as I believe with future developments and improvements they will be useful to composers. In many ways, they are part of the sound of the 20th century — and if they exist, why not use them? (at one time, they were saying that the organ was just a 'machine').

JEAN EICHELBERGER IVEY: As director of the electronic music studio (which, I founded in 1969) at Peabody Conservatory (the music school of Johns Hopkins University), I am exploring the possibility of adding some degree of computerization to what is now quite a well equipped 'traditional' tape studio. I think this is an important trend of the future which we perhaps owe it to our students to offer, at least to some extent. But in terms of my own composition, writing for live performers interests me most (especially singers) and when it comes to tape composition, the handcraft method suits me better than computerized methods — at least, so far.

KARL KORTE: No reasonable person at this point should doubt the computer's potential ability to accomplish almost anything. The question is do we yet have the ethical knowledge to program it to do the right things? We really don't know very much about the nature of the 'musical experience' or the 'creative act' itself. Perhaps someday we will. The music I've heard from computers so far has been of very limited interest.

ANDREAS MAKRIS: This technology so far has not attracted me and therefore plays no role in my music. Just the same, the future is open to young composers to use whatever they wish to create new music. So far, I have not been impressed, but there is no reason for any composer to abandon anything which produces sound for possible music creation.

BARTON MCLEAN: I see no essential role in digital technology in my future until it travels from, as Jack Fincher says in *Human Intelligence,* a 'left brain' to a 'right brain' approach. As Sid Hodkinson so eloquently says in a forthcoming *Radiofest New American Music* program we are currently producing, "I have had some of my best successes in composing when I really didn't know what the hell I was doing." The idea of completely thinking out everything beforehand smacks of sterility.

PRISCILLA MCLEAN: I have used a digital-to-analog converter, which was in the Synthi 100 Real-time Sequencer, from which I created my two large electronic works, on CRI and Folkways Recordings. The more 'musical' the computer becomes, i.e. the more I can approach it from a performance standpoint, the more interested I will become in using computers. As with synthesizers, computers will have to become less expensive and more manageable before they will become more mainstream.

VINCENT PERSICHETTI: The electronic medium is a valid medium. When enough composers conceive music for a medium, a meaningful literature results.

ELLIUT SCHWARTZ: The new technology doesn't interest me much at this point. My very limited experience with computers has led me to believe — perhaps inaccurately — that one can't easily fiddle around with them and improvise. I consider that a deficiency. Devices that could give me real-time instant gratification, or that could 'process' one medium via another (e.g. film to dance to sound to light) *would* be nice to explore. I've always been more interested in the mystery, magic, and confused ambivalence of technology than by any tightened control it might offer. For me, the important fact of electronic music has been the loudspeaker — sounds miraculously coming out of a little box — rather than the kind of material the loudspeaker deals with.

HALSEY STEVENS: I see no role in my music for computer technology nor — do I envision a brilliant future for computerized music 'in general.'

FRED TILLIS: No direct creative role in my music. As an aid in music reproduction (score and sound), significant breakthroughs are possible.

#4. What role does and should a large organization of composers have in contemporary society (e.g. ASUC)? Do you belong to one or more? Should such groups strive for political power and would you join (if not now a member of one) if more efforts for financial and political strength were made through such groups?

T. J. ANDERSON: I am a member of BMI and consider its relationship to the contemporary composer similar to ASCAP. The recent development of ASUC represents a move toward solidification of our diverse interests. I personally believe the concept of unionization might be more fruitful.

LESLIE BASSETT: Composer organizations serve many functions, among them the important one of getting to know one's colleagues and the reinforcement of one's self respect in his true profession. The organizations are not effective in reaching the public at large, however, and this must be done to overcome the composer's present sense of isolation. The American Composers Orchestra would seem to be a fine example of efforts in that direction.

WARREN BENSON: A large organization should represent the bulk of the best composers of the society at a political level in the sense that it is a powerful lobby for better pecuniary recognition. No, I do not belong to one or more because I have found them in the past to be more concerned with 'one-upmanship' than in developing programs for the general financial good of composers everywhere, and see no strong mutual support system at present.

WILLIAM BOLCOM: The only association I've belonged to for a long time is AMC, and this because they help on copying costs. I got impressed into ACA because Fran Thorne, who is one of God's people, asked me to join and help. I don't really believe in composer's self-help organizations. This is one area where I don't believe in a democratic attitude. Some composers are simply better than others; if less-good ones want to lean together, let them. I also vowed never to join ASUC 1) because of the acronym, and 2) because I don't want to be typed — least of all as a University Composer!

FARLE BROWN: 'A large organization of composers' should primarily devote itself to bringing about performances of broad-minded, inclusive programs, very well rehearsed, in very important concert halls, frequently, within the regular 'commercial' musical society, as confidently and convincingly presented as a concert of Beethoven in Bonn. With sensitive and intelligent programing, clear-headed and unpretentious articles and the above 'professional' conditions, the critics and public will finally pay attention and enjoy. Narrow-minded doctrinaire programming and timidity (lack of real conviction) (and ghetto mentality) is very destructive to contemporary music in this country. I belong to ACA and NVIC, not ASUC.

JOHN CAGE: I am not interested in political power. I have more confidence in individuals than in institutions. I belong to ASCAP and music is published by the Henmar Press of C.F. Peters Corporation. But these connections are practical rather than part of an ongoing struggle.

ROBERT CEELY: ASUC should become militant and start demanding performances from University ensembles as well as soliciting performances from the larger non-university performance groups. At present — though I have been a member of ASUC — I cannot justify the thirty-five dollar cost to become a member. Further, I find the organization worthless as far as being a force to fight for better conditions for the composer. The feeling within the organization seems almost one of apology: apology for being so rude as to wish time to compose, apology to constantly be asking for money, apology for asking the resident violist to look at his new viola piece. I suppose if I taught at an affluent institution that paid for trips to meetings of ASUC I might consider remaining a member.

For now, the three page newsletter announcing the doings of the same seven composers and out of date composition contests is not enough to justify the bread. What is needed is ASWC (American Society of Non University Composers) a group that would demand that BMT pay decent guarantees, that would demand that the BSO which cost 12 million a year to run, spend a minimum of $120,000.00 on Commissions for new American Composers' works each year, that works by living composers be required on the programs of any organization receiving tax free status, that Public Radio which survives as a cultural disc jockey be required to pay decent royalties for playing recordings of living composers, and that — finally — ASNUC would fight for a place for us in the economic structure of this great land of ours.

BARNEY CHILDS: Large outfits as ASUC are worth while, and I'm happy to support them. I'm for more music being played and heard, more opportunity to get together and listen and discuss, more interchange of sounds and ideas. What's all this 'financial and political strength' business? That kind of political power? We live today in an opulence and sloth that a few centuries ago was limited to the nobility, yet one hears perpetual complaint about financial paucity. The word *politics* has been rendered meaningless by its attachment to practically every other substantive in the language. Those whose intent is more money, more reputation, more power, more more more! have inevitably found means to turn possibilities to these ends.

NORMAN DELLO JOIO: I do not belong to organizations in general.

DAVID DIAMOND: I am a non-joiner. I believe in democratic aristocracy of the spirit as e. e. cummings defined it for himself. Political involvement in the Arts is part of the Ego trip of the ambitious.

The quietest and loudest noises are organized by them. Money is important for survival (stomach). ASCAP gives me that money for what I have given them to control. That is all I am interested in.

DAVID EPSTEIN: I do belong to several composer-organizations (ASUC, AMC, ASCAP). I find them valuable in many ways — rights, protection (ASCAP), conferences, folloquia, publications and journals, newsletters, and — very important — working in numerous ways to advance the collective health of the composing profession. To the extent that these goals are advanced, I find these organizations a constructive political force. To the extent that they themselves may become political in their inner workings, I find this bothersome and time consuming. But then, that's life.

ROSS LEE FINNEY: De Tocqueville in *Democracy in America* comments on the fact that Americans organize societies — a hat. There is no reason why composers shouldn't respond to this national urge. There is always a tendency for such an organization to support some aesthetic 'principle' and to stand in the way of younger composers who don't subscribe to that 'principle.'

LUKAS FOSS: Composers have unions in Russia and in Hollywood. The product (the music) reveals some significant parallels. Composers, poets, painters must not organize.

JAMES FULKERSON: I don't know about ASUC — except for the jokes about its anagram. Maybe they'll change theirs like Cal Arts did — remember CIA (California Institute of the Arts)? I do belong to the German performing rights society — GEMA and I have a German publisher, Edition Modern. GEMA has a full pension at age 65 for those composers who are elected to full membership which is a real tangible result of its workings. As to political power, what would composers do with political power? I can't think of too many composers who would make particularly good American presidents can you?

GEORGE HEUSSENSTAMM: Composer organizations serve a valuable function in bringing composers together in a society where meaningful interchange of views may take place and a forum for performance is offered, even though the audience is made up essentially of colleagues. I belong to ASUC, ISCM, and NACUSA, and take delight in the activities rendered by them.

Some of what it does bleeds out into the general public, but we could do much more In that direction. I don't believe in private, closed sessions or concerts. We could use some good PR and some Madison Avenue techniques to improve our image, to make the idea of what we do more attractive to a general audience. A lot of money would help! Let us be political if it can procure more financial support.

KAREL HUSA: I am not sure if political strength is an asset to organizations of composers; we see it in some countries and if you are not a member of *that* politic, you are out. I think *freedom* is the most important matter for the composer. I am a member of several organizations of composers for various reasons: I like their ideas, aims, directions, and through meetings and magazines the exchange of information. But also, because each society of composers needs our support, because in some way we all are contributing and making things happen and thus keeping new music alive.

JEAN EICHELBERGFR IVEY: Personally I have found memberships in professional societies valuable. I have been a member of ASUC since it started, and was the first editor of its Newsletter. I have also been for many years a member of the American Music Center and the Southeastern Composers League. Such societies offer a composer various opportunities: their newsletters are usually full of helpful information, and their meetings offer performance possibilities and personal contacts with other composers and musicians. "They are also one of the ways — not the only one, of course — in which one can *contribute* to one's profession, and try to help make conditions better for composers as a group. Currently I am a board member of the League of Composers — ISCM.

KARL KORTE: I am a member of ASUC (albeit a somewhat reluctant one). It is a good organization that is developing some political clout through its broadcast and recording series. However, I am still intrinsically opposed to the idea of separating 'new music' from the mainstream of other musical activities. For me, the idea of several hundred composers sitting around passing judgment upon one another is not a healthy spectacle.

ANDREAS MAKRIS: I have been a member of A.S.C.A.P. for sometime and I do believe that composers should come in contact with each other in one or another capacity. Just the same, I think a composer's life by nature is non-political and the phrase of 'strive for political power' does not inspire me in the least. I feel A.S.C.A.P. is as good an organization as any a composer could join.

BART MCLEAN: As with every such organization, you get out of it what you put into it. Composers I respect the most, in a certain sense, are those that have worked hard to make life a little better for all of us — the Leo Krafts, the Ed Londons, and the Aaron Coplands, not to mention my teacher Henry Cowell. We all realize that there are some of us have paid our dues, and some who have not.

PRISCILLA MCLEAN: I feel one of the most important ways a large composer organization can affect society is in the awareness-raising of the composers' music, via concerts at regional and national conventions, journals and recordings of new music, radio broadcasts , etc. Also this brings composers in contact with each other, something much needed in our spread-out society. I think political strength could not hurt, especially today when the nation is becoming much more conservative and cautious; during such times the arts always suffer. I have been on the executive committee of ASUC since 1976, and a member since 1971 (I joined when a piece of mine was accepted for the newly-formed ASUC Radio Series). I have not joined any women's organizations yet because I have been so busy in ASUC. I am a member of the American Music Center.

VINCENT PERSICHETTI: The composer's efforts should be directed to his composing.

ELLIOTT SCHWARTZ: I've been a member of ASCAP for many years (now in the process of switching to BMI), and also belong to ASUC, American Music Center, and the College Music Society. They're valuable as 'lobbies' to make government and the musical public aware of special needs and the interests, as a forum for the exchange of ideas, and as an annual excuse to meet and visit with old friends from across the U.S.A. I'm not sure what's meant by 'political power' since composers as a class don't produce anything that anyone wants or really needs (like wheat, or postal service, or a cure for cancer) or anything that people fear (like weapons), threatening to withhold (or use) our services — which is the only kind of political power there is — won't scare anyone.

HALSEY STEVENS: The only organizations of composers I belong to are ACA (charter member) and NACUSA (a legacy from the old NAACC). The former is concerned with stimulating the performance of its member's music and (through BMI) the collection and distribution of performance fees, etc.

The latter is interested also in performance, but it has traditionally concerned itself with the innocuous and the expedient. I retain membership largely through inertia. I am not convinced of the efficacy of such organizations as ASUC, etc., nor of the need for them; hence I have not been seduced into joining them so far.

FRED TILLIS: a) modest, b) yes, c) composers are not likely inclined to build such a sophisticated political network.

#5. A recent survey showed over 200 new music performing groups in America today. This would undoubtedly overshadow available groups to any composer or set of composers in history. Is this an indication of current successes of 'new' music in this country? Are you contacted by such groups for pieces? Are groups you are aware of performing premieres of many new pieces or performing the older 'masterworks' more often than not? What role could such groups perform in fashioning a future for contemporary music in America?

T. J. ANDERSON: I have not been contacted by any 'near' music groups and therefore have not felt them instrumental in the development of career. These groups, however, are important in promoting the music of local composers and reinforcing the concept of a masterwork (whatever that might mean). It seems to me that a group committed to contemporary music must have a sense of dedication to the diversity of the society as opposed to the above limited scope. To be successful in the broader understanding of contemporary music requires a far greater knowledge of musical styles and a diversity of performance skills.

LESLIE BASSETT: Many of these groups are active and committed, doing fine work. Many have a small yet loyal audience and perform works by American composers. I have had fine performances by them. They are a vital part of our musical life and must be preserved as a crucial link with the public at large. None of them may be perfect, but they all mean well and account for many performances of composers which would otherwise not be heard. Onward and upward.

WARREN BENSON: I think part of the development of new music ensembles today is due to the fact that they can be a handy outlet for the *young conductor* who does not have the money or backing available to form a full size orchestra. Knowing that there is a large number of composers wanting to have their works played, forming a flexible small group to provide this service gives them something important to do as conductors though they often end up with full size orchestras and standard programs. Some of them are vitally and validly interested in our music.

Occasionally I am contacted by such a group for pieces, but not often. I think more of the groups who perform premieres should perform some of the twentieth century *masterworks* and curios more often than they do. By masterworks I would include works of the early part of this century which are generally not done, particularly works of the '20's and '30's from all the Americas, among other interesting places. Fundamentally, though, I am opposed to all-contemporary (all new works, very recent works) concerts as I am bored by meals consisting entirely of meat, or pickled squid.

WILLIAM BOLCOM: I am often asked for pieces by contemporary-music-performing groups. I note, however, that many concentrate on music at least 10 years old. Then we had our most 'avant-garde' period. Now that 'avant-garde' is old-hat, I find that these groups mostly play my old music, and that groups that concentrate on wide varieties of musical styles want my newer stuff (e.g. Orpheus, Saint Paul Chamber Orchestra, CMS of Lincoln Center). I am personally bored with ghettoized modern-music associations and welcome a more catholic attitude toward programming in concerts.

EARLE BROWN: Do you mean that there are over 200 *new* music groups, or 200 new *music groups*? The 'large organization of composers' addressing themselves to suggestions in 4 could do a lot for 'a future for contemporary music in 'America,' as well as for American music in the *world*!

JOHN CAGE: I am glad that there are in the USA so many groups performing new music. I think that many of them are not connected with universities, so that one can say that music is beginning to take place in the country itself. Part of this is due to the fact that concerts are now given in other places than concert halls (though also in them): art galleries, churches, lofts, streets; and part to the munificence of foundations which enable some young composers and musicians to work with their arts even though they are no longer in school.

ROBERT CEELY: Not knowing the source of your survey I will only say there are mighty few really good new music performers or performing groups. We need them; they could best serve composers by giving superb performances of a wide range of composers now living as well as occasional performances by other composers from the 14th century on up to our day. The problem now is that too few organizations are willing to really put in the time and effort to master the problems associated with learning a new work. We have all known conductors who continue with a performance after one or more of its performers are lost. To stop would admit defeat, and what the conductor wants to do is win.

BARNEY CHILDS: I'm not sure that new music is having successes, but the implication is that people are becoming marginally more interested in it, just as the implication from the increased number of 'new music' compositions on recordings. I have been contacted by, and commissioned by, groups for new pieces from time to time.

I'd agree that the 'new' music programmed by many groups tends to include a solid chunk of earlier 20th-century 'masterworks' and, too, that the immediately current music performed is in most cases in fairly specialized idioms based on the particular group's preferences. Mention should be made of not only professional level new music groups but also of student new music performance ensembles, and the value of these above and beyond the dissemination of new music is the acquaintanceship of student musicians with new music, musicians who are not only the audience of the next decades but the teachers and performers also. Further, many of these ensembles do not limit their programming to new 'art' or 'concert' music; we see the inclusion of more and more music from other creative areas. Many student players bring, for example, contemporary stage band and studio band experience to new music groups. I enjoy having my work performed by student ensembles; maybe the professionalism and polished of a pro performance won't be there, but it is often more than compensated for by the enjoyment and enthusiasm which animates many student performances.

NORMAN DELLO JOIO: Groups playing contemporary music reflect the need for performers to find outlets on an expanded scale. I see no evidence that this has anything to do with the 'success' of new music.

DAVID DIAMOND: Did you ever attend those '200 new music performing groups' performances with 200 the maximum attendance and 50 the more usual, accompanied by bears, pony tails, dark glasses, marijuana, and vapid expressions of visage and non-conversation at any point of human contact?

In the Twenty and Thirties there was a League of Composers, and a brilliant diversity in their programs! And public. They were not appellate avant-garde. They were truly a League working in behalf of the *Present* not the *Future*. Schoenberg admitted to his Private Readings society only those who cared or who could pay admission in order to become acquainted with the new music. The word avant-garde or show biz, smartalecism was unknown to him and his colleagues. Varèse conducted Monteverdi and made no disciples. When will a collective avant-garde work be written called *Judas*?

ED DIEMENTE: Singly, or in groups, performers are my best friends. Yes, I have composed for such contemporary music ensembles. Whether groups play all first performances or a combination of 'new' and 'masterworks of 20th century literature' depends a great deal on resources. A group may want to perform *Pierrot Lunaire* but not have the players to do it. If contemporary ensembles were funded, if they could broadcast and record, the face of music in our society would be revolutionized.

DAVID EPSTEIN: The existence of so many of these groups is a healthy sign, in my opinion. Many of them have grown up as a counterforce to the 'established' musical organizations that for various reasons serve new music poorly or not at all. This is the way new groups should arise. The fact that they are so numerous and spread so widely over the country certainly indicates an interest in new music that is also spreading around the U.S. — significantly so, I suspect, for these groups could not survive if there were not audiences to play for. I am contacted by such groups for pieces and have had some gratifying experiences in being performed by them. As to the balance of 'new vs. older masterworks' performances: I strongly favor a mixture of this kind on any program (or most programs). Concerts must present audiences with a mix of pleasure, challenge, stimulation, and — let's face it — 'fun.' A blend of older and newer contemporary works with new music points in this direction.

Concerts exclusively of new works can be pretty tough going for all of us at times, certainly for the general public. I'd go even further: mixtures of baroque or classical works with new music can enhance new music, particularly if some consistent thread of style, approach, structure, whatever, can help to unify such a program. Program building is an art, whether the content is new music or otherwise. And always a public (if not 'the' public) must be considered — it is for audiences, after all, that all of this exists.

ROSS LEE FINNEY: These new performing groups play a very important role in our contemporary musical life. The performers are often extremely skillful and perform new works with real authority. Many have developed audiences for contemporary music that are both large and loyal. These groups have had an impact on older organizations such as the symphony orchestra and the band. They have encouraged performers such as percussionists who have had little chance to appear publicly. They have become an outlet for young conductors who understand the inflections of American music. They have used electronic and multi-media devices more easily than larger organizations. I would hope that in time they will help the economic position of performers and composers and spread our culture geographically in a way that large organizations cannot do.

LUKAS FOSS: Performing groups, a chamber music of virtuosi, that is what is new and promising in new music (besides electronics). The earliest example is *Pierrot* — then came *Histoire*. These two milestones mark the beginning of our new music. They created the need for performing groups.

JAMES FULKERSON: Over 200 new music performing groups means just over 4 per state (when averaged). To eyes, this is precious little activity, and I hope there is much more going on than that. A greater problem is that they are (philosophical differences aside) open to John Cage, George Crumb, Morton Feldman, or Charles Wourinen, but to the proverbial Art Smith from Decatur they are really a closed shop. Having started out with the Buffalo group and been active in New York before going to Europe, I have enough visibility that those groups do my works, but it's because of my visibility more than anything else which leads to more performances.

One finds a basically healthier scene in the universities, I think, because they are almost always the result of a collaboration between the local musicians and the local composers who are often also performers or conductors. Ties, unlike the groups you mention, are not concerned with the financial prospect of programming and undoubtedly give a wider fare of the compositional work being done today. "This interaction, happening quietly and consistently without media coverage, is what makes contemporary music. The idea of a future for contemporary music is somewhat odd — there will always be contemporary music, be it jazz, classical, folk, or what have you. Music is bigger than any of us and it is alive, well, and prospering as it has done through the ages. The groups you refer to are only one of several catalytic agents in a vast system of 'classical art' music, which is itself only a portion of a vast musical world.

GEORGE HEUSSENSTAMM: Surely there are many more than 200 groups found in your survey. For me, it signifies that young performers like to play new music, to accept the challenges it offers. Experience has been that they are quite eager to perform new works rather than established ones. But do not burden them with the responsibility of snagging audiences. Be satisfied they are playing the music, and enlist others to populate the concert hall.

KAREL HUSA: Surely these groups are very important for the future of American music, because they are forums for composers. Certainly not all works performed will become masterpieces, but from the large amount of compositions some will be outstanding and few hopefully will one day stand as 'great works of the past.' We read how difficult it was for Beethoven to get his *Missa Solemnis* performed and published; or how Berlioz and even Schoenberg had to beg supporters to finance performances of their music. We are so much more grateful for the 200 new music performing groups in America today. I think that there are several reasons for the existence of these ensembles. There are many more composers today than 30 years ago and also there are many more performers, and many of them are interested in the writings of their colleagues. Especially when they are young and students in schools, they are sympathetic to the cause of the young composer, who does not know where to turn. Also, young people today have incredibly inquiring minds; they link music to life and sense that composers perhaps say in tones what they feel.

Also, most of the 'classical' literature is in the hands of the super-virtuoso stars and relatively difficult for a young performer to enter the circle. Many of them became known by performing new and musical works. Same in the recording business; all classical music is on records (some works in 50 versions in Schwann). We composers are grateful to these performers for their interest in us. If we look at the statistics today and take performances of all music, the new music — speaking in percents — is not as much performed today, as it was in the 1900s (in Europe) or in the time of Mozart, Haydn, or, going back to the 18th century and renaissance.

JEAN EICHELBERGER IVEY: The large number of new music groups is probably proportional to the large number of living composers in the U.S. I'm not sure it greatly enhances the performance possibilities of any one individual. So many groups do not want to pay the composer, or his publisher, anything!

So what they offer is chiefly exposure. Small wonder if publishers are unwilling to take on much new music, and if composers work long hours at non-composing jobs when so many expect to play new music free of charge. If these groups will support the music they play financially, and also commission works, they can make a real difference on the American scene. But this is all part of a large, and complex, financial and social problem, to which I know no easy answers.

KARL KORTE: Your statement that 'over 200 new music performing groups in America today' undoubtedly overshadows available groups to any composer in history — and (that) this is an indication of current success of 'new music' is simply not true. If this country's major opera houses premiered ten new operas a year, as Venice's did for decades, or if all concerts in this country consisted of mostly new music, as was the case during the 18th and 19th centuries, then we would have something.

Let's be honest. Many of those 200 'new music' groups exist exclusively for someone's or group's private 'hobby riding.' I've been at too many 'new music' concerts that accomplished far more in the way of harm than good. There are exceptions, of course. I think the idea of programming older masterworks alongside of brand new pieces is healthy. If third rate performances and doctrinaire programming can be avoided, such groups can play a role in 'fashioning a future for contemporary music in America.'

ANDREAS MAKRIS: The new musical performing groups in America are definitely a major plus for new music as well as for the young composer. I have been contacted by some of these groups and have been asked to compose for them. Generally speaking, while these musical groups do not ignore older 'masterworks' they are concentrated more on performing new music. These musical organizations are becoming the back-bone for the so-called young and not established composer. They have two elements that are often lacking in the traditional symphony orchestra. 1) It is their own musical group, it is new, they feel enthusiastic, and as a result more daring. 2) Their budget usually is not the astronomical budget of a symphony orchestra and therefore are more capable of taking greater risks with the audiences. Furthermore, because of the fact that they themselves are not known, they may have more empathy for the unknown young composer. Perhaps the only irony of these new groups is that they themselves are strongly inclined to come in contact with the more known composers. While this is understandable, they should not forget that scouting younger unknown composers is more rewarding and more in the spirit of their group.

BARTON MCLEAN: It is true that more and more music is being performed today. But, who is listening?

PRISCILLA MCLEAN: If our own group (The McLean Mix) is an indication, many new music groups have been formed by composers anxious to have their music heard and to interact with a live audience. It may be a reaction against the impersonal media situation existing today and a desire to get out and touch the audience at close range.

I feel this is healthy and exciting. There are a wide variety of groups of all kinds, and I have been asked by many for pieces. Often groups who are billing for a substantial amount of money or appealing to large audiences perform more 'masterworks' than premieres. Only a few composers can perform only their own works and premieres and draw a large fee and crowd, unless, of course, they are commercial (pop) artists.

VINCENT PERSICHETTI: New performing groups premiere works. Not until they perform works that have been premiered will they be serving this century through selectivity.

ELLIOTT SCHWARTZ: Weren't there hundreds of opera houses by the early 18th century, or court orchestras during the Mannheim-Esterhazy years? I don't think our situation is so unusual historically. I'm contacted by new music ensembles every now and then for my pieces — usually about the possibility of performing an existent work rather than commissioning a new one, probably because money is becoming tighter every year. I also compose music for groups that *don't* specialize in new music, that would include a piece of mine on a program with Schubert and Vivaldi. I can't say which is the 'better' situation: certainly the audiences are very different! Even though a survey does indicate the existence of 200-plus new music groups in America, we should also realize that many groups are concentrated in a few urban (and university-based) areas; many have identical instrumentations (and often share performers, free-lance from one group to the next); many stress music by established name composers and 20th-century classics rather than *local* talent. We could do with a few less of these, and a lot more encouragement of composition at the grass roots level, nationwide.

ROBERT STARER: I do not see the future of music in the expansion of groups devoted to very special areas. I rather believe we should try to regain our audience.

HALSEY STEVENS: 'New music performing groups' is ambiguous: does it mean *new groups* for the *performance of music* or *groups for the performance of new music*? If the latter, as I suspect, I do not view the end resultant with optimism. Nor do I take the establishment and continued existence of such groups as confirmation of the health of the art. So many groups are ephemeral, put together for a few concerts, with little likelihood of their survival for more than a brief season.

Certainly there is more interest on the part of performers in some of the least traditional music of the present century, and far more technical *expertise* for its performance . . . I am little interested in the premiere for premiere's sake: if the music is worth hearing, it is worth re-hearing, or should be . . . naturally the older 'masterworks' will (and should) continue to be played; new scores should be weighed against them in performance and take their chances — a few of them may become in their turn 'masterworks.'

FRED TILLIS: A) no, B) occasionally, C) most often the *masterworks* are being performed, D) by including a percentage (25% to 50%) of American music on each concert presented to the public, much could be accomplished.

#6. What literary work(s), if any, have influenced your musical thoughts, concepts, and art output?

T. J. ANDERSON: I have been very much influenced by the poetry of M.B. Tolson, Arna Bontemps, Pearl Lomax, Pauline Hanson, Robert Hayden, Milton Kessler, and Leon Forrest, and have set music to their poetry.

LESLIE BASSETT: Songs need texts, as do choral works, and many instrumental pieces have a quotation as genesis. Poetry and quotations are rich and important resources. I have used many: Milton, Shelley, the Bible, Burton, Blake, Tagore, Van Doren, Hammarskjöld, etc., etc.

WARREN BENISON: My work is influenced, I am sure, by what I read. Poetry has certainly influenced work in ways that I cannot significantly document, but I know it's there. In addition, the world of visual arts has had a significant role to play in the way I think about music. The whole question of form can be enriched by a knowledge of poetic and visual formal concerns, and I'm sure that has seeped into my work at some level or another.

WILLIAM BOLCQM: Poetry has had a great effect on me, mostly Blake, but also many contemporary poets ranging from Roethke, Kunitz, to Christopher Logue, Starbuck (whose work attracts me because perhaps it's a little like my music), Arnold Weinstein, and others not particularly attracted to people like Lowell or Ashbery, fine as they are. Other great influence has been theater; I respond to a large variety of writers and have done stage music for many of them — I might like O'Neill or Albee less than I might respond to Behan or Joe Orton, speaking only of a few 20th-century writers.

I love the borderline between comedy and tragedy, between hilarity and terror . . . I know that you want to know if I have ever been influenced by any body of work on music as far as compositional techniques is concerned. If I was at any time, I am certainly not now. I distrust word-oriented impetuses to composition.

EARLE BROWN: Literary works, influenced by: the Symbolist poets (Rimbaud, Valery, Mallarme especially); Surrealist theories and writings; Gertrud Stein (everything); James Joyce (everything); Kenneth Patchen; Buckminster Fuller; Beckett; Ionesco; Marinetti (selected writings); William James; Bergson; writings by and about visual arts (not to mention the art itself) . . . etc. It would be an immense list and I see that I have mentioned names and not the works (mostly), but I take it that this will suffice. A most important recent (10 years) influence is *Centering*, by Mary Caroline Richards, and also her, *Crossing Point*; and her entire way of being.

JOHN CAGE: Recently I have been deeply involved not only with the writings, particularly the *Journal*, of Henry David Thoreau, but also with *Finnegans Wake* of James Joyce, *Score with Parts* and *Renga, Mareau and Empty Words*, and also various graphic works (not musical) including the current *Changes and Disappearances* and an edition of unique prints by the Crown Point Press are all made by means of Thoreau's work; and now *Roaratorio* and the several *Writings through Finnegans Wake*, are only possible because of what Joyce wrote.

ROBERT CEELY: Everything I read or have read. Or none of it.

BARNEY CHILDS: A tricky question to answer for me, since with my education through the doctorate having been in literature I've read exhaustively for the last 35 years. Much of my present view of music and how it works, for example, has been conditioned by an extensive familiarity with poetry and poetic theory of the last forty years, and an exposition of this would require far more space than this questionnaire allows. Again, the definition of 'literature' in the question is pesky. Certainly books, as R. Murray Schafer's *The Tuning of the World*, Lawrence Halprin's *The RSVP Cycles*, Dick Higgins' *A Dialectic of Centuries*, and Morse Peckham's *Man's Rage for Chaos* aren't I suppose really 'literature,' as others have had major impact on my thinking about, and thus on my writing, music.

Finally, even the way in which literature can influence one's composing is a question here. I'm sure we have all read books which were vital in shaping our thought, even though this thought had little or no direct musical application. I have of course been directly stimulated to write specific music from specific passages in literature on occasion, from works as disparate and unlikely as Michael Ayrton's *The Maze Maker*, Harvey Allen's *Anthony Adverse*, the fantasies of E. R. Edison, and translated Navajo poetry. But I'm thinking now of those major readings in one's life as defined above: surely these do have an effect, no matter at what remove, on one's creativity, but how to explain how this works? For me, several of these have been some early short stories of Paul Goodman, James Agee's *Let Us Now Praise Famous Men*, Geoffrey Winthrop Young's *On High Hills*, and John Masters' *The Road Past Mandalay*.

NORMAN DELLO JOIO: The poetry of Walt Whitman, English poets of the 18th and 19th century, the Bible, and Catholic liturgy have influenced my output.

DAVID DIAMOND: Santayana's *The Sense of Beauty*, Pater's *Marius*, Gide's *Counterfeiters*, Cummings' *Notebooks* (and friendships), Melville's *Moby Dick* and *Pierre*, Valery's *Poetry* and *Monsieur Teste*, Michelangelo's *Sonnets*.

ED DIEMENTE: *Phenomenon of Man* by Teilhard de Shardin, *Diaries* by Paul Klee, *Autobiography of Malcolm X*, *Notebook* by Robert Lowell, *Collected Poems* by Wallace Stevens.

DAVID EPSTEIN: I've been specifically influenced by several poets, whose texts I have set in song cycles and choral works — Emily Dickinson, Keats, Gerard Manley Hopkins, and most recently the biblical psalmists. In a more general sense I've been influenced by literature per se. Aspects of my music have counterparts in literature — the dramatic, the lyrical, the philosophical. While none of these have had specific connections with music, they have provided a general stimulation that often gets musical imagination going.

LUKAS FOSS: When I was 19: Carl Sandburg (*The Prairie*); When I was 30: Rainer Marie Rilke (*The Parable of Death*); Since then: Kafka and Beckett have left their mark.

JAMES FULKERSON: The work of Doris Lessing has been very stimulating for me.

GEORGE HEUSSENSTAMM: I read a great deal but cannot in fact single out any specific works which have influenced my musical thinking as such. But some of the work being done in the sciences — astronomy, for example — has surely had an impact on my music. Living conveniently close to the California Institute of Technology offers an advantage in that much of the content of high-level lectures given on that campus is converted into stimuli for musical ideas.

KAREL HUSA: This is a rather immense question; many literary works, first Czech, German, French, Russian, but also American, Indian, Chinese, Japanese, etc. When I reach for names, these come to mind (with regrets for those I forgot at the moment): Sophocles, Shakespeare, Goethe, Thoreau, Eluard, Dostoyevski, Cummings, Camus, Strindberg, James Baldwin, Huxley, Kafka, Rilke, and Czech writer Karel Capek, and poet Brezina. I think, though, that painting and sculpture with drawing have influenced musical thoughts too.

JEAN EICHELBERGER IVEY: Literature plays a big role in my thinking generally; in my dreams, and also in musical thinking. Since I am particularly fond of writing for the voice, the choice and setting of texts occupies me a good deal. I sometimes write my own texts, as in *Testament of Eve*, mentioned in question #1, and *Solstice*, a vocal chamber work commissioned by Sigma Alpha Iota.

I have set Shakespeare, Whitman, the modern American poet Carolyn Kizer, and many others. Also, some of my music without texts is linked up in mind with literary or programatic ideas. I am just finishing a work for orchestra and tape, with no text, called *Sea-Change,* a word derived from Shakespeare's *Tempest*, which play also inspired my piece *Prospero*, for bass voice, horn, percussion, and tape. (The latter has recently been recorded for Grenadilla records.)

KARL KORTE: None that I would care to talk about.

ANDREAS MAKRIS: I really don't know. A composer is constantly influenced from everything he reads, hears, or comes in contact with. But contrary to some novelists and biographers would have us believe, I feel these impressions and influences come to us in small doses and constantly not, 'all at once.' It is very impressive to read in a biography that this great composer read 'that' and instantly all his musical thoughts and output took a drastic new direction. In my opinion, this is simply more spectacular than a truthful event.

BARTON MCLEAN: Ancient, pre-Columbian Nahuatl poetry, Jack Fincher's *Human Intelligence,* and Edward Hall's *Beyond Culture.*

PRISCILLA MCLEAN: Usually everything I write is influenced by literary or artistic works. *Beneath the Horizon* for tuba and whales was influenced by Eugene O'Neill's one-act play *Beyond the Horizon* (in mood), the poetry of e. e. cummings inspired a recently completed set of songs: *Songs for Adults and Other Children*, Carl Sandburg's poem *Isle of Patmos* Inspired my title for my electronic work *Invisible Chariots*.

VINCENT PERSICHETTI: Poetic, biblical, scientific, and mythological writings.

ELLIOTT SCHWARTZ: Literature and music don't combine easily in my work. I've always felt much more comfortable with music that had no words or programmatic scenarios, relying instead upon the abstract 'drama' of the concert ritual itself. I have been influenced by certain concepts in painting, architecture, and experimental theatre, however, in creating various pieces.

HALSEY STEVENS: None that I know of.

FRED TILLIS: Poetry by Afro-American poets.

#7. Do you copy the final copy of your own scores? Your own parts? If not, do you assign the responsibility to a student, professional copyist, your publisher, the commissioning body, or the performing group? Who is responsible for the copying costs (you, your publisher, commissioning organization, performing ensemble)?

T. J. ANDERSON: I personally copy all of my scores and will continue to do so regardless of financial condition. For parts, I usually rely on professional copyists.

LESLIE BASSETT: Yes, I always do my own scores, but will have the parts copied professionally unless there is no time. Sometimes I will do the parts if there are special problems in cueing or page turns. I often use an Italian professional, supplemented by students and UC copyists. Copying costs are normally included in the commission fee.

WARREN BENSON: I do not usually copy the masters of my own scores or parts. I have professional copyists who are paid by the commissioning body.

WILLIAM BOLCOM: I transmit my scores directly from sketch onto ozalid, pencil on front with orange carbon backing, and make ozalid copies or xeroxes from those. Usually there is provision in commission for copying costs; most often I hire professionals. (I have used the same copyist since 1963.) Sources vary for copying costs; I've never experienced a publisher putting in much money on that.

EARLE BROWN: I copy the final copy of my manuscript but my publisher makes a 'final copy' of that for publication; which I of course correct. Like everyone (I assume) I copied my own parts but it is now done by publisher, unless it is very unusual, in which case I copy them (or have them copied under very supervised conditions). The copying costs are most frequently handled by the publisher; sometimes including the commissioning fee, but seldom by the performing ensemble.

JOHN CAGE: I no longer copy scores or parts except when the final score is the first one (as is the case in *Renga*, *Child of Tree*, *Branches,* etc.). I engage a professional copyist and consider myself responsible for the costs though, occasionally C.F. Peters has shared them with me.

ROBERT CEELY: Yes. Usually. Sometimes. ME.

BARNEY CHILDS: Yes, I make my own final copies of both scores and parts.

DAVID DIAMOND: Yes, I make my final copies. Publishers pay 50% parts costs. If I do not have these means I can always hope for the generosity of wealthy friends. Besides, I do not compose as much as I use to. There is so much that is still unperformed.

ED DIEMENTE: Yes, I copy my own scores. Sometimes I do the parts too if there are notational problems or if I do not have the funds to pay a copyist. If I can get someone else to do it, I'll take anyone who is good at it. (I am fussy.)

DAVID EPSTEIN: I generally do the fair copy of my scores — the one that emanates from sketches or short score. I find it a miserable chore for which I have little talent, and the time demands are enormous (one or two hours per page in a musical hand that will win no prizes).

Whoever invents a practical and quick system for doing this work will find me lining up at his door as the first customer. I've been fortunate to have a publisher for many years now who handles the extractions of parts and also the publication preparation of scores. (Of course I, like any composer, must read proofs, but this concerns musical substance, not mechanics). The best arrangement concerning copying costs connected with a commission is to ask that the commissioner set aside money toward these expenses. When publishers oversee this work, they generally work out arrangements with the composer.

LUKAS FOSS: It depends. If my publisher doesn't do it, I have a professional or student copy. In that case I am stuck with the cost, except when the American Music Center helps out.

JAMES FULKERSON: I have used a professional copyist for nearly all of my work for the past 3 years, including parts. I hate copy work more than words can describe — and my results look like it. I include the estimated copying costs in the commissioning fee.

GEORGE HEUSSENSTAMM: You struck a nerve center with this question! I have always copied my scores and parts out of sheer economic necessity. Consequently, I've developed a concern that manuscripts should be written neatly, properly, and efficiently — to the extent that I've written a book on the subject, entitled *MUSIC COPYING A SELF INSTRUCTION* in which every technique and trick I've learned over the past twenty years is presented to the reader, along with a thorough exposition of basic musical notation. As far as I'm concerned, music copying should be a required course for every music major, let alone composition major, and it should comprise a full 3-unit course, not merely a one hour per week, one-unit, token course.

KAREL HUSA: I used to copy the final scores myself; it took weeks, as I wanted to have a nice looking print. Now, I write score legibly, so that they can be used for the time being, with hope that they will soon be published. The parts are either copied by the publisher, or a student, or a professional copyist. When I was young, I did the parts copying myself too (parts to my first and second string quartets, *Evocations of Slovakia* and others including orchestral parts to *Concertino for Piano*, *Divertimento*, etc.). I think it was a good experience and helpful too. I have realized, mostly as a conductor, how important good copied parts are.

Only excellently written parts can give an excellent performance. On the other hand, badly copied parts bury any possibility of a good performance. Performers feel they do not need to make a great effort of trying, if the composer did not care about the parts. Responsibility for the cost of copying has been with me, or with my publishers, commissioning organizations, etc.; it depends.

JEAN EICHELBERGER IVEY: I *always* copy orchestral *scores*, combining this with the final revision or editing of the piece. Sometimes I have the parts copied, if I can afford it. I am glad to say that I have had two grants from the American Music Center for orchestral parts. Otherwise, if I have the parts copied, I'm the one who pays — which is why I have often copied my own parts! I have occasionally had small chamber scores copied, when particularly pressed for time.

Sometimes I employ a student, if I have one who has a particularly good hand, but more often I use a professional copyist if I use anyone, because with students I often spend a disproportionate amount of time instructing them in the process. I might say in passing that organizations who give grants and commissions might take a closer look at copying costs. All too often the total commission given the composer — for which he is expected to create the work and furnish all the materials — is far *less* than a professional copyist would charge to copy it. These so-called commissions are more in the nature of token honorariums.

KARL KORTE: Scores? Always! Parts? Almost never! Whenever possible the commissioning body (which is often the performing group) should be responsible for the composer's costs.

ANDREAS MAKRIS: I compose first in my mind (just like any other composer) but contrary to many other composers I do not write my sketches on paper. When I have a substantialized idea I put it directly on the score. While I am very aware of the general musical direction, nothing is written any place except directly on the score.

So, in an essence I have no final score, my first 'is' the final. All the parts are extracted by a professional copyist and of course checked by me. The cost is paid by the commissioning groups, the performing artists, or the publisher. By the way, a word of advice; do not try to save money by copying your own music. The success of the performance naturally depends on many things, but a clear professional copy holds a considerable share for that success.

BART MCLEAN: No. I usually assign them to a young, starving, talented composer (of whom there seem to be many in Austin lately). I usually get University research grants for copying expenses.

PRISCILLA MCLAEN: The dilemma of copying has been a problem with me for years. I have for years copied all my own scores and parts, but I find myself with less and less time to do that. Right now, I am leaning toward copying in pencil a fairly neat just-finished score, getting the piece performed and revised (as it always needs to be), and then hiring a copyist I trust to do a final ink score. Since scores are somewhat bizarre, I will have to work with the copyist closely. I received a grant in 1975 for copying costs on my orchestral piece (American Music Center Copying Grant), but other than that, I have to pay the costs myself.

VINCENT PERSICHETTI: I copy my own scores. My parts are prepared professionally at cost.

ELLIOTT SCHWARTZ: Many of my more recent scores are used as 'parts' (i.e. the players all read from copies of the score), even in works for chamber orchestra. I like the idea that each performer can see what everyone else is doing, and in certain aspects of my music — rhythmic synchronization and freely overlapping non-synchronization — it may be essential. So in these situations there are no individual 'parts' at all. In other cases, such as large orchestral or band pieces, I have parts copied by a student. The scores are always in my own manuscript.

ROBERT STARER: My publishers, with whom I have worked for years, either publish or rent my larger works and get parts copied unless the commissioning organization does so. At their request I write some more saleable pieces, such as technically simple and musically accessible works for piano, chorus, and band. I take pleasure in being performed by amateurs or students.

HALSEY STEVENS: For most of my creative life I have preferred to copy my own work, finding it more accurate and often more legible that that of even professional copyists. Unfortunately, a neurological impairment has made it impossible for me to produce the kind of fair copy that I should insist upon as a performer, and therefore the task must now be assigned to other hands. Who pays for what should be stipulated in contracts and commissions; so long as there is no ambiguity, equitable treatment is quite possible.

FRED TILLIS: 1) sometimes, 2) no, 3) student or professional copyist, 4) copying costs have varied from commissioning organization, to performing ensemble, and my absorbing of the expense.

#8. Do you feel the communication and dialogue between performers and composers are closer today than ever? What comments would you make in your association and work with performers of your music?

T. J. ANDERSON: Any performer that commits their talent to a contemporary piece is usually most willing to work with the composer. I personally view this relationship as humanistic and therefore a joint venture rather than my imposing a set absolute standard.

LESLIE BASSETT: Same as ever. There are always performers to whom we feel close and who are supportive and alert. Other seem to have no interest in new music or our music, even though we are good friends in eve1Y other respect. It would seem that some groups of instrumentalists are more inclined to be interested than others winds and percussion more than strings, for example. But there are always good people in any classification, for which we remain grateful.

WARREN BENSON: I think the communication and dialogue between performers and composer is what composer and performers make of it. I'm sure it's always been reasonable, though narrow. With the resident studentship that occurs in American universities and colleges today, the physical closeness of today's performer and composer (often they live in the same building while they are studying) makes a great difference in the amount of time they spend together, the growth they achieve together, and the interest they have in each other's work at every level over a period which might extend to six or seven years at the most, and for four years as a kind of standard. This should improve things.

All of my music has been written for specific people and/or specific organizations with whom I have had some acquaintance, if not long term professional awareness. I have depended on these people for information regarding the competence of their organizations, technical details about their own performance abilities, and any special requests they might have for a work that they have commissioned.

WILLIAM BOLCOM: I have no idea whether dialogue between composers and performers is actually closer or less close than ever, as you put it. It sounds like a leading question. I enjoy working with performers and I think we work well together. My usual approach is directly to the performer's understanding of the piece; I like to work as if I were a stage director of the best kind, not telling everyone what to do so much as asking them to understand what I want. My approach to musicians is like my approach to actors.

EARLE BROWN: I think that 'the communication and dialogue between performers and composer' was probably closer in pre-classic times, before things became so formalized and 'official' and performance because such a business of pleasing the public and the concert managers, subscribers, board of directors, etc. A lot of performers and groups are rather afraid of communicating with composers of 'new' music because the people who book and/or hire them are afraid that the music will not be popular.

This attitude stands unnecessarily and unfortunately (for everyone) in the way of our having a broad LIVING art of music and an exciting dialogue with the public elements of the culture . . . visual arts, literature, philosophy, etc. I do think, however, that there is better communication at the present time than in the 40's or 50's generally speaking. (We all have our *special* performer contacts i.e. Schoenberg and Kolisch; Boulez and the Parrenin Quartet; Cage and Feldman and I with Tudor; Carter with Oppens and Jacobs; myself with Bruno Maderna, etc., but obviously the music, if it is any good, must (will) make it's way out of just personal devotions and into the more objective world.)

There is a lot of prejudice and fundamentally wrong information about mY music but with personal contact and *correct* information I have very good contacts with performers. My 'open forum' works for orchestra, (usually in time-proportional notation) were obviously very radical and new for musicians in the early 60's. There was an initial fear of the unknown and (comparatively) unpredictable (form) but with sufficient sensitive and intelligent explanation and rehearsal the orchestras almost always found themselves enjoying the proceedings and results.

My work actually provokes and extends the potential of 'dialog' between myself, and the performers; and, thank God, they usually respond sensitively and positively. I have always had much better 'communication' and understanding with the performers and the public than with the musicologists who somehow think that I'm being 'irresponsible' or trying to shoot down the musical past and future, which I am not. I *am*, however, trying to add another dimension; the score as ICON is not the only serious endeavor.

JOHN CAGE: I think there is a coming together of musicians so that it matters less than it did whether one writes, plays, or listens to music if, that is, the activity is characterized by an attention to each event and to all of its characteristics.

ROBERT CEELY: Having only lived at this time in history, it is difficult to comment on the relationship between composer and performer in any other time. Today it is completely dependent upon the circumstance and the people involved. Curiously, today there exist side by side excellent performers and absolute charlatans. An occasional superb performance is more apt to come from a small chamber group than from a Symphony Orchestra; in the same way that a good performer is most likely not a member of an established large orchestra, he is a 'free lancer.' The charlatan is that person who cannot play well in any ensemble, but by playing a certain kind of contemporary music can fake his way — if not to the top a lot further than he has any musical right to do. This fellow cannot play a dotted eighth followed by a sixteenth, but he sure can play chance music. The trouble with the charlatan is that he gives modern music a bad performance.

BARNEY CHILDS: I don't think any kind of universal judgment is possible about the degree of interaction of performers and composers, but I'd suspect that yes, there is more than before. Of course part of this has been through the breakdown of the traditional separate encapsulating of these groups, with an increased number of composers who are strong performers who compose. I have always got on well with performers, although perhaps this is a loaded answer since people who don't like my music don't usually play it, and those few who find themselves compelled to do so are professional enough to keep quiet about it.

I like to think that music (and much of it is after all written at the direct request of specific performers) gives a player a chance to enjoy the instrument, to demonstrate through the music not only the pleasure of performing but also his own skill with, and affection for, the Instrument — and in occasional passages, to challenge himself with composer demands that will stretch him a little. I'm much more pleased by a performer telling me that the piece lies well for his horn and that he enjoyed playing it than by audience or critic approval.

DAVID DIAMOND: The performers who used to perform music are now almost all dead. The younger performers are almost all lazy or interested only in first performances or in the newer notational garbs and trends. Since most are learning the standard 'chestnuts' as they make their thousands, they permit themselves performances of those new works of composers resident in cities or countries who sponsor the commissions. It is a kind of Mafia all its own. One has to examine how Glock ran the BBC in the fifties, Strobel and Boulez and the Polish Autumn Festivals, then go back and examine the programs of the ISCN. What a difference!!! My music is almost wholly ignored by the younger performers of big international contracts. I am blessed with the small communities of performers who perform what they love.

ED DIEMENTE: No. When composer/performer were one, the integration was complete. I have good, professional relationships with performers. I have learned much from them. Most of what I write is fashioned for a particular performer.

DAVID EPSTEIN: Because I've led an active second life as a conductor, I have had close and continual contact with performers, and I find this a rewarding part of being a professional musician. I've also found, in preparing performances of music and that of other contemporary composers, that accomplished performers have a very high sense of professional responsibility and standards, and are concerned to do right by a work, which also means doing right by themselves. Obviously I value these associations, and I've found that carefully planned rehearsals of new works, coupled with clear and realistic expectations of players, produces good results in the moment of truth. This is not every composer's experience, and for various and complicated reasons too numerous to go into here, except perhaps for one continual and overriding condition present whenever new music is prepared. This is the tension composers naturally feel their musical ideas, so clear and precise in their ears, don't come out that way.

On the other side of the fence, performers are under considerable pressure under these circumstances. They feel exposed, and they have not the standard of a well known style to help them play a part as the composer may have heard it. This is an unavoidable tension, and only patience and constructive work from both sides can turn it into a fruitful one. We've all seen situations where the opposite has happened. For my own part, I find this one of the challenges and pleasures of performing, as well as one of the challenges to compositional craft — to fashion music that can be facilitated and played successfully. Being involved with these situations is one of the most rewarding sides of being a musician. I thrive on it, and it has worked for me.

LUKAS FOSS: 10-15 years ago it was closer than ever. Now, composer-performer teams are less prevalent.

JAMES FULKERSON: No. It has always been close. I don't think music-making has differed too much in real terns of struggles, cooperations, collaborations, etc. through the ages. Of course, many of us are/have always been composer-performers which means that we know 'in our bones' the possibilities and shortcomings of the various instruments and instrumentalists. Still, I spent 1978 and part of 1979 as composer-in-residence at the Victorian College of the Arts in Melbourne, Australia where I collaborated extensively with cellist Sarah Hopkins; conductor, John Hopkins; and many fine players among the staff and students. For me, it was a prolific and inspiring time which I wish could go on forever. Contemporary music-making happens among players irregardless of when the music was composed or improvised. It's that magic in the moment which imparts the import . . . (almost quotable).

GEORGE HEUSSENSTAMM: Composers and performers should see themselves living in a symbiotic relationship with one another. I have the greatest respect and admiration for performers, and when I place a score before them, I think of it as an act of friendship, not the instigation of a bitter fight. I suspect that the composer/performer relationship is on better footing than in the past. Performers seem more willing to communicate, willing to join in exploration with you, willing to take chances with you. I recall with pleasure the many sessions I have had with performers, hashing out the problems of performance technique and listening intently to their well-directed advice.

KAREL HUSA: I am not sure if communications today are closer, as I believe devoted performers existed in times of Mozart, Brahms, Janacek, Ives, and others, but I have the feeling that the relations between the performer and composer are on a more democratic, friendly basis. We can see the change in today's orchestras: the conductor and players have a different relationship than in the past. I am not criticizing those conductors, on the contrary, I am impressed by their achievements, but it seems impossible today to work the same way. I find myself getting more when I work in a friendly atmosphere and in mutual respect and understanding. After all I, as a conductor and composer, am grateful to the performers when they devote their energy and enthusiasm for music they do not know yet.

JEAN EICHELBERGER IVEY: I think this is an individual matter. Teaching at Peabody, where we have many excellent performers both faculty and students, I find my contacts with performers much better than they used to be — and living in New York helps in this regard too. In the past I have lived in some geographically isolated places where I had much less contact. I find working with groups very rewarding. I like to write pieces for particular performers or groups, tailor made to them, to participate in rehearsals, to get the performers' comments and reactions, and so on. I think this kind of interaction is very important for composition students too, and the possibility of its taking place is one of the values of studying composition in a professional school as opposed to doing so in a school that does not stress performance. I also think it is important to be, or have been, a performer to some extent at least. I view with misgiving any would be composer who has not become proficient in any performing medium, because I think he is missing important insight into performance problems and is less likely to write well for performers.

KARL KORTE: Are communication between performer and composer closer? I'm not really sure. There are many fine performers commissioning new works but frequently they seem most interested in works that primarily demonstrate their virtuosity for special effects. Musically this is often self-limiting. On the other hand we don't seem to have many conductors (like Koussevitzky) championing our cause through the constant commissioning, performance, and, more importantly, repeat performance of new works.

ANDREAS MAKRIS: No, I feel they are further apart than ever. In the old days a composer was first a musician and because of his unusual talent he became creative by composing, but without leaving his original occupation of playing an instrument, singing, conducting , etc. Presently, one finds quite often young students occupied with composition without proving themselves as having any ability or unusual talent in playing and performing an instrument. The result is usually a tragic event of isolation between composer and performer, and the tower of this isolation is built by the composer himself. He begins to write theoretical music, something that is often called by the professional performer a 'paper music.' Then the schism of the relationship begins. The composer takes the position that the performers 'have not reached the intellectual level to understand his music' while the performers complain that the composer does not have the sufficient knowledge of the instrument he is writing for. In my personal experience, some 90% of the isolation between composer and performer is the result of the actions of the composer rather than that of the performer. As for the second part of the question, I must say that I personally have had the finest relationship with performers of music. Perhaps this is so because of unique position. Presently, I am Composer In Residence of the National Symphony Orchestra as well as a first violinist of that group, and most of my works have been premiered by the National Symphony Orchestra. Naturally the musicians feel a special empathy to premiere a work composed by one of their colleagues, and I have found them most cooperative. Furthermore, because of the constant contact I have with the orchestra, I think I know what the complications of the instruments are as well as the possible problems which I try to avoid. Quite often, if I have questions in one of my passages about its practicality of being performed, I am not ashamed to ask colleagues to play it for me backstage before I put it in my score. I have found that this not only expands knowledge, but also gives a pride to the performer who eventually gives his best in the premiere.

PRISCILLA MCLEAN: Only recently have I lived in a location where good performers were either plentiful or available. I like to explore new sound possibilities on instruments, which means having the performer there with me experimenting. I have been heavily into electronics the last few years, and am only now getting back to instruments, now that I live in Austin where there are some eager performers.

VINCENT PERSICHETTI: I write for the angels above.

ELLIOTT SCHWARTZ: Yes, I feel that composers and performers are closely allied (assuming we're speaking of the kind of performer who enjoys 20th-century music to begin with!) . . . many composers (myself included) are performing more and more frequently as touring artists, and a number of outstanding avant-garde performers — Bert Turetzky, Allen Blustine, Jerry Bunke, Jack Glick, Dwight Peltzer, and other soloists. Ensembles from the most distinguished new music groups to junior high school bands, have also been great fun to rehearse with. If their response is positive, that's probably the most gratifying aspect of my work as a composer.

HALSEY STEVENS: My association and work with performers have generally been amiable and reasonably productive. I like to be present at rehearsals of a new work; once it has been 'set,' there is no longer a need for the composer's presence.

FRED TILLIS: I) no, 2) I prefer a close working relationship between composer and performer.

#9. What sources of funding are you aware of for composers (commissions, foundations, federal and local government grants)?

T. J. ANDERSON: In addition to those listed in your question the largest source of funding continues to be at the sacrifice of the composers themselves.

LESLIE BASSETT: Funding can come from BMI and ASCAP, grants from various endowments (federal, state, and private), commissions, awards (National Institute of Arts and Letters, for example), income from publishers, fees for public appearances, speeches, guest composer visits, conducting one's own music, appearing as soloist in one's own music, salaries as teachers, professors, publishers, editors, professional performers, film writers, etc., copying grants.

WARREN BENISON: Sources of funding listed such as commissions, foundations, federal and local government grants might be supplemented by the faculty study grants that are given at certain state universities.

WILLIAM BOLCOM: I can tell you what I've been granted: (as far as I can remember)

    2 National Endowments

    1 New York State CAPS grant

    A Koussevitzsky Fdtn. Award

    Several from organists: AGO, Holtkamp, private sources

    American Choral Foundation

    A commission given jointly by the Seattle Symphony and PONCHO
      (a Seattle-based fund)

    Fromm Foundation

    Rackham Foundation (Univ of Michigan)

    etc. etc.

Many times a performing organization or player will find funds and not tell me how they are found, or I won't make a note of it. My W2s go to the taxman so quickly that I don't look too carefully at them.

EARLE BROWN: The same sources you mention.

JOHN CAGE: It seems to me that there are many more sources of funding than there were formerly. I sit on several boards. Many institutions are actively interested in supporting cultural life in America, and do so without being asked.

ROBERT CEELY: Every composer has the same list. Why bother to ask for it? A silly question.

BARNEY CHILDS: The usual: NEA and Guggenheim; one's state arts council (if one lives in such a state.); smaller foundations; university, group, and individual commissions. I believe there are occasional business firms that have commissioned music. Unfortunately the Bicentennial used up about ten years' worth of commission funds!

DAVID DIAMOND: National endowment. In general, a fiasco.

ED DIEMENTE: I have had very little success in funding from foundations. I, therefore, do not think I am the best person to answer this question.

LUKAS FOSS: All of these.

JAMES FULKERSON: Commissions and university funded chairs of composition (or composer-in-residencies when no teaching is involved). There are various grants but I don't really know what they are.

GEORGE HEUSSENSTAMM: The NEA was kind enough to confer a Fellowship grant upon me in 1976. That, hopefully, will continue to be a source of assistance. Then there are Guggenheim, Fromm, Alice M. Ditson, a couple of colonies, then I begin to run dry. The Ford Foundation was active in the early '70s funding the recording of contemporary American music; it's a pity they aren't doing more in the way of direct aid to composers today. The State of California, regrettably, has not yet become aware of the composers living on its soil.

KAREL HUSA: There are numerous sources of funding for composers today. It would be long to enumerate them, they are listed in many music magazines, notices are given periodically by American Music Center and other composer's societies; Musical America lists them in the annual issue, etc. I think possibilities for American composers, especially young artists, are very good and it should be so. What a difference, compared with some seventy years ago, when there were practically no commissions and not many grants .

JEAN EICHELBERGER IVEY: I think I'm aware of most funding sources. I applied for the National Endowment Grant every other year since they started, till I got one in 1978 for <u>Sea-Change</u>, the orchestra piece mentioned in #6. The grant, for a work for large orchestra lasting between 15 and 20 minutes was a somewhat unrealistic $3,000. Not enough to take a year off from teaching — which I had hoped for — or to have the score and parts both copied; still, good to have.

I've also applied for a NY State grant every year since they started, and the Guggenheim about 10 times, so far to no avail. I've applied for the advanced Fulbright several times and was named an alternate this year, but did not get it. I cannot help observing a strong tendency to favor men in all of these. This year, for instance, as so often in the past, not one Guggenheim grant in composition went to a woman. Since we have many fine, well-qualified women composers, and since not one item or service costs any less to a woman than to a man, I hope these grantors will soon recognize that a group comprising half the human race should be represented by about half the grants. Women, like men, need money!

KARL KORTE: None that everyone else isn't aware of as well.

ANDREAS MAKRIS: In this country there are many fundings for the composers, starting with the National Endowment for the Arts, Symphony Orchestra commissions, small local competitions, etc. which I am not going to list here. One can find such information through libraries. I would say though that the healthiest contact for a composer and perhaps the most successful as far as hearing his music is a commission from the Symphony Orchestras. If one receives money from some source to compose, fine, but one is not guaranteed that he will hear his work performed unless a Symphony Orchestra asked him to compose.

PRISCILLA MCLFAN: Probably the same ones that everyone else is aware of! NEA, Guggenheim, American Music Center copying grant, Martha Baird Rockefeller. A few ones for woman composers are popping up — read the AMC Newsletter or ASUC Newsletter (wouldn't this question be better if all answers were consolidated as in a survey??).

VINCENT PERSICHETTI: All sources.

ELLIOTT SCHWARTZ: Those I'm most familiar with include the state and federal agencies that support new pieces (such as the NEA Composer-librettist program), the big foundation grants — Guggenheim, American Academy in Rome, etc. — that provide full income for a fixed period, the 'colonies' which offer room and board you're working on a project, either free or for a small charge. The latter include MacDowell Colony, Yaddo, and the Composers Cottage at Wolf Trap (all of which I've attended); the Rockefeller Foundation's Study Center at Bellagio, Italy (where I will be in 1980); estates run by the Camargo foundation in France, Wurlitzer Fund in Taos, N.M., Sweetbriar College in Virginia (where I've not been).

The 'Meet the Composer' Fund of New York will support your appearances (to lecture, perform, attend rehearsals, etc.) on a matching basis, but only in certain eastern U.S. states. I wish that were a national program! Martha Baird Rockefeller Fund will support publication or recording projects, up to a limited amount. And the American Music Center has just established a program to support, on a matching basis, the commissioning of works for solo performer. (The soloist applies for the grant, I believe.) This is hardly a complete list, but it gives some idea of the total support available. It says nothing about outright commissions, or prizes awarded at festivals, or fellowships for study!

HALSEY STEVENS: I have no knowledge of sources for funding other than those that are common knowledge — HEW, Guggenheim, Rockefeller, etc., etc. One thing provides a note of optimism: I conclude that far more individuals and performing groups, from small ensembles to orchestras, are commissioning music for their own use. That can be only beneficial to the art.

FRED TILLIS: National Endowments for the Arts. Rockefeller and Ford Foundations and many others.

#10. What was a recent performance, composition, or recording that you found particularly special, unique, and/or exciting?

T. J. ANDERSON: In the spring of 1978, I had a retrospective concert of my music performed at Richard Hunt's studio in Chicago, Illinois. That following fall a 50th year celebration of my music was performed at the Longy School of Music in Cambridge, Mass. Both concerts were well received and participating performers were excellent.

LESLIE BASSETT: I've been much attracted to Bill Bolcom's *House*, Bill Albright's *Five Chromatic Dances*, Maxwell-Davies *8 Songs for a Mad King* to name just a few. There are many others, since a lot of fine music is being written now — whether or not the critics know it or not.

WARREN BENSON: I found all of my most recent performances particularly special, unique and exciting, although not always in ways I had predicted nor even in ways that I liked. I always view the next one that's liable to be the most special, unique, and/or exciting!

WILLIAM BOLCOM: The most recent performance is always the most exciting. Recently I've been happy with several, so I'll single out one: on a McKim Fund from the Library of Congress I wrote a violin and piano sonata, which Sergiu Luca and I premiered at the Coolidge Auditorium. We were very nervous (January 12th was the date) and the tape, which has been broadcast, shows this, but all in all I am happy with the performance. Luca is not only capable of the technical side of his part, his interpretation was rich and satisfying.

EARLE BROWN: The most recent "special, unique and/or exciting" performance was a "retrospective" of my work, presented by Radio France (Paris), by the 'Nouvel Orchestre Philharmonique,' on Jan. 27, 1979. Performances of *Available Forms I* (1961); *December 1952* (1952) with orchestra; *New Piece* (1971); *Sign Sounds* (1972); *Corroboree* (1964); and *Twenty Five Pages* (1953).

JOHN CAGE: I live, at least I try, from day to day and my work is generally in many directions all at the same time. For instance: I write this from Köln on the 31st of May. Tomorrow I go to the Hague to give 3 performances with the Merce Cunningham Dance Company as part of the Holland Festival; then I return to Germany for the Festival of my music in Bonn, June 6-10, which will include the first complete performance of *Empty Words* ($11^{1/2}$ hours through the night) and the first performance of *Hymns and Variations* and the first European performance of *Renga with Apartment House 1776;* then I go for a month with John and Monika Fulleman to collect ambient sounds and music in Ireland; then to IRCAM in Paris with the Fullemans to make *Roaratorio* (a radio play with music) for the West German Radio, The Dutch Catholic Radio, the South German Radio, and IRCAM; then I return to New York to continue work on the violin etudes. Then the etudes are finished I plan to make others for recorders with Pete Rose.

ROBERT CEELY: Every recording is unique, some are special, and a very few are exciting.

BARNEY CHILDS: David Maslanka's *Concerto for Piano, Winds, and Percussion*.

DAVID DIAMOND: The re-issue of my *Fourth Symphony* on New World Records.

ED DIEMENTE: An informal gathering in a home near Ivar Mikhashoff played the piano. His selections varied from Debussy, Ravel, to Feldman, Wolff, and the contemporary waltzes from the C.F. Peters volume. Many of the works were provocative. The playing was magnificent.

LUKAS FOSS: Performances of *Speculum Musicum*, by the American Composers Orchestra and by the Brooklyn Philharmonic often excite me. As to my own work, the Group for Contemporary Music did a beautiful performance of my most difficult piece *Echoi*. The Buffalo Evenings for New Music gave a masterly reading of my recent *13 Ways of Looking at a Blackbird,* and the Cleveland Orchestra performed brilliantly in the premiere of my *Quintets for Orchestra*.

JAMES FULKERSON: Real highs for me have been 1) attending 6 weeks of masterclasses by the Dutch cellist, Anner Bylsma; 2) rehearsing and conducting the premiere of my own *Concerto for Amplified Cello*; 3) attending the final piece of mine which was about to be recorded; 4) listening to a recording of the Debussy *Sonata* to be by Rostropovitch/ Britten, and 5) hearing a new recording by Demetrius Stratos — vocal solo — terrific experience (Cramps, Milano, Italia).

GEORGE HEUSSENSTAMM: Probably the premiere of my *Brass Quintet No. 3*, as performed by the American Brass Quintet concert of the 75th Anniversary Season of the Coleman Concerts in Pasadena. The work, written on a fine commission from the Coleman Association, was magnificently performed, and was followed by a smashing banquet honoring the players and the composer. That one will stick in the memory.

KAREL HUSA: I assume you mean a performance of my composition? This past spring, 1979, I have conducted the performance of *An American Te Deum* for chorus, baritone solo and wind ensemble with the Eastman Wind Ensemble, Cornell Choruses, and Mark E. Johnson, soloist. It was finally the performance, the way I have imagined when I wrote it, and, under the best circumstances. Not that the preceding performances were not good, but it is rare that all factors come together to make it nearly perfect; sometimes the hall is not satisfactory, another time the chorus is small, or not sufficient rehearsal time is available, microphone for the narrator not properly adjusted, or performers — including the conductor — make too many mistakes, etc.

At the end of each of the eleven performances you say to yourself: 'This was not my music,' or 'this was far from what I wrote', or 'this is what I thought it should sound like.' It reminds me what Stravinsky said to Dr. Heinrich Strobel (Director of Music at Sudwestfunk Radio in Germany): 'only one out of ten performances of compositions is *very* good.'

JEAN EICHELBERGER IVEY: Last fall I heard *Déserts* live for the first time, on an all-Varèse concert given by the Peabody Contemporary Music Ensemble conducted by Frederik Prausnitz, a conductor who was closely associated with Varèse in his lifetime. Also present was Otto Luening. Both these men spoke on the occasion about Varèse as they remembered him. *Deserts* is, of course, a classic. I have heard it many times on records often playing it for my classes, and also heard the NY Philharmonic play it on the radio years ago when I was living in Kansas. As with any work that combines live performers with tape, it made a lot of difference to hear it live. It was also wonderful to note that a work once considered quite inaccessible was now being well played by student performers, and seemed perfectly accessible to an audience consisting largely of Peabody and Hopkins students.

KARL KORTE: Too many to list.

ANDREAS MAKRIS: Listening and seeing for the first time in my life, Rostropovich conducting a Tchaikovsky Symphony, it was such a unique and exciting emotional experience which I shall never forget.

BARTON MCLEAN: Wow. Glad you asked that. My wife Priscilla and I are currently putting together 13 NEA-funded programs, and I am also submissions coordinator for ASUC radio, recording, journal of scores projects, all of which means that we get a large number of new pieces. Curtis Curtis-Smith's *Unisonics* sax and piano is outstanding — a strong original, compelling piece. Leslie Bassett's *Concerto for 2 Pianos and Orchestra* is dynamic. John Watt's *Chimney* for trumpet and tape is incredibly sensuous, and his MAS based on Gagaku oriental sounds is sensitive and beautiful. Dave Cope's *Glassworks* done at San Diego for two pianos is shattering, especially with multimedia effects.

Priscilla McLean's *Invisible Chariots* is, in my opinion, one of the great electronic works of all time. Works by students Reed Holmes (*Nova* for quad tape, winner of the Jersey State festival), Kevin Hanlon (*Piece for Alto Sax and Tape Delays* and *Through to the End of the Tunnel* winner of the Sonevera competition (*Suite* for 12 flutes) are first rate.

Karl Korte's *Fibers* for wind ensemble is powerful and strong. Reynold Wiedenaar's *Tinsel Chicken Coop* and its *Sequel* are among the most works since the best of Spike Jones. Sid Hodkinson's November *Voices* is deeply moving. Berio's *Concerto for 2 Pianos* is a masterpiece, and Stockhausen's *Signs of the Zodiac* featuring as it does single instruments in a suite-like fashion is mind boggling for the freshness and sheer invention that he imparts to a form that is rather worn. I could go on and on. This is the most exciting time for creating music in the whole history of man.

PRISCILLA MCLEAN: David Maslanka has just written a new piece for the Arthur Weisburg Ensemble finished at the MacDowell Colony in July where I saw the score, which looks very interesting. Also his *Concerto for Piano and Symphonic Wind Ensemble*. Some new exciting piano works I have heard in connection with the radio series I produce are: Ann Silsbee's *Doors*, Samuel Pellman's *Silent Night* for prepared piano and Stephen Scott's *Music for Bowed Strings III*. I have been very impressed with the CRI recordings of Curtis-Smith, and the 2 piano concerto of Leslie Bassett when it was played in Kennedy Center in May. Also Barton McLean's *Dimensions II* (piano and tape) and his work-in-progress *Mysteries from the Ancient Nahuatl* for large chorus, electronics, soloists, narrator, and ensemble. And William Albright's *Organbook III,* performed at the University of Kansas Symposium in February. I could continue on and on — there is so much new exciting music!

VINCENT PERSICHETTI: The New-Art String Quartet's recording of my four *String Quartets*.

ELLIOTT SCHWARTZ: This spring (1979) I attended the premiere of a work for winds, brass and percussion called *Scatter*, commissioned and performed by a terrific wind ensemble at Bishop Ireton High School in Alexandria, Virginia, conducted by Garwood Whaley. Those were really very talented, responsive, and openminded kids. Later this spring and summer, I've been recording my own music in New York and California with good friends Bert Turetzky, Jerry Bunke, Leonard Raver, and new friend Allen Dean. The musicianship and high level of creative energy were outstanding at those sessions; we hope those qualities shine through the finished records.

ROBERT STARER: The most enjoyable recent experience with performers was working on my new opera with members of the Minnesota Opera Company, an excellent group devoted to producing new works.

HALSEY STEVENS: Question ambiguous. Does this refer to recent performance of music of mine, or of others? In any case, I have no special nomination; I derive satisfaction from music of many kinds, having no preconceived notions as to style or content.

I do not measure music by its speciality, uniqueness, or excitement, though of course all of these contribute to the whole effect. Of my own music, I am generally stimulated most by the most recent work, especially if it comes hot off the draughting table and has not had time to cool before performance.

FRED TILLIS: Monks of Tibet.

19.

INTERVIEW WITH GORDON MUMMA
David Cope

Gordon Mumma was among the first composers to employ circuitry of his own design in composition and performance. A prolific composer and a virtuoso performer on French horn, his work is known for the integration of advanced electroacoustic principles. Mumma has termed his approach "cybersonic" and has applied it to a wide range of compositions including *Hornpipe*, ectroacoustic music for cybersonic French Horn, and *Arbivex*, a surrogate myoelecfronic telemetering system with pairs of performing appendages.

"Hornpipe is an interactive live-electronic work for solo hornist, cybersonic console, and a performance space. The hornist performs with various techniques on a valveless waldhorn and a standard "French horn." These techniques include a traditional embouchure, and the production of multiphonics with special double-reeds.

The cybersonic console, attached to the hornist's belt, has microphones with which it 'hears' the sounds made by the hornist and the acoustical resonances of the space. The electronic circuitry of the console analyzes the acoustical resonances of the space, and responds interactively with the hornist. The console is connected by an umbilical cable to a stereophonic sound system, so that its responses are heard from loudspeakers.

The cybersonic console has several functions. First, it makes an electronic map of the acoustical resonances of the space. This is achieved during the first few minutes of the performance by eight electronically resonant circuits that become automatically tuned to the acoustical resonances of the space.

Second, each circuit has a memory that accumulates information about its resonant condition. Technically, this condition is determined from the frequency (f) and the resonant efficiency (Q) of the circuit.

Third, when sufficient information is obtained, a VCA (voltage controlled amplifier) for each circuit is gated on, sending its electronically resonant response through the umbilical to the loudspeakers. Because each of the eight resonant circuits is somewhat independent, and has different memory and gating characteristics, these responses can occur in many different combinations.

A performance of Hornpipe begins as a solo, without electronic sound. When the responses of the cybersonic console are heard from the loudspeakers, the hornist can then interact with the electronic map of the cybersonic console. By playing sounds which reinforce the electronic map, the hornist can increase the responses of the cybersonic console.

The performer's choice of anti-resonant sounds strongly influences the continuity of a performance. Without the reinforcement of its original electronic map, the cybersonic console gradually makes a new map representing the hornist's anti-resonant sounds. In other words, having interacted with the responses of the cybersonic console, and learned the electronic map of the acoustical resonances of the space, the hornist can choose sounds which deceive the console into thinking it is in a different performance space. After the cybersonic console has developed a new map (of the hornist's anti-resonant sounds), it no longer responds to the natural acoustical resonances of the space. The performance of Hornpipe has evolved from an introductory solo, through an ensemble between hornist, cybersonic console, and performance space, to a concluding solo section for horn.

20.

INTERVIEW WITH STEVE REICH
Andrew R. Brown

Brown: What is the order of commissioning and writing in your process?

Reich: *The Cave* had seven co-commissioners. Basically *Three Tales* is Beryl Korot's and my second video opera and many of these same people were interested in it because they were interested in the previous work. With a few exceptions, I have been writing for the last twenty odd years or so what I wanted to write and then trying to find people to commission it. I don't really write pieces I wouldn't otherwise write just because of a commission. If someone asks me for a piece I have no interest in, I simply don't accept the commission.

Brown: To what extent does your understanding of the commissioners' expectations guide the work you write?

Reich: If I write for the Kronos Quartet or Pat Metheny or Richard Stolzman, these musicians and their performing style inspire what I write for them. As to organizations and festivals, these are generally people who are going to trust me. I think I've got to the point where people will know what I've done and expect that hopefully I'll do something that they will like, although they're not going to know the details until it's finished.

I've also become aware of how I work and how to keep my own fires burning. I want to keep those fires stoked because that's in everybody's best interest.

Brown: So you've developed a level of trust that you won't do something quite different from what you've previously done.

Reich: As a matter of fact, I always do something different from what I've previously done. I don't think that if you listened to *Piano Phase* that you would have predicted *Music for 18 Musicians*, and I don't think that if you listened to *Music for 18 Musicians,* that you would have predicted *Different Trains*, and so on. As a matter of fact, commissioners hope for that. I'm not the only one. As an artist interested in other artists, I'm interested in them for their body of work. For instance, I want to hear whatever new piece Arvo Pärt or Michael Gordon does. I'm interested in their music and if one piece comes along that I don't like, well I'm interested to hear the next one.

Brown: Do you have a clear idea of the intended audience for your work?

Reich: I don't have any intended audience, I never had an intended audience. When I'm writing music, I'm pleasing myself and I've always hoped that if I love it, you'll love it too, and thank heavens that's worked out to be the case. When I was very young I could have told you who my audience was. In 1967, I could have told you which people came to the Park Place Gallery to hear my first concerts there in New York City. They were mainly dancers, choreographers, painters, and sculptors, with very few composers, mostly jazz and downtown types. But now I can't possibly tell who is in the audience and I'm delighted that that's the case.

Brown: So you write to please yourself?

Reich: Any composer works from this basic principle. Are they going to do market research? In their studio they're doing what they're doing and if they're excited about it and they love it, and if they're fairly normal human beings and their receptors are in more-or-less working order, then hopefully there will be some other people who feel the same way.

Brown: Can you describe you compositional environment?

Reich: Well, I have two studios, one in New York and one in Vermont. They are both very similar and both small. I'm sitting in the one in Vermont now and there's a Baldwin Hamilton upright piano in each of them, and a vibraphone and marimba in each, a sampling keyboard in each. Then on the other side of the room is a Macintosh computer. Basically that's about it. I have a MIDI time piece AV that I use to keep synchronization when I'm working with Beryl. When I'm writing pieces of music by myself I don't need it. I also have a set of loudspeakers, amplifier, and mixer.

Brown: And you've been working with the Finale software for some years now.

Reich: Well, actually I still work with pencil and paper, I go back and forth between the computer and the piano where there is a music notebook. But the music notebooks take a lot longer to fill up now than before I started working with computer. I got my first Macintosh in 1986. A couple of years earlier, my son, who I guess was about eight years of age at the time, wanted an Apple II because all of his friends had one.

So we finally broke down and got him one and it was the first computer that entered the house. When I was looking for software for him, I noticed that there was a little music program that did four part notation and I bought it and fooled around with it and thought "Well, you know, it's pretty lame, but it's interesting and maybe one day it will really be something." I actually got to know Christopher Yavelow who was a kind of Mac fanatic and at the time wrote some articles about explaining what a Macintosh could do, and in those days there was Professional Composer.

I began in 1986 with Professional Composer to save money. I had just finished *Desert Music*, and the entire commission fee had gone from my bank account to the copyist's bank account. I didn't like losing all that money and I can't stand proofreading. He [Yavelow] said, "Look, if you get the score correct in Professional Composer, then when you're extracting the parts you don't have to proofread them."

I could hardly believe that, but I printed out some parts for *Four Sections*. I used Professional Composer for *Four Sections*. In those days, the ties were so poor and the printing was so poor that I simply put the score in without any curved lines, no slurs, and no ties, and had my copyist fill those in by hand so it was a kind of hybrid. But when the San Francisco Symphony played it, the principal second violinist came up to me and said, "Man those are beautiful parts, who published them? No mistakes and gorgeous." Well I said, "That's it, I'm hooked."

At that point I was simply using the notation program, and then someone else said to me that the same company makes this terrific program called Performer which you can use like a tape recorder for MIDI. I'd been basically working with multitrack tape from the beginning.

When I did *Piano Phase*, I was literally recording myself on piano, playing back a tape loop, and then playing with the loop, so it goes way back. So I became interested in Performer back around 1987 or 1988. Then, of course, one thing leads to another and I guess the real breakthrough was *Different Trains*, where I realized that if I worked on it on tape I'd still be working on it, my fingernails would be bleeding.

It was really a piece to be done on computer, and I did that on a Mac Plus running Professional Composer and occasionally Performer, and using these samplers that Casio had given me. So that was a real eye and ear opener. *Different Trains* gave me the idea of doing an opera that I actually believed in. Commissions for operas had been proposed to me in the late 70s and early 80s, first by the Holland Festival and later by the Frankfurt Opera. I was very flattered, but I didn't have an opera in me. I don't care for that form, and nothing to say there. Then I thought to myself "This is insane, how come I don't at least have some alternative?"

But I really had nothing, so I simply shrugged my shoulders and went about doing what I did those days. With *Different Trains* I thought, well if you could see the people that you were hearing, if it were on video tape instead of audio tape and you could see the musicians on stage playing the speech melody of what was being said, well then there would be the possibility of the kind of opera I would be interested in. And since I knew this extremely good video artist Beryl Korot, and since she was willing, *The Cave* resulted. Syncing with video, of course, put me heavily into using Performer at that point. I switched from Professional Composer to Finale for scoring and I am still using it.

Brown: So it's clear that technology, both computers and video, has had an influence on your direction in terms of the possibilities they afford.

Reich: Yes. I came to be known to the public in the late sixties through two recordings, one was *Come Out*, a tape piece which came out on CBS Odyssey in 1967. Then they did a record of my music on Columbia Masterworks in 1969 which included *Violin Phase* and *It's Gonna Rain*, both of which involved tape. So my involvement with technology in the sense of tape goes back to the beginning of my public life. Obviously, I was a music student. I didn't know about tape recording. Then I was far away from technology.

After the tape pieces I felt that I didn't want to spend my life making tapes and if the process of phasing didn't work with live human beings playing instruments, then it was merely a gimmick; which is something I still believe. So the result was *Piano Phase* and all the other pieces leading to *Drumming*, which was the last of the phase pieces. The whole phasing process was basically discovered with technology, taking the differentiation in speed between two tape recorders and transferring that to human beings, which is an unusual way of composing different direction than people mostly move.

Brown: There is more often a desire to have technology imitate a human action or process, but you have done the reverse with performed phase pieces.

Reich: I began to realize that the phasing process was just like *"Row, Row, Row Your Boat"* or "Frere Jacques." It's a round or canon except that the distance between voice one and voice two is flexible, constantly in motion. That then expressed itself in a lot of live pieces up to *Drumming* in 1971. I really felt that the only electronics I was interested in were microphones, amplifiers, and loudspeakers.

Basically that's all I worked with from 1971 to 1988.

I did *Four Organs* in 1970 for the four electric organs, and that was a pain in the neck when we were touring. We knew the marimbas would work, the glockenspiels would work, the drums were fine, but the electric organs were always broken. We carried five of them so we could get four that worked, but sometimes two of them would be broken. That kind of thing gets to you and I began to move further and further away from technology.

I have a dislike of synthesizers; there's not a synthesizer that's been built that I can stand. I would occasionally use a DX7 as a marriage of convenience to double the brass in *Desert Music* so that when they were taking a breath there wouldn't be a hole in a long-held chord. I used them in *Sextet* because I knew I was going to tour the piece and if I used English horns and clarinets then I would have had four more musicians, ten instead of six, so I made do.

It was a marriage of convenience not a marriage of love. If I want something that sounds like a violin I use a violin, I don't want to use an electronic imitation. The *sampler* is another whole world. The *sampler* allows you to bring your voice, my voice, the sound of slamming doors, or what-have-you into the music. Because the interface is a keyboard, it's easy to bring it in on the 'and' of three of the fifteenth bar by just playing. So that was tremendously exciting, and that resulted in *Different Trains*. *Different Trains* was like a line in the sand. *Different Trains*, in one sense, goes back to the early tape pieces, and at the same time, instead of it being speech that almost sounds like music, it was actually doubled and developed by string quartet. That piece was done at a time when I also decided I was not going to write for orchestra any more. Indeed, I haven't and I don't plan to. That piece was a real turning point for me. In a sense I went back to a lot of the things I had been interested in when I was younger, with the sampling keyboard as the sort of open sesame.

Brown: In your work, there is still a performance going on, even when players trigger samples.

Reich: That's what interests me; performance. My music is written overwhelmingly for standard western acoustic instruments that are just amplified. But sometimes I write for a MIDI percussion pad which is an instrument which has no acoustical sound except a thud which sounds like a very metallic marimba or xylophone. That's still performance, but quite different than even *New York Counterpoint* played on clarinet.

Brown: You have an early history of purely electronic tape phase pieces that influenced later live performance works.

Reich: Well I did tape pieces in 1965 and 1966 and never again. I think what interests me is that electronic music can be seen as a kind of stream feeding into the live music river. There are a lot of new ideas that one would never have by pursuing the history of performed music east or west, which can be suggested by electronic equipment and then fed back into live performance.

Brown: How do you find working with sampled speech where timing is quite set, compared with a musical phrase which is unrestricted?

Reich: *Three Tales* is much more oriented to the music throughout. So even if I have some sampled material I change it to fit the key, and so on, even to fit the timing. The music comes first and the sampled material is made to fit the music. I slow down a radio announcer's voice in *Hindenburg* to 12 times its original length, and that floats over the music which stays in tempo.

Now, I'm not letting the music be determined by the speech. Earlier, in *The Cave* and *Different Trains*, whatever the speech sample was, the music had to come out of that. In *Three Tales* it's just the opposite, music first.

Brown: In the same way that the tape machine influenced your work, would you say that the sampler influenced it in similarly powerful ways?

Reich: Without the possibility of sampling, I wouldn't have done *Different Trains*, and without doing *Different Trains* I wouldn't have thought of any solution to music theatre that I would have been interested in. So the idea of working with video was opened because of sampling. There can be a really tight synchronization between the sound and music. To put it in movie terms, when I go to movies I'm not interested in the mood music; I'm interested in the synchronized sound track — the traffic, the people talking, the clicking of heels off the pavement, that's my sound track — as to the movie music, that doesn't interest me at all.

Brown: So the computer is used for note-by-note details and sound manipulations. How do you work with large scale structures and form?

Reich: Well, it depends. In *Three Tales*, Beryl and I had meetings and we sketched out the entire piece. Earlier on, I remember with *Music for 18 Musicians*, the macro level was done when the eleven initial pulsing chords were done, and I said 'This is the basis for a short section of the piece. I'm going to take each one and make it a middle register drone.' When I did *Desert Music*, I finally got the text extracts that I wanted and I literally arranged the text pages on the marimba until they were in an order I liked and I said 'that's the form of the piece.'

Similarly with *Telhillim*, I took the psalm fragments and arranged them. Any piece of mine that is set to text uses an arrangement of the text as the form. However, *Proverb* was different. But I wanted *Proverb* to be different. I wanted to go to something that would use a very short text that would be more musically developed; in the case of *Proverb*, a long augmentation canon. In the last few years I'm less interested in the discursiveness in a piece. I mean, *The Cave* was the extreme of discursiveness, and now I want to get back *Three Tales* to a more aphoristic, oblique treatment of text so that less is said, and it is developed over a longer period of time and therefore more meanings come out of it.

Brown: So what are the techniques you are using for developing meaning in *Hindenburg*?

Reich: An augmentation canon as in *Proverb*. The first movement of *Hindenburg* is basically taking one short text, it could not have been a technical matter, setting it one way, setting it another next way, then setting it a third way. The third way begins and ends by expanding rhythmically and I've found that to be enormously interesting. What happens with the augmentation canon in *Proverb* and in *Hindenburg* is a slowing down of the text. I knew very early on (in the 1970s) that slow motion sound was going to be interesting, but I've finally figured out exactly what that is: augmentation canon, and a parallel augmenting of the sound material to go with that. I'm very interested in that, and *Hindenburg* will end the way it began with a radio announcer's voice from those days saying something like, "Hindenburg is gone, but from her ashes will arise the knowledge." Which says a lot, you know, the tone of voice and everything. And the singers will probably be singing some part of that text as well. I'm very fond, as you know, of arch forms, and this piece will also be an arch.

Brown: Do you think of composing in terms of uncovering music or constructing music?

Reich: I am totally a composer in the traditional sense of the word: I mean, using my volition. But even when you're using your volition, for instance, the first thing that anybody does may have a lot going for it, and it may not. But the first shot, you never want to dismiss too easily.

There have been isolated instances of the other alternatives you were talking about, of discovering something, and making that be the "guiding light" as it were. That was true in *The Cave* in the sense in which the tonal center of the first two movements is in A minor, because of two happenstances. Number one, the drone inside *The Cave* space (that large empty Mosque space) is, because of its physics, its construction, reinforcing A and when you're in there has an A minor feel to it. Then after recording the chanted phrases from the Koran I got back to the piano and found out that the voice was, low and behold, in A minor. So I said, "Well that's it" because the aesthetic in *The Cave* and in *Different Trains* was, "Whatever people say I have to follow what they say." If I don't like it I can get something else, but I can't change its pitch. So that gave me the information since I knew that both first and second movements would take a trip to that place geographically. I figured that was my target, A minor. That's the exception which proves the rule. I am not the Marcel Duchamp of music. Maybe John Cage is. The early tape pieces, *It's Gonna Rain* and *Come Out*, are they found objects? Yes they are. But I must have gone through ten hours of tapes to find "come out, to show them." At times it's like picking up a pebble on the beach. But it's like hours and hours on the beach to find exactly what you're looking for. Then once I found it, it went through a meticulous process and there were lots of rejects that went either too fast or too slow. So, yes, it's accepting some things and also working out a lot of things as well.

There was tension in the earlier pieces between letting it be and doing something to it, and there was more letting-it-be up to about *Music for 18 Musicians*. My composing gets more volitional with *Music for 18 Musicians* and after that. I'd say *Pendulum Music* was my piece closest to Cage. It's audible sculpture, it's whatever happens. But again the situation of the pendulums is highly set up.

Brown: How does the sampled material relate to the musical direction in *Three Tales*?

Reich: There are a lot of levels. What's really interesting me the most about this piece in a purely musical sense is that it is not like *Different Trains* and *The Cave*. In them, I worked as follows: I used either archive recordings of the Holocaust survivors or early recordings I made of my governess in *Different Trains*, and in *The Cave* all the recordings were made in Israel, on the West Bank, in New York, and in Dallas, Texas. Because of the nature of the pieces — *Different Trains* is kind of an homage to the living or the dead, and because *The Cave* deals with religious subject matter — I just accepted the speech melody of people as it was, and if it wasn't the right notes for what I needed, I had to go find another sample, that was the rule I set for myself. In other words, I was the faithful scribe. It also meant that, musically speaking, in *Different Trains* and *The Cave* every time you get a new speaker you get a new tempo, which was of course very different from the way I'd worked before that. I always had very long stretches of unbroken tempo.

In *Three Tales,* I thought I'm not dealing with religious subject matter, I'm not making an homage to the living or the dead, I'm just dealing with radio announcements and all sorts of people who happened to be alive when the Hindenburg existed, and so on, and so forth.

And I wanted to be able to structure the piece harmonically the way I would structure a piece which was not using samples, where the harmony would be worked out the way I wanted to work out the harmony independent of the sampled material. I wanted to set up a tempo and get a head of steam going rhythmically the way I did with my other pieces. So I decided that in this piece I will change, drastically if need be, any of the sampled material to fit the music.

So I start off in three flats and if Herb Morrison is not in three flats, and he's not, then I'm going to change him to three flats, and when I want to stretch his voice out, then I just stretch it out. So the whole aesthetic is different and the whole technical means of working is different — it harkens back to the way I was writing before I was working with samples. I can make musical decisions. It's like having your cake and eating it too, I can use the samples and also write the music I want to write. It turns out that Digital Performer, the new incarnation of it, has this really superb pitch shifting which you can apply to spoken voice beautifully because it doesn't shift the formants when it shifts the pitch. You don't get the chipmunk effect, you don't get the Darth Vader effect, you really can move easily in thirds and sometimes more and neither I nor the speaker themselves is the least bit aware of it.

Brown: Would you say then that most of the larger-scale structural decisions are made away from the computer?

Reich: In general I would say that was the case. The computer is the scene of detailed working out. The larger things happen in discussion in dramatic work. Harmony and melody happens at the piano and then I bring my music notebook to the computer and start working out the details.

Brown: Would it be reasonable to characterize that as similar to a sort of orchestration-like process?

Reich: No, it's not at all the same as that. For a long time, my orchestration and my composition have been one and the same thing. A couple of the orchestra pieces were orchestrated, including parts of *Three Movements*, parts of the *Four Sections*, and *Desert Music*, but that is rare. Usually the musical ideas and the instruments that are going to be playing those ideas are one and the same thing.

Because I composed from the very beginning by overdubbing on tape, I compose now using instrument samples so I can hear the timbre. Especially now with Sample Cell which I load with very good actual recordings of musical instruments, there's no need for orchestration later on. Occasionally in the old days I used to change some details, but I find now that if I'm writing for the percussion family and for keyboards, strings, and woodwinds, I rarely have to change anything. One of the quintessential difficulties with orchestration was, do you put the clarinets above the oboes or the oboes above the clarinets? I found that in the early days I would simply have a woodwind player, who doubled, come over to my house and bring an oboe, English horn, and a Bb clarinet and we would simply try it a number of different ways and record it. But then when I got Sample Cell for *City Life* I thought, "well let's see how good this thing really is. I'll see if what I up with using Sample Cell will prove to be reality in rehearsal." I went ahead with Sample Cell and wrote it out that way and when I went into rehearsal with Ensemble Modern, bam, it was right there. So now I know I can trust the computer mock-up for even as subtle a question as that.

Brown: So the computer's feedback is close enough to the final product that you can make those fine judgments.

Reich: If it sounds good in the sampled mock-up, it sounds good in the instrumental performance, period. In fact it sounds better because in performance you have all those little extra added richnesses and irregularities. My rhythms in the MIDI mock-up are exact. An eighth note is a computer accurate eighth note, but it's just a mock-up. When it's actually played it always feels better.

Brown: Do you have a favorite analogy for the composing process, such as painting on a blank canvas, or sculpting with sound?

Reich: It's very much like an architect, who makes drawings and then he makes a maquette, a model. It's almost exactly like an architect's model. You can call the client in and have them take a look at it, and you can alter it. I send my MIDI mock-ups to conductors with the score. It's very much analogous to an architect's model of a finished building.

Brown: How do you judge the success of the composition as you work on it?

Reich: By how I feel about it. If I think it sounds good and it moves me, then it's right. If it doesn't, then it's wrong. If it doesn't, I try to find out what the reasons for that are, and the reasons are technical, but 'Das Affect' is what I'm looking for.

Brown: Who are your biggest influences and major influences?

 Reich: We can start with Perotin, back in the 12th century, he's definitely up there. J. S. Bach, Béla Bartók, Igor Stravinsky, Ravel, and Debussy . . . I think those are the major ones. And on the jazz side, John Coltrane and to a lesser extent, Miles Davis and the drummer Kenny Clark. Then African music, specifically that of Ghana, gamelan music specifically that of Bali, and Hebrew cantorlation with which I spent several years.

Brown: Do you see yourself as continuing the orchestral tradition?

Reich: People who write for orchestra generally are people I'm not interested in. Concertos, symphonies, and so on. I don't know anyone writing stuff like that, that I'm interested in.

Brown: Is that because you don't like the textural density of orchestras?

Reich: Well, there's a whole lot of things that go with the orchestra, with its traditions of the forms that were written for the orchestra. There's the fatness of the sound you talked about — I don't need 18 first violins, I need one which is amplified. There's the sociology that goes with it; the fact that those people themselves are preoccupied with Beethoven, Brahms, Mozart, and Haydn. I'm more interested in ensembles that when they play a piece of old classical music, they play a piece of Schoenberg or Stravinsky. Like the Ensemble Modern, or the Ensemble Intercontemporain. I am going to be in Belgium in March with the Ictus ensemble and in the same month I'm going to be in England with the London Sinfonetta. So my lot is cast entirely with those ensembles, which are similar to my own.

These are people who also, at least the better ones, have a member of the ensemble who is the sound engineer and runs the mixing board, and they are frequently or constantly amplified. They work with samplers and they work with computing equipment. People who don't do this at all I don't find their music very interesting. It It isn't because I love the sound of any particular device, it's because people who aren't interested in those devices aren't very interesting people. Maybe it's because they aren't in touch with their own time, they're too preoccupied with a time in which they are not living. I think that's the key to it.

Brown: So where do you find your works well received?

Reich: I would say in England, France, America, Belgium, and Japan. With the emphasis in Japan at the moment. It varies. I get an enormous amount of work in Germany. The German public likes it. The musical establishment, the critics take me seriously even though I have no interest in German composers. In Holland, Louis Andriessen has been influenced by my work. Pierre Boulez has sort of wiped out other composers in France. There's no one really whose strong. But there is a great deal of interest in what I do in France, as there is in England, too.

Postview

Some readers of this book will no doubt praise it for the wide range of its mix of American and European avant-garde music. Other readers will damm it for its lack of composers whose names do not appear here. For example, Igor Stravinsky, György Ligeti, Béla Bartók, Edgard Varèse, Terry Riley, Frank Zappa, Laurie Anderson, Diamonda Galás, La Monte Young, George Antheil, Luigi Russolo, Luc Ferrari, and the many others that don't appear in this book. Some of those composers, of course, died before they could be interviewed or were unavailable due to performance dates. Others were unwilling to appear in these pages due to not enjoying the 'avant-garde' name attached to them or their compositions. All that said, *The Composer Magazine* did its best to spread the information about the musical avant-garde with as much honor and interest as possible. We hope that you too enjoyed this books contents and appreciate the value that the composers herein gave their best to make the world around them more interesting and new.

David Cope

Composer Index